Embracing Cultural Competency

*A Roadmap
for Nonprofit
Capacity Builders*

Praise for *Embracing Cultural Competency*

"This book guides readers to a better understanding that cultural competency is not a soft skill but a core issue, requiring work and time. The information has relevance wherever people of various backgrounds need to come together to accomplish common objectives."

—Yvette Larkin, Senior Program Officer, Associated Black Charities

"Many different audiences can find lessons in this information. It reinforces the importance of examining and dismantling institutional inequities, rather than focusing solely on interpersonal development."

—Adrienne Mansanares, Program Officer,
Inclusiveness Project at The Denver Foundation

"I appreciate how this text helps readers become aware of racial privilege and how it influences one's work, often in subtle ways. Capacity builders who work across many types of nonprofits, foundations, and community groups will find this book accessible and helpful."

—Katherine Pease, Principal, Katherine Pease & Associates

"Real world, first person examples in this book help personalize issues that might otherwise appear abstract to some people. This collection of voices does a great job of providing diverse perspectives and tools. This book is long over-due and goes a long way in addressing many challenges that keep organizations from becoming more successful."

—Elissa Perry, Principal, Think.Do.Repeat

"An impressive breadth and depth of perspectives are offered in this book. Readers will find tools to help them gain greater cultural competency in working with communities—and become more inclusive in their organizational processes."

—Scot T. Spencer, Manager of Baltimore Relations,
Annie E. Casey Foundation

"Great personal stories and perspectives can be found here. This text will motivate readers to start their own internal conversation about issues related to cultural competency."

—Suzanne Bronheim, Senior Policy Associate, National Center
for Cultural Competence, Georgetown University

Embracing Cultural Competency

*A Roadmap
for Nonprofit
Capacity Builders*

Patricia St.Onge   *Lead Author*

Contributing Authors:

Part One: Beth Applegate
Vicki Asakura
Monika K. Moss
Alfredo Vergara-Lobo

Part Three: Brigette Rouson

FIELDSTONE
ALLIANCE

SAINT PAUL
MINNESOTA

800-274-6024
www.FieldstoneAlliance.org

Manufactured in the U.S.A.
First printing, June 2009

Cover image: © Sirylok/Dreamstime.com

Library of Congress Cataloging-in-Publication Data

Embracing cultural competency: a roadmap for nonprofit capacity builders
    p.   cm.
    "Lead author: Patricia St.Onge; contributing authors: Beth Applegate . . . [et al.]"— P.   .
    Includes bibliographical references and index.
    ISBN 978-0-940069-68-8
    1. Nonprofit organizations—Management.
2. Intercultural communication.
3. Communication in management.   4. Diversity in the workplace—Management.   I. St.Onge, Patricia, 1953–   II. Applegate, Beth, 1961–
III. Fieldstone Alliance.
    HD62.6.C85 2009
    658'.048—dc22
                       2008034010

This work is dedicated to my life and work partner, Wilson Riles, and to our daughters and grandchildren who make the work have meaning. I also dedicate it to Frank J. Omowale Satterwhite, who showed me the way, and Diana Marie Lee, Dahnesh Medora, Brigette Rouson, and all those who journey with me.

—Patricia St.Onge

About the Authors

Beth Applegate is the principal of Applegate Consulting Group (ACG), an organization development (OD) practice that assists national and international nonprofit organizations, government agencies, and socially responsible for-profit corporations with developing human and organizational capacity and building a more just and equitable society.

Using systems theory and a well-established action research model, ACG helps diverse organizations adapt to changing environments, identify priorities, strengthen leadership, and facilitate continuous learning. Working collaboratively with each client, ACG employs a series of planned change processes that strengthen organizational effectiveness and increase capabilities. ACG's work is inextricably linked to advancing democratic processes and humanistic values. Through shared responsibility and effort with each client, ACG

- Develops leaders who are intentional, proactive, and clear about their visions
- Supports the development of diverse workplace cultures where all employees feel invested and valued
- Helps individuals understand the significance, power, and importance of their contributions
- Clarifies strategic direction and facilitates effective collaboration
- Supports the development of sustainable organizations that are socially responsible

Beth Applegate can be reached at Beth@applegateonline.com.

Vicki Asakura is a third-generation Japanese American who grew up in the ethnically diverse Central Area of Seattle. Her life experiences have had a strong influence on her passion for racial justice and capacity-building work in communities of color and refugees and immigrants. After graduating with a bachelor's degree from the University of Washington, she started her professional career in a newly formed community-based organization providing employment services for Asian Americans in the Seattle area. Through this job she became a community advocate for programs and funding in support of

English as a second language (ESL) and other bilingual services for the growing immigrant and refugee communities.

After seventeen years at the Seattle-King County Private Industry Council, where she managed federal and state-funded grants providing employment and training services for refugees, Asakura joined the newly created Nonprofit Assistance Center (NAC) in 2000, where she currently serves as executive director. Under her leadership, NAC has created new models for effective and culturally competent capacity building and leadership development for organizations and leaders based in low-income, refugee, immigrant communities and in communities of color and has implemented new strategies as part of a race and public policy agenda.

Asakura chairs the Alliance for Nonprofit Management Cultural Competency Initiative and the United Way of King County Employment Impact Council. She is past chair of the King County Refugee Planning Committee, which advocates on local and state refugee issues, and is a member of the Minority Executive Directors' Coalition of King County (based in Seattle) and the Asian Pacific Directors' Coalition. She is also involved in various community-building efforts, including Making Connections, an initiative of the Annie E. Casey Foundation and BuRSST for Prosperity, an initiative of the Northwest Area Foundation.

Monika K. Moss, president of MKM Management Consulting, has worked as a master mapper and business consultant for twenty years. She has dedicated her talents to helping organizations and individuals create powerful road-maps to their vision. As founder of MKM Management Consulting (www.mkmmanagement.com), Moss is committed to partnering with others to make a difference by supporting the transformation of individuals and organizations. A scholar and practitioner, Moss was published in the International Association of Facilitators' *Group Facilitation: A Research and Application Journal* (Spring 2004) and wrote the book *Life Mapping: A Process of Self-Discovery and Path Finding* (Keys for Life Publishing, 2007).

Moss is a regular presenter and trainer at regional and national conferences on issues of effective meetings, facilitative leadership, strategic planning, Gestalt organizational systems development theory, nonprofit management, cultural competency, and diversity. She is on the faculty of the Gestalt Organizational Systems Development Center and a partner with the Center for Nonprofit Policy and Practice at Cleveland State University's Maxine Levine College of Urban Affairs. Moss has bachelor's and master's degrees from Howard University and Columbia University, respectively. She is a 2007 graduate of Leadership Cleveland, a member of the National Black MBA Association, OD Connection, and the Alliance for Nonprofit Management. She is involved with numerous community, business, and civic groups.

Brigette Rouson brings more than twenty years of experience as a consultant, public policy attorney, grant maker, board member, and scholar-activist. Her leadership signature is advancing social transformation through attention to cultural identity. She is senior consultant with Mosaica: The Center for Nonprofit Development and Pluralism. Rouson previously served as program director for the Alliance for Nonprofit Management, the premier national association of capacity builders devoted to improving nonprofits' management and governance capacity.

She directed the three-year startup of the alliance's Cultural Competency Initiative, building the knowledge, will, and skill of nonprofit capacity builders to address cultural dynamics in their work. As a board member of the Nonprofit Sector Workforce Coalition, she promotes recruitment and retention of non-profit sector workers and leadership under age forty. In the alliance, she is a member of affinity groups focused on people of color (which she co-founded with Monika Moss), board governance, executive transitions, and faith-based capacity builders.

In her consulting capacity, Rouson provides expert guidance to numerous funder initiatives, community-based organizations, and national groups. For the Washington Area Women's Foundation, she serves as a donor-organizer to the African American Women's Giving Circle and a grant reviewer for its capacity-building fund. Previously, she led grantmaking for girls and young women at Ms. Foundation for Women, including a $4 million collaborative. A graduate of Howard University and Georgetown Law Center, she completed coursework toward a Ph.D. in communications and culture at the University of Pennsylvania. She is proud to be among alumni of Shannon Leadership Institute, as well as Stone Circles and Vallecitos retreats for activists. She has published work on African American women in traditional African spiritual practice, news coverage of interethnic conflict, and low-power TV as a community medium. The mother of a jazz percussionist and spouse of a librarian and music educator, she resides in Washington, D.C., and is a member of the D.C. Bar.

Patricia St.Onge (Six Nations) is a partner in Seven Generations Consulting Company, providing coaching, training, consulting, and technical assistance in the areas of community organizing, social change advocacy, organizational development, cross-cultural effectiveness, consensus building, and executive, spiritual, and personal coaching. Seven Generations works with public agencies, nonprofit organizations, foundations, academic institutions, congregations, and communities.

The name *Seven Generations* comes from the Six Nations tradition that reminds us that we honor the generations who have come before us and make decisions that are mindful of their impact on seven generations to come.

St.Onge is the former director of education and training and current affiliate consultant at the National Community Development Institute, a technical assistance intermediary working in grassroots communities of color. She has served as executive director of several nonprofit agencies, including Habitat for Humanity at affiliates in Boston, Oakland, and San Francisco before becoming western regional director. She serves on several community boards. St.Onge also performs ceremonies and rituals. She is a contributing author to *Collective Wisdom*, edited by Donald Gerard, Inward Journey Press, Oakland, California.

St.Onge has a degree in human services from Southern New Hampshire University and a master of divinity degree from Pacific School of Religion. She has completed the coursework for co-active coaching and is certified in spiritual direction from the Chaplaincy Institute for Arts and Interfaith Ministries. She is of Six Nations (Mohawk) and Quebecois descent. She reads, writes, and makes jewelry. Between them, she and her life partner, Wilson Riles, have six daughters and seven grandchildren.

Alfredo Vergara-Lobo, principal at Vergara-Lobo Associates, has a background in education, social work, organizational change, and recreation. He brings years of experience with nonprofit and public entities domestically and abroad to his practice. A popular speaker and presenter, Vergara-Lobo has trained and presented to hundreds of audiences throughout the country and abroad in English and Spanish. He received his master of social work degree from the School of Social Welfare at University of California-Berkeley and his bachelor's degree from San Francisco State University.

Vergara-Lobo has taught in public and private schools in the United States and Latin America and is a guest lecturer for the schools of Social Work and Social

Welfare at San Francisco State University and the University of California-Berkeley, respectively.

An expert in nonprofit partnerships, Vergara-Lobo was a funding consultant for the Strategic Solutions project, a national initiative to advance the field of nonprofit partnerships and fine-tune knowledge and practice in that area. He has co-authored *The M Word: A Board Member's Guide to Mergers—How, Why, and Why Not to Merge Nonprofit Organizations* (CompassPoint Nonprofit Services, 2005).

Vergara-Lobo has consulted with dozens of nonprofit organizations, foundations, and government entities domestically and abroad, in English and in Spanish, in the areas of strategic planning, board development, strategic partnerships, and cultural competence. He has co-authored *Crossing Borders, Sharing Journeys: Effective Capacity Building with Immigrant and Refugee Groups* (Fieldstone Alliance, 2006).

Contents

Acknowledgments

Lead Author

Patricia St.Onge

Contributing Authors

Beth Applegate
Vicki Asakura
Monika K. Moss
Brigette Rouson
Alfredo Vergara-Lobo

Doug Toft served as the content editor for this book. His vision and thorough attention were extraordinary. Heather Iliff and Vivian R. Rouson made valuable editing contributions to earlier manuscripts. Wilson Riles contributed to the writing, particularly the section on internalized oppression. He also edited the first draft. Emily Gantz McKay was a reader for a part of the book manuscript, and Michele Robinson provided editing assistance. Previous Fieldstone Alliance staff helped shepherd the book in important ways. Finally, special thanks to Dr. Roni Posner and Dr. David Maurrasse, who provided crucial early support in their roles as Alliance for Nonprofit Management leaders; to former Alliance staff, especially Maratha Iraheta; and to members of the People of Color Affinity Group and allies.

Sponsors

The Alliance for Nonprofit Management is thankful for the generosity of the UPS Foundation, Annie E. Casey Foundation, Citi Foundation, and Charles Stewart Mott Foundation.

Alliance Cultural Competency Initiative Advisory Group
Chair: Vicki Asakura, Nonprofit Assistance Center

Advisory Group Members

Margo Bailey
Melwood

Ignatius Bau
California Endowment

Cherie Brown
National Coalition Building Institute

William Buster
Mary Reynolds Babcock Foundation

Lauren Casteel
The Denver Foundation

Fernando Cuevas
Southern Partners Fund

Anushka Fernandopulle
CompassPoint Nonprofit Services

Sharon Gary-Smith
Consultant to Foundations

Tawara Goode
National Center for Cultural Competence

Karen Johns
Diversity Pipeline Alliance and
Volunteer Consulting Group

Mercedes Martin
InPartnership Consulting, Inc., and Ernst and Young

Virginia Martinez
Mexican American Legal Defense Fund

Ricardo Millett
Ricardo Millett and Associates

Leroy Moore
National Minorities with Disabilities Coalition

Cynthia Parker
Interaction Institute for Social Change

Katherine Pease
Katherine Pease and Associates

Howard Ross
CookRoss, Inc.

Patricia Talton
IntegritySource

Makani Themba-Nixon
The Praxis Project

Peter York
TCC Group

Research Participants

We thank the many people who participated in, collaborated in, and supported our research (names and affiliations listed were current at the time of the research dates shown):

PEER DIALOGUE: SAN FRANCISCO (JANUARY 2006)
Janeen Antoine, American Indian Contemporary Arts
Anushka Fernandopulle, an independent consultant who was with
   CompassPoint Nonprofit Services at the time of the dialogue
Diane J. Johnson, CompassPoint Nonprofit Services
Helen Kim, Building Movement Project
Diana Marie Lee, National Community Development Institute
Dahnesh Medora, National Community Development Institute (currently
   Technical Assistance to Community Services)
Ana Perez, Global Exchange/VISIONS Inc.
Lisa Russ, Movement Strategy Center

PEER DIALOGUE: CHICAGO (MARCH 2006)
Claudette Baker, Donors Forum of Chicago
Dr. Michael Bennett, Egan Urban Center, DePaul University
Patricia Canessa, Ph.D., Salud Latina/Latino Health
Victor Chears, Chears and Associates
Leticia Escamilla, United Way of Metropolitan Chicago
Jean Hardy Robinson, JHR Resources
Virginia Martinez, International Center for Health Leadership
   Development, University of Illinois
Alyson Parham, Partec Consulting Group Inc.

PEER DIALOGUE: ATLANTA (APRIL 2006)
Aparna Bhattacharyya, Raksha Inc.
Fernando Cuevas Jr., Southern Partners Fund
Sharon Gary-Smith, Consultant to Foundations
Tina Graf, Flourish! (consulting practice)
Cappy Harmon, National Coalition Building Institute Atlanta
Eleanor Hooks, Ph.D., Georgia Center for Nonprofits
Janice Robinson, United Way of Metropolitan Atlanta
Loretta Ross, SisterSong Women of Color Reproductive Health Collective
Monika Moss, MKM Management Consulting
Host: Janine Lee, Arthur M. Blank Family Foundation

GRANTMAKER ROUNDTABLE: CHICAGO (MARCH 2006)
Shelley Davis, Chicago Foundation for Women
Andrea Foggy-Paxton, Annie E. Cassey Foundation
Ada Gugenheim, Chicago Community Trust
Beth Ann Hester, Social Venture Partners Chicago
Ngoan Le, Chicago Community Trust
Leslie Ramyk, Chicago Community Organizing Capacity Building Initiative
Toya Randall, Grand Victoria Foundation
Kimberley Roberson, Charles Stewart Mott Foundation
Artavia Berry Roberson, Public Allies Chicago
Host: Kassie Davis, Chicago Community Trust

GRANTMAKER ROUNDTABLE: ATLANTA (APRIL 2006)
Lynette Bell, SunTrust Bank
Birgit Burton, Georgia Tech CEISMC
Milano Harden, the Genius Group
Muriel Hepburn, National Black Arts Festival
Zenith Houston, Stevie Wonder Foundation
Stephanie Hughley, National Black Arts Festival
Charlotte King, Snowden and King Marketing Communications
Janice Robinson, United Way of Atlanta
Hubert Sapp, Bert and Mary Meyer Foundation
Host: Janine Lee, Arthur M. Blank Family Foundation

Interviewees

(SPRING/FALL 2006)

Omisade Burney-Scott, Ananse Consulting
Juan Cruz, Cultural Dynamics
Milano Harden, the Genius Group
Frank Lopez, Nonprofit Enterprise Center
Jan Masaoka, CompassPoint Nonprofit Services
David Maurrasse, Marga Inc.
Barbara Meyer, Bert and Mary Meyer Foundation
Leroy Moore, Harambee Education Council of California
Andrea Nagel, Interaction Institute for Social Change
Cynthia Parker, Interaction Institute for Social Change
Kaki Rusmore, Community Foundation for Monterey County
Frank J. Omowale Satterwhite, National Community Development Institute
Sojeila Silva, Northern California Community Loan Fund
Julie Simpson, Cricket Island Foundation
Bo Thao, Asian Americans/Pacific Islanders in Philanthropy
Makani Themba-Nixon, the Praxis Project
Dick Trudell, American Indian Resources Institute
Thomas Watson, Southeastern Organizational Development Initiative

(WINTER 2003–2004)

Ignatius Bau, California Endowment
Tom Bailey and Jennifer Henderson, Strategic Interventions
Tawara Goode, National Center for Cultural Competence
Kien Lee, Association for Study and Development of Community
Christine Robinson, Stillwaters Consulting
Frank J. Omowale Satterwhite, National Community Development Institute
Suganya Sockalingam, Consultant

PEER REVIEWERS

Bob Agres, Hawai'i Alliance for Community-Based Economic Development
Juan Cruz, Cultural Dynamics
Mercedes Martin, InPartnership Consulting
Guadalupe Pacheco, Office of Minority Health, U.S. Department of Health
    and Human Services
Cynthia Parker, Interaction Institute for Social Change
Lisa Russ, Movement Strategy Center
Bo Thao, Asian Americans/Pacific Islanders in Philanthropy

FIELD REVIEWERS

A. Adar Ayira, Core Concepts

Suzanne Bronheim, Georgetown University

Vivian Jackson, National Center for Cultural Competence,
    Georgetown University

Yvette Larkin, Associated Black Charities

Adrienne Mansanares, the Denver Foundation

Katherine Pease, Katherine Pease and Associates

Elissa Perry, Think.Do.Repeat

Scot T. Spencer, Annie E. Casey Foundation

Foreword

You started your journey toward cultural competency long before you picked up this publication, and your journey will continue long after you have read it. *Embracing Cultural Competency: A Roadmap for Nonprofit Capacity Builders* is intended to deepen your exposure to an analysis and way of thinking about working cross-culturally. This is not a "how-to" manual; rather, this book reflects how this work is an ongoing journey. There is no checklist to complete that will make you culturally competent.

The Alliance for Nonprofit Management is committed to advancing effectiveness in the nonprofit sector across a wide range of areas. Through our research, as well as the extensive experience of our members, it is clear that to be effective, capacity builders and nonprofits must understand how to fully embrace and benefit from diversity. This book is part of the Alliance's Cultural Competency Initiative that includes research, training, publishing, and standards to advance the field.

The Alliance's ethical standards call on capacity builders to "continuously seek to develop and improve their understanding of cultural competency and apply that learning to all processes of capacity building in which they are engaged." We have found that there are simply no shortcuts. It is not easy to deal with racism, classism, ableism, and a range of other "isms" that undermine our effectiveness as organizations and as a society, and it can be emotional and frustrating at times.

We invite you to think of cultural competency as an adventure and this book as a roadmap. Our destination is a just society. Whether you are just beginning to think about what it means to be culturally based in your practice or you are a seasoned practitioner who lives and breathes this question, we hope that somewhere you will find, in the chorus of voices reflected in this book, words that encourage you and inspire you to keep moving in your ongoing cultural competency journey.

Together, we can work toward a vision of all nonprofits becoming more inclusive, more connected, and ultimately, more effective by gaining needed knowledge and skills. Because people and human systems are culturally based, we will be more effective in achieving our mission impact by paying attention to culture.

Tangie Newborn
Former Executive Director and CEO
Alliance for Nonprofit Management

PATRICIA ST.ONGE

Preface

As we put the final touches on this book, the United States had just elected Barack Obama, the country's first African American president. Like many of us, I am giddy with the possibilities of change. I am truly hopeful. At the same time, many parallels exist between the election and the efforts of many other White-dominated organizations. We are changing demographically, and young people have very different attitudes about race and culture. Those two factors made it inevitable that early in this century we would elect a person of color or a woman to the White House. This does not mean that our politics or our society is "post-racial" or "post-gender." Ideally, it means that marginalized groups are finding a voice in our electoral system in a way they haven't before, and we have the numbers to shift some elections.

Still, the changes we need to make are much deeper than changing some faces in important places within the government. Until we acknowledge the foundation on which the United States was built—the three-legged stool of conquest, slavery, and misogyny—we can't fully appreciate and live out the other values that we espouse of justice, equality, and freedom. The following statistics illustrate which racial groups hold elected positions in Spring 2009 in Congress.

COMBINED STATISTICS FOR THE HOUSE AND SENATE

Category	*Number of Members*
African American (8%)	42
American Indian (less than 1%)	1
Asian (1%)	7
Caucasian (85%)	456
Hispanic (5%)	25
Not Stated (less than 1%)	2
Vietnamese (less than 1%)	2

For complete demographic information, including age, gender, and other factors, please refer to http://www.congress.org/congressorg/directory/congdir.tt.

President Obama's move to the White House meant there were no African Americans in the Senate for a time. Roland Burris was then appointed for Illinois.

When an organization seeks to become more diverse, a common tactic is to fill particular slots with people of color; lesbian, gay, transgender, bisexual, and queer (LGTBQ) folk; or other historically marginalized group members. Once these slots are filled, the organizational leaders often think their work is done. They are surprised when conflicts arise later. I would caution that, as a country, we are similar to organizations that are grappling with questions of equity, race, class, gender, and other forms of oppression. Hiring is a limited first step; it is not the last step in the process of becoming more inclusive and open.

Another common practice among organizations and communities is to hire or elect people of color who are fully bicultural and comfortable navigating the dominant culture. This requires far less of a community or organization in terms of its own introspection. There is little need to address the systems of oppression if enough of the faces in the front of the room look like the communities who are being oppressed. We need to move to the point where the communities and organizations are themselves bicultural or multicultural.

My definition of what multicultural means goes way beyond "one of each" in leadership positions. We can point to former President George W. Bush's first cabinet, a classic example of filling slots with people who made his administration one of the most diverse in history. Many of those appointments made no difference to the communities from which they came. Real culturally based leadership means doing the hard work of opening the organization to be affirming and welcoming of multiple realities and working together as a whole community or organization to determine the points of oppression.

I am excited about the presidential election because it is a giant leap in the right direction. We still have a long way to go. There is still much to do. As we begin, as a nation, to address real issues of injustice, it is important that we do it through the lens of culture. We need to understand all of the complexities that inform who we are as individuals and as a nation. President Obama is up to the task, but he can't do it alone. In fact, he shouldn't do it alone, and we shouldn't expect it of him. He can't even do it with a great cabinet. We can take advantage of this special moment in our history and use it to advance the cause of justice and peace. Yes, we can!

Introduction

Conversation as a Tool for Transformation

For the hundredth time, I stand in the front of the room and ask, "What is the most important question we're addressing in a changing world?" For about the sixty-fifth time, people answer with the words *diversity* or *changing demographics* or *cultural sensitivity* or some variation on the idea of cultural competency. While some eyes light up, I see others roll. Even as it is pressing, this is the topic that people find most exhausting to deal with.

As I reflect on that too familiar scenario, it occurs to me that one of the reasons that cultural competency is both compelling and so exhausting is that we haven't figured out how to have conversations about it. Or the conversations we typically have are ineffective. Too often, people walk away feeling angry, depressed, or guilty. If the facilitation is especially poor, they might feel all three.

Why This Conversation Is So Challenging

Cultural competency is a topic that is close to my heart for so many reasons, the most compelling of which is that I can only imagine a just society as one that pays attention to the cultural richness of all of its members. Culture is a wonderful vehicle for embracing those who differ from us.

Yet grappling with culture is exhausting. The concept of culture can be one of the most effective means for exclusion. We yearn for conversation about culture, and we fear it at the same time. There are several reasons for this.

First, paying attention to culture is considered by some to be among the "soft" skills that are often seen as less important than "hard" skills, such as fiscal management, fund-raising, and governance. We make the necessary investments, often with a combination of dedicated staff and outsourcing, for each of the "hard" functions. We recognize that it will be difficult for organizations to survive if these are neglected. For those of us who work to help organizations thrive over the long term, however, experience reveals that neglecting "soft" skills is equally dangerous. In fact, cultural competency can now be counted as a core competency.

Second, *this conversation takes time.* It is not unusual for an organization to call me with a request for support in dealing with challenging cross-cultural issues, including race, class, gender, sexual identity, and religion. Often, the conversation starts like this: "Hello, we're the Merrily We Roll Along Foundation. We've had a few situations come up lately where people are having a hard time getting along. We need some cultural sensitivity training. We've set aside two hours, one week from Thursday. Can you facilitate our meeting?" Here, too, experience tells us that it is impossible to build healthy, strong relationships— which are at the heart of cultural competency—without a deep investment of time and energy.

A third reason that talking about cultural competency is challenging is that *it is a largely emotional interaction.* We tend to be more comfortable in the realm of intellect. As a concept, cross-cultural effectiveness is a great idea, and as long as the conversation stays conceptual, we feel safe. When it turns to our experience and our practice, the anxiety level rises. Most of us do not jump boldly into the spaces that make us uncomfortable. For these and many other reasons, people working with and within nonprofits often limit the conversation to our ways of thinking.

This book is about having the conversation in a safe way, one that honors both intellect and emotions. Our work acknowledges and attends to the person, the organization, and the community as an integrated whole. We are not only a mind, or a body, soul, or heart. When we are healthy, we are integrated. We hold all of our parts as sacred. This applies not only to individuals or groups but also to organizations and communities. They are not just the people who make them up; they are the systems, the relationships, the structures, and the spirit of the place where they function.

The only way that capacity builders can understand this and function as helpers is for each of us to bring our whole self to the process. This is hard if we come from a culture that overvalues the mind and undervalues the heart. We can engage fully in cross-cultural effectiveness only if we jump in with both feet. Experience shows that when we do jump, we are surprised by the many treasures we find in the uncomfortable unknown.

Fourth, our experiences are so different—based on our race, class, and culture—that it is hard to imagine that someone else can understand and appreciate them. Even though we think we're likely to understand someone else's experience, the thought that we might not is unsettling. Rather than make a mistake, we often don't do or say anything.

In my home, we talk about "magical thinking." This happens when we know something is true but act otherwise. For example, I think that after a full day's work I can get my grandkids from school, take them to dinner and to powwow practice, *and* be fully attentive at the powwow committee meeting going on in the next room. This is magical thinking.

So, too, with culturally based practice. We can't know everything about every community, and so we decide that the gaps in our knowledge are unimportant. This magical way of thinking persists despite all evidence to the contrary. In reality, lack of cultural competency is a root cause for broken relationships, for organizations that don't fulfill their mission, and for communities that have a hard time achieving social justice.

A fifth reason is that many communities of color (and other marginalized communities that contribute significantly) tend to be weighted down by internalized oppression.[1] At some point, you come to believe the message that you are not worthy of consideration and that you don't have the capacity to be your whole self. You engage in life from the perspective of what those around you suggest is your real self. You can no longer see the possibility of living from the place of your power, strengths, and talents. Your eyes are locked on to your deficits. Systems are designed to reinforce this message to people, organizations, and communities. From that vantage point, every view is clouded.

Even though the conversation about cultural competency is so challenging, it offers multiple benefits. In an opening keynote presentation for the Alliance for Nonprofit Management's 2006 conference in Los Angeles, Manuel Pastor presented a slide that showed a group of people, all of them with raised hands and smiling. The caption was "victory always looks good in the end." Cultural competency can be a muddy road, but it is also a road filled with treasures along the way.

Use the Power of Language to Unleash Capacity

We begin discovering these treasures when we remember that language has multiple layers of power. We can use language as a vehicle for communication.

We can use it as a weapon of exclusion and hurt. We can use language as a tool for transformation.

In their book *How the Way We Talk Can Change the Way We Work,* Robert Kegan and Lisa Laskow Lahey give helpful tips for shifting the function of our language from utilitarian to transformational. According to these authors, new forms of conversation can open up fresh perspectives and create new options for action:

> The forms of speaking we have available to us regulate the forms of thinking, feeling, and meaning making to which we have access, which in turn constrain how we see the world and act in it. Some language forms concentrate more individual and social energy than others do; they provide more focus, increase direction, and enhance capacity. . . . In our experience, these novel language forms do not spring up on their own. They require intention and attention.[2]

For people who work in the nonprofit sector, one of these novel language forms involves a shift from solving problems to unleashing capacity.

At one point, I was executive director of a program that served homeless women and their children. Rather than doing the usual intake—asking them to share their problems—we asked each woman to identify three skills, gifts, or talents she brought into the household.

Not one could answer the question at first. We invited the women to dinner, and during a conversation where they told their stories, we helped them see the skills they had cultivated—sometimes, just to survive. One woman lived in a car with two children under age four. She knew where everything was that she needed to care for her children. I suggested that this was a skill. Another woman found clothes at free clothing closets and sewed them by hand to make beautiful outfits for her twin girls. As the women discovered that they did have skills and gifts, their participation in the program changed. They saw themselves as resources for the community rather than needy women taking from the program.

For some of us, our whole lives are about reaching a point where we can voice our needs, whether it's for subsidized housing or child care, cash benefits, or food stamps. We can get what we need only if we state what's *wrong* with us. Others of us are trained from birth to share our *strengths.* Private schools, good jobs, and college admissions are all platforms where we get to say how great we are. Is it any wonder that those who mostly learn how to speak of their needs fall prey to "charity providers"—and that those who mostly speak of their skills have a hard time cultivating empathy for those who are "needy"?

The framework of problem-solving tends to stem from mainstream thinking. Funders and others less familiar with the field of cultural competency often function in this framework.

As you read this book, you will find that we approach the issue more from the perspective of what capacity can be *unleashed* if we speak in new ways that honor and value people as their whole selves, as part of their own cultures. This is an alternative to problem solving.

When I work with groups in this way, I find that what is unleashed is power. We often think of power in relational terms—power *over,* power *with,* or power *within.* In the context of cultural competency, we mean something like the power generated by an engine. This is a force of energy that enables people to move in the world in the ways that they desire and to create a just society. (For more about this conception of power, see chapter 8.) In making this distinction we move from charity to justice:

▪ *Charity says:* You have problems and I have resources. I will bring my resources to bear to solve your problems. (If I have a progressive angle on charity, I will acknowledge that you have value and can help me to help you.)

▪ *Justice says:* The system we're operating under is broken. Let's identify what each of us can bring to changing the system. We can share power, leadership, and access to resources. The result can be a quality of life that enriches all.

Cultural competency means that each practitioner is part of the whole and works to unleash the power and performance of everyone involved in nonprofits. Strategies to bring about change around race and power are considered. These include using a team-based approach, a dialogue process, and a diversity priority for executive searches.[3] We discover where *systems* are broken, not people. We understand ourselves and the institutions we participate in to be multidimensional. This is the heart of a process that builds a just society.

Clarify the Conversation with Definitions

Definitions are more than words. Embedded in them are assumptions, attitudes, and potentials for behavior. To set a foundation for our discussion, we will share some of our definitions and see how they guide our conversation about cultural competency in capacity building. (For more definitions, see "Key Terms for Cultural Competency" in the Resources on page 147).

Take *culture,* for example. The King County, Washington, Department of Community and Human Services defines culture as "an integrated pattern of human behavior which includes but is not limited to thought, communication, languages, beliefs, values, practices, customs, courtesies, rituals, manners of interacting, roles, relationships, and expected behaviors of a racial, ethnic, religious, social, or political group; the ability to transmit the above to succeeding generations; dynamic in nature."[4]

This definition implies two dimensions of culture. First, there is what we see above the surface, which gives us one set of data. In addition, there is everything below the surface, which reveals deeper meanings.

The "iceberg" metaphor is often used to describe this dual nature of culture. Above the surface are the visible, outward signs of culture, such as food, dress, music, art, dance, literature, language, and celebrations. Below the surface are the more subtle and invisible ways that culture influences our worldview. Here is where we encounter attitudes and values—for example, notions of modesty, concepts of beauty, and relationships with nature. Here is also where we find competitive or cooperative ways to engage with people, patterns of emotional response, relationships to time and space, and styles of nonverbal communication (such as eye contact and gestures). We could each give many more examples.

This view of culture has two key implications. One is that when we focus on only the tip of the cultural iceberg—visible differences between people—we limit our ability to be aware of, and to engage deeply with, individuals and communities. Second, our conversations about race, religion, geography, age, sexual identity, and other cultural markers tend to focus on marginalized communities. This reinforces the false notion that the dominant, or mainstream, culture is the norm rather than a culture like other cultures.

For example, a participant in one of our workshops described a time she was named on a list of resource people in her field. Next to her name were the words *African American.* Other people of color on the list were identified as *Asian* or *Latino.* Also included were names with no such identification, the assumption being that someone was White unless otherwise noted. Practices such as these impair our ability to recognize and respectfully engage with groups and communities.

Competency is a measure of knowledge and skill in a particular field of practice. At its deeper level, competency is also a commitment to something more than the cultivation of a skill set.

We chose this term to frame our work, recognizing that *cultural competency* is a term that has been used to exploit communities' frustrations over the challenges of engaging with each other with integrity. Some people who identify themselves as *diversity* or *cultural competency trainers* provide a series of parlor tricks that, at best, amount to superficial tools. When they do most harm, these trainers nurture stereotypes and open up fissures between people or groups without healing them.

In my experience, cultural competency is a way of being in the room. This means bringing my whole self to the encounter and seeing everyone else in their complexity. For me, cultural competency also means delighting in that complexity.

Capacity building is the "process of developing and strengthening the skills, instincts, abilities, processes, and resources that organizations and communities need to survive, adapt, and thrive in the fast-changing world."[5]

Culturally competent capacity building is, of course, the subject of this book, which we also refer to as *culturally based work* by capacity builders. We start with a definition created by the People of Color Affinity Group of the Alliance for Nonprofit Management:[6]

> Culturally competent capacity building is a community-centered process that begins with an understanding of historical realities and an appreciation of the community's assets in its own cultural context. The process should enhance the quality of life, create equal access to necessary resources, and partner with the community to foster strategic and progressive social change.

This definition is distinctive, emphasizing "three Cs" of effective capacity building:

■ *Context:* understanding historical and cultural realities that relate to the current situation

■ *Community:* using a process that stays centered in a group of people who face their own unique challenges and possibilities

■ *Change:* altering conditions in ways that advance equity for people and communities of color

What holds these three threads together is recognizing that this is a time-consuming journey. The journey itself is at least as important as the destination.

What You Can Gain from This Book

This is not a how-to manual. Rather, this book frames several key issues related to cultural competency in capacity building. Here you will find a set of principles and way of thinking. Use this book to guide your journey as you pay attention to culture in all aspects of your work with nonprofit organizations.

We hope that this book will help you meet the challenges of cultural competency and move the conversation in a positive direction. In these pages you will find examples of culturally based capacity building with individuals, organizations, and communities.

Our audience includes capacity builders in all their forms. Some of you already pay significant attention to race, class, and culture in your work. For others, this book may be an invitation to take a first look. In either case, we provide fundamental knowledge that nonprofit capacity builders—particularly, consultants and funders—can use to become more effective.

Write Your Own Definition

Take a minute now to write your own definition of cultural competency:

_____

_____

_____

_____

_____

_____

_____

_____

_____

_____

Welcome back! How did it go? E-mail us your definition at *culturalcompetency@allianceonline.org*

We encourage you to identify your own understanding of cultural competency and other key terms used in this book, and to do so in a way that celebrates and transforms your practice. Our aim is to support you as you identify your own cultural locations and the impact of culture in your work.

Reading this book will not make anyone proficient in culturally competent capacity building. Rather, this publication offers one way to begin or continue a long journey of changing the field—building awareness, commitment, and demand for a way of working that pays attention to culture. With this offering, our hope is to release the power of the capacity-building field and deepen its positive impact on communities of color and society as a whole.

When it comes to cultural competency, there is no entry by default. People of color are not culturally competent simply by virtue of birth or upbringing. During roundtables at the 2005 conference of the Alliance for Nonprofit Management, we learned that when a group talks about capacity building through the lens of culture, the exchange reveals deep insights about every community. This is an open field. No one is automatically entered, and everyone can participate if they are willing to make a significant commitment and do the hard work.

This is the first in a series of publications that the Alliance set out to develop, as an organization or through its members. Our hope is that publications that follow, online or in print, will apply cultural competency to many aspects of capacity building, such as generation change and executive transitions, coaching, strategic planning, and board development.

We expect that publications sparked by Alliance for Nonprofit Management's Cultural Competency Initiative (CCI) will be of particular interest to consultants and other technical assistance providers, grantmakers, and philanthropic organizations. We believe that nonprofit capacity builders who play other roles—nonprofit executives, researchers, communications professionals, coalition builders, and the like—will find this work useful. We expect that the framework, the perspectives, and the literature review will be helpful to leaders of *any* organization, business, or community that is serious about increasing its cultural competency, even if it is not in the nonprofit sector.

There are many organizations and individuals whose life work is addressing the challenge of cultural competency. This book adds one more voice to the community. We hope it will be a springboard for many conversations within the capacity-building field and the nonprofit sector as a whole.

In the following chapters we articulate the values that shape a culturally based approach, including knowing and appreciating the tremendous wisdom that exists within the individuals, organizations, and communities with whom we do this work. That includes an assumption of the wisdom that you hold as you read this book. The Alliance for Nonprofit Management looks forward to a long-term dialogue within the capacity-building field related to strengthening our cultural competency. Please send your ideas to culturalcompetency@allianceonline.org.

The Process behind This Book

In many cultures, a product is only considered to be as good as the process by which it is developed. We believe this to be true of this work. Throughout the text, we will share insights into our process so that you can "walk the walk" with us.

This book brings the rich experience of a life's work from many capacity builders. That process began when the Alliance for Nonprofit Management launched a Cultural Competency Initiative (CCI). This involved a team from the People of Color Affinity Group that aimed to document culturally based practices and proposed a book project to the Alliance.[7] (More information about the Cultural Competency Initiative is available online at www.allianceonline.org.)

Our methodology included gathering and sharing stories. Through a range of methods—literature review, personal interviews, peer dialogue, insights of contributing authors, and workshops—we have unearthed some of the most important advances in culturally based capacity building.

One of the results was our choice to focus on race and ethnicity as the primary dividing line in the United States. At the same time, our commitment was to remain mindful of intersections between topics. Our overall analysis of power includes other important aspects of identity, such as gender, sexual orientation, class, religion, and geography.

It is impossible to completely convey the power of cultural dynamics in a publication. Nevertheless, I jumped at the chance to work on this project with the Alliance for Nonprofit Management. Besides me, this collaboration involved other authors and members of the Alliance's People of Color Affinity Group, Brigette Rouson, Heather Iliff, and others who were on the Alliance staff. We could not have done this work without strong support from Roni Posner and Tangie Newborn (both former executive directors of the Alliance) and from supportive board members, including David Maurrasse, Frank J. Omowale Satterwhite, Natalie Abatemarco, and Alan Bromberger.

How This Book Is Organized

One goal of this book is to underscore the complexity within ethnic communities. Part One embodies this perspective. It presents the landscape of five major ethnic communities in the United States. You will note distinct voices in these chapters, which were contributed by different writers. That difference is due to writing styles *and* to a larger cultural milieu. Note the richness of these voices and the beauty in their differences. After you read each chapter in Part One, take a minute to think about the multiple layers of insight that come to you.

The perspective of any writer can represent only one element of a community and by no means the whole. We hope this book will dispel notions that any community is monolithic. There are overlapping boundaries between communities, and readers may identify with a racial or ethnic group not named in this book. Even so, Part One offers a way to start appreciating the distinctions among and within groups, along with the complexity of cultural identity and organizational change.

Note that this part of the book includes a White, or European American, voice. This was done to acknowledge that White identity is not neutral or the default setting for conversations about cultural competency. We can better understand the dynamics of difference by paying attention to this voice as one among many others.

About the Organizations Involved in This Book

This book comes from the Cultural Competency Initiative (CCI). In order to advance a high level of cultural competency in nonprofit and other sector leadership, CCI offers practical approaches for honoring cultural identity. The focus is on promoting racial equity as well as intersections among identities. CCI generates awareness through online resources, conference sessions, and a series of publications online and in print. The purpose is to set standards of practice, facilitate peer dialogue, and provide training.

CCI was created by members of the People of Color Affinity Group from the Alliance for Nonprofit Management. Formed in 2001, this group offers a forum for capacity builders of color to share experiences and expand the presence of people of color in the field. Most important, the group serves to catalyze change in the nonprofit sector and ultimately the larger society.

By gathering people of African, Asian, Latino, Native/American Indian, and Arabic ancestry, the People of Color Affinity Group accelerates peer learning and challenges business as usual. Recognition, resources, multi-ethnic collaboration, mentoring, marketing, and partnership are tools for doing that. The group seeks to turn nonprofit capacity building into a force for progressive social change.

Part Two of this book offers a framework for cultural competency in capacity building. The chapters in this part of the book are based directly on the "three Cs" included in our earlier definition of cultural competency:

- Cultural competency as discovering *context*
- Cultural competency as a *community* process
- Cultural competency as *changing* institutions

Part Two concludes with an invitation to continue the conversation about cultural competency.

Part Three is the resource section of this book. Readers will find material to support insights of the authors and ways to apply the concepts. This section points to resources already published, current perspectives, needs and possibilities, documented strategies, and a bibliography for further reading.

Again, each part of this book is based on the imperative for social change. We expect that engaging with the cultural competency framework will be more than an exercise in skill building. It is a journey toward building a just society. We can arrive at a just society only if we have practiced justice along the way.

Some Questions and Answers about Cultural Competency

Why is the Cultural Competency Initiative dedicating resources to creating and sharing tools?

"Nonprofit/philanthropic organizations and leadership have not kept pace with the dramatic cultural change in the world around us. To some extent, the tools we are using are like typewriters in a world of Internet cultural competence. As a field, we must become more deliberate about our preparation for the future."—*Ron McKinley, project director, Fieldstone Alliance Kellogg Action Lab*

Why is moving beyond "diversity" essential for nonprofit leaders?

"Diversity may vary the faces, but not necessarily the thinking or the outcomes. As the community-building field matures, it becomes more apparent that culturally based capacity building is a fundamental prerequisite for achieving genuine social change in communities of color. Conventional technical assistance programs are not effectively addressing the complex capacity-building needs of these communities."—*Frank J. Omowale Satterwhite, founding president, founder and senior advisor, National Community Development Institute*

I'm not a person of color; how does cultural competency relate to my work?

"The Cultural Competency Initiative addresses the simple fact that everyone is a cultural being. This work cultivates a cross-cutting skill set to bring out the best of all the cultures that influence nonprofit organizations and communities."—*Roni Posner, principal, Posner Associates*

What is important to understand about how cultural competency affects my work?

"As nonprofit leaders and technical assistance providers, we need to understand how group dynamics, race, power, and privilege influence organizations both internally and externally. We also need to challenge ourselves to remember that things that work for mainstream or large institutions may not necessarily work for grassroots organizations or communities of color."—*Vicki Asakura, executive director, Nonprofit Assistance Center*

Part One

Practitioner Perspectives from Five Major Ethnic Communities

Overview

Our goal in this section is to help you, the reader, see the complexity of each ethnic community. We hope this will move the field closer to dispelling whatever notions are still out there that communities are monolithic. Even what we've shared with you has come through the lens of each writer, who represents one element of a community and not the community itself. You will note distinctly different voices in each section. That is not only due to the individual writing styles of each person, but it reflects the cultural milieu within which he or she writes.

Each of us was asked to write a piece with these guidelines:

- Describe the landscape of a particular community.
- Look at the implications for capacity building in particular communities.
- Document the writer's journey through the topic.

I was delighted to get a chance to read each piece. The differences in style are more than personal. They are embedded in the cultural ways of the author and reflect a cultural perspective.

We recognize that we limit the discussion to some extent by focusing on these particular communities (African American, Asian American, European American, First Nations People, and Latino/Latina). There are many people in the United States whose cultural identity doesn't fit neatly into one of these racial or cultural boxes. Arab Americans are an example. In addition, we didn't pull out specific perspectives from the disability community, LGTBQ community, or other cultural groups. We also didn't focus specifically on gender or age, each of which could be the topic of a whole paper. The primary reason for this decision is that in the U.S. social system and power structures, race is still the major fault line. As you will read in the contributors' sections, race has been at the heart of the taking and growing of this country. In each of the categories we mention, there are people who are bi: biracial, bilingual, bicultural, bisexual. This increases the complexity of our work and makes it richer at the same time.

Other important factors to consider as we work in multicultural settings include the unfamiliarity with notions of "race" to many immigrants; even when they come from countries that are multi-ethnic. Most other societies don't form themselves around this issue the way the United States does. I was facilitating training for consultants who were discussing the definition of race. As I roamed around the room, catching tidbits of conversation, I overheard one particular conversation where a woman who is an immigrant from East Africa said: "We don't talk about race in my country. We have ethnic struggles, but the basis for the struggle is not framed as ethnic or cultural." Another member of the group, from South America, concurred: "It wasn't until I came to the U.S. that I was a 'person of color.' At home we all share the same national identity and don't make the distinctions that you make here in the U.S."

In addition to the implications for capacity building that are laid out in each section, I think it's important to look at two dynamics that may be going on within communities that are rooted in the racialized systems we've created over time. The first is internalized oppression. For each segment of each community, internalized oppression has a different face. It can look like anger or rage. It can look like despair or hopelessness. It can also look like hyper-achievement or bravado. Whatever it looks like, it has deep roots in every community and is often overlooked when we examine contributing factors to a person, an organization, or a community's identity. *As a capacity builder, we might ask ourselves: What does my internalized oppression look like? How am I dealing with it? How can I engage this particular person, organization, or community to address its own internalized oppression? What are the strategies they need to develop for dealing effectively with internalized oppression?*

Another implication for capacity building is the temptation of the *hierarchy of oppression,* or as the Generation X'ers say, Oppression Olympics! One of the consequences of a racist structure is that it pits one marginalized group against another to ensure they don't create power in solidarity. This is so inculcated in the process of creating and maintaining a racist system that it doesn't have to remain a conscious process. It's in the water, as they say. One of the unfortunate consequences is that we have created pressure on everyone to engage with the structure through the lens of their oppression. Once that is done, the race to the bottom begins. It's where each community of color lays claim to having been most oppressed and can't see the connections with other forms of oppression. It is also where the charges of reverse racism come from. In the nonprofit world, we have seen funders fuel this phenomenon by looking to see where the *greatest needs are* in determining funding priorities. Nonprofits often respond by describing communities from a deficit perspective, trying to prove their constituent group is more disadvantaged than others. We have seen a wedge drawn between immigrant rights and racial justice, reinforcing rigid racial hierarchies (Quiroz-Martinez, pp. 18–12, *The Nonprofit Quarterly,* 2002).

It's deadly to the process of social change.

We invite you now to listen to the voices of these particular writers, each of whom represents a portion of a community. Note the richness of the voices, the beauty in their differences. *After you read each one, take a minute to think about what you've read and how it was written. See the multiple layers of insight that come to you from that reflection.*

Caucasian perspective: Beth Applegate
Asian American/Pacific Islander perspective: Vicki Asakura
African American perspective: Monika K. Moss
Indigenous perspective: Patricia St.Onge
Latino perspective: Alfredo Vergara-Lobo

Chapter 1

My Journey Is a Slow, Steady Awakening

There is no single defining moment in my childhood or adulthood based on my race that stands out positively or negatively as *the* experience that shaped and deepened my commitment to racial and social justice. Rather, my journey continues to be a slow, steady awakening about what I fail to notice and the connection to my own White privilege.

As I consider what my fellow contributors will share about their personal journeys as people of color, it reminds me once again: I spend little time thinking about myself as a White person. Unlike my colleagues, and because of White privilege, I experience the truth of James Baldwin's observation that "being White means never having to think about it."[8] White space is not racialized as it is for people of color.

I am a White person working in organization development (OD) and non-profit capacity building. I am also committed to racial equity, social justice, and the conscious, intentional use of myself as a means to effect systemic social change. I offer organization development services to the nonprofit sector in the United States to intentionally create an equitable society and improve the human condition. This core value frames my client engagement and supports me in my role as "critical friend."

In this role, and based on my core values, I partner closely with each client to understand not only what the organization intends to accomplish but also the organization's readiness for change. From there, I co-design inquiry and action processes with them. I recognize and deeply value my clients' own expertise in their fields of work and their direct understanding of the challenges that their organizations face. In this way, I build on clients' perspectives as I help them move forward. I am also, however, prepared to challenge clients' assumptions and norms as a "critical friend."

Finally, throughout my OD work with clients, I strive to support my clients' abilities and willingness to bring underlying social identities and the dynamics of internalized dominance and internalized subordination into collective awareness. The purpose is to challenge oppression and privilege and make visible the underlying assumptions that produce and reproduce organizational, societal, and global structures of domination. As a result, clients' systems are more prepared to engage in alternative possibilities, create equitable organizational change processes, and make more informed choices that advance fair organizational structures and systems, promoting racial justice and social responsibility.

Coming to Terms with "Double Consciousness"

It was hard at first to admit that despite being committed to racial equity, I have beliefs, behaviors, and assumptions based on *internalized racist superiority*. This is defined as

> A complex multigenerational socialization process that teaches White people to believe, accept, and live out superior societal definitions of self and to fit into and live out superior societal roles. These behaviors define and normalize the race construct and its outcome: White supremacy.[9]

As a White antiracist, I experience a *double consciousness*. This term comes from W.E.B. DuBois, who described a social and spiritual split experienced by people of color.[10] My experience as a White antiracist cannot be directly compared to the kind of double consciousness that he describes. Yet I must, as Christine Clark suggests, "become and unbecome White, and own and disown my racial identity."[11] I must stay aware that I operate from the filters imposed by my racial identity as a White person—and from the beliefs, behaviors, and assumptions of White supremacy.

Just as I learn to manage a double consciousness as a White antiracist, so I remain vigilant as a White organizational development practitioner and capacity builder. While I work to create an equitable society, I am also influenced by theories of the field. These explanations of reality have been largely shaped by the dominant racial group and, mostly, by White men. Often, however, these theories are promoted by White men *and* women throughout the nonprofit sector. Examples surface during conversations about common concepts in the field: discussions about best practices, about what is professional, and ways of knowing that are not linked to formal education. In the end, it is about deciding which experiences count. In each case, organizations operate out of a mainstream worldview—that is, a White worldview.

Understanding the systemic nature of White supremacy affirms that I can be the subject of discrimination based on gender and sexual orientation. Being a White lesbian raises my awareness of oppression. Society's ideas about what is normal—its beliefs, rituals, institutional rules, and rewards—all extend privilege to heterosexuals while denying basic civil rights to same-sex couples. Proposed laws do the same, including the Defense of Marriage Act. Much like White privilege, heterosexism reinforces heterosexuality as the norm and other sexual orientations as inferior.

At the same time, I can be an agent of the dominant racial group, which discriminates based on race. Even though I may be the subject of discrimination based on my sexual orientation, I remember that "privileging" simultaneously occurs because I am White. Because of their membership in a racialized group, women of color who are lesbians will experience additional oppression in different ways from me.

Managing a Lingering Fear

I use sociopolitical and scientifically based tools and methodologies to gather information and to inform dialogue. The approaches I formulate are designed to achieve as comprehensive a picture of the organization's situation as possible, making practical use of available resources. I assist clients to meaningfully interpret the data and apply new knowledge to envision their options and to advance their long-term aims. I am also attentive to the importance of substantive, flexible, and transparent planning processes for promoting stakeholder buy-in and commitment.

Part of my role is to ensure that methodologies for assessment, outreach, communication, and implementation have credibility to diverse stakeholders both within and outside the organization. I help clients approach change through sound, evidence-based analysis, and decision making that considers many perspectives and potential impacts.

My work can be laudable, and I can point to positive effects. Yet at a personal level it remains difficult for me to address racism in the nonprofit organizations I serve. Each day I muster the courage and energy to interrupt the White privilege and racism in myself and with other White people. I must, as Peggy

Macintosh talked about at the ninth annual White Privilege Conference, "load new software every day" in order to, as Barbara Love said at the same conference, interrupt the patterns of thought and behavior that I learned through an oppressive socialization process. Simultaneously, I must also interrupt my fear of "being seen and seen-through" by people of color.[12] Especially when we talk about race, the fear that Robert Jensen describes is visceral for me:

> What if People of Color can look past my anti-racist vocabulary and analysis and sense that I don't know how to treat them as equals? What if they know about me what I don't dare know about myself? What if they can see what I can't even voice about my fear?[13]

In April 2008 at that conference I co-designed and facilitated a session called "The Critical Liberation of White Women—What Are We Fighting For?" The focus was to create a place for White women to talk about the dynamics of internalized dominance and internalized subordination and how those dynamics keep us from effectively partnering and building coalitions to dismantle racism and other forms of oppression. It was also a time and place to develop our thinking as and for White women about what it means and what it will take to develop critical liberation praxis.

We made fifty copies of our handout, and conference organizers closed the session doors to a room of nearly seventy-five White women of all ages, sizes, gender expressions, and sexual orientations. Who knew that other White women besides my co-presenter and me needed and wanted to gather and share our experiences, struggles, and hopes as White allies?

My colleague and I developed a set of handouts based on our own patterns of behaviors, attitudes, and feelings that create divisiveness. We asked participants to notice where they did and did not resonate with the list of patterns, to reflect on the multiple self-identities that might be operating and at risk in the room, and to notice where they felt threatened or scared. Items for reflection included the following:

White Women among White Women:

1. _____ If confronted on White privilege and racist attitudes or behaviors, I focus on sexism and other subordinated group identities.

2. _____ If it gets too hard, I withdraw, shut down, or claim that I am not feeling "safe" as a way to avoid doing the work.

3. _____ I focus primarily on the individual level and not the group level: *They don't like me. I'm not likable or competent. I'm a bad person.*

4. _____ It takes vigilance and is exhausting to track myself and interrupt racist attitudes, thoughts, and behaviors; it's easier to not pay attention.

5. _____ I often work alone or as the only White woman on staff.

White Women among People of Color:

1. _____ I seek approval/validation from people of color: *Am I doing it right? Am I OK? I'm a good White person, right?*

2. _____ I seek relationships with people of color, not White women allies.

3. _____ I use people of color as confessors: *Here's what I did/said/thought; is it OK?* Meaning, *Am I OK?*

4. _____ I struggle to develop an internal sense of what is just and right and use people of color as the measuring stick.

5. _____ It is an ego boost for me to be included by men of color and women of color in their circles.

This experience reinforced another one of my core values: We often lead where we most need to learn. To practice "inserting the new software" and to manage the fears I shared above, I consciously seek opportunities like the White Privilege Conference and my ongoing White Women's Caucus to re-examine myself and the way I am within my immediate family, community, and client systems. As a result, I better understand some of the themes that flow through my life. These have made me the sister and daughter, friend, partner, and organization development scholar-practitioner that I am today. Some of the learning experiences make me proud and some bring up shame, but all have been instructive.

My current learning edge involves practicing daily enactments, which means making constant and intentional choices. One example is based on my awareness of the dynamics of oppression and my awareness of the roles played by each individual in the maintenance of that system. When I find myself in assessment or judgment, my daily enactment is to name the fear of connecting with the other or myself as quickly as possible. Then I intentionally choose to reframe the patterns of thought and behavior (learned through an oppressive socialization process) by being intentional about my role and choices in working toward liberation.

At times this journey is scary and painful. It is also a boundless gift, giving me the inspiration and courage to continue my journey better able to embrace my human imperfections. What I know for sure is this: The more I learn about White privilege, the more I learn what I *don't* know about White privilege. Claiming the identity of a lifelong learner, I remain a work in progress. I continue to fine-tune. I continue to use myself as a positive instrument for change.

White Privilege in the United States— A Historical Framework

In her keynote speech at the 2006 White Privilege Conference, Barbara Love made this point: "No White people came to this country. . . . They were French, Spanish, German, Jewish, and Irish, etc. The construction of Whiteness was specifically created to dominate and oppress."[14] Europeans only began to think of themselves as White and superior to people of color during the slave trade. For hundreds of years prior to this, Europeans did not think in terms of race.[15]

The United States government used laws and policies to establish intentional systems of advantages and rewards. These successfully institutionalized racism, ensuring that White people benefited over people of color. A prominent example is the U.S. Constitution. The founding fathers drafted a document based on equality, liberty, the rights of men, and the pursuit of happiness. At the same time, this document excluded native peoples and defined African Americans as real estate (counted as three-fifths of a person for purposes of taxation).[16]

Emancipation was followed by one hundred more years of institutionalized White privilege through the enactment of Black Codes, Jim Crow laws, and convict leasing. The Triangular Trade—commerce in sugar, slaves, and manufactured goods that linked Europe, West Africa, the West Indies, and the eastern seaboard of the United States—created unprecedented wealth. In the United States and allied nations, the industrial revolution was backed by the slave trade.[17]

During the New Deal in the 1930s, government-sponsored programs and policies supported White privilege and racism. These included the Social Security Act, which was set up primarily to benefit White male workers during the Depression. While many people with jobs could contribute to Social

Security, millions more were not eligible. Among them were people of color who earned too little to participate. The unprecedented transfer of wealth from the U.S. government to White people as individuals has never again been matched.[18] The whole system of invisible and unearned assets still benefits White people today.

Taking Responsibility for Privilege and Moving Beyond It

At the 2008 White Privilege Conference, the theme was "Critical Liberation Praxis—Creating Transformation for Social Justice." The focus was on clarifying, describing, and creating practice/praxis that focuses on where we are going (liberation) rather than where we are coming from (oppression, White privilege)—on what we want (liberation) rather than on what we don't want (White privilege, White supremacy, oppression).

I was involved in several conversations about the need to find the words for understanding and moving beyond the racial categories and system of oppression without perpetuating White privilege. We identified the need to answer questions such as, How do we stop identifying on the basis of race without denying race? We deepened our awareness and understanding through organized sessions and casual conversations about what it means to study White privilege—not to learn more about White privilege, but rather to see what it can teach us about liberation.

Further, there was a strong sense of urgency about antiracist White people overtly reclaiming pride in being White as a means of furthering the liberation struggle. We were challenged to define what it means to be White so that White extremists do not continue to co-opt and define Whiteness and what it means to be proud.

As a result of attending that conference, I was reminded that my power comes from fully understanding and taking ownership of my White privilege and then using it to continually interrupt racist practices where I find them. I can do this while remembering, in the words of Audre Lorde, that "the true focus of revolutionary change is to see the piece of the oppressor inside us."[19] According to Beverly Tatum,

> Cultural racism is the cultural images and messages that affirm the assumed superiority of Whites and the assumed inferiority of people of color. It is like smog in the air. Sometimes it is so thick it is visible,

other times it is less apparent, but always, day in and day out, we are breathing it in.[20]

I believe we must clear the smog before our eyes. Instead of relying on people of color to do the work for us, we as White people can take full responsibility for educating ourselves about the impact of White culture, White privilege, and racism. We also need to educate ourselves about other cultures. Then we can more effectively join with people of color as partners, change agents, and fellow self-liberators.

Think Beyond "Diversity"

The praxes of the various models used to examine difference have been shaped by evolving mental models over time. For example, multiculturalism often seeks to acknowledge the appreciation of differences through periodic cultural celebrations. Diversity takes a step forward, albeit primarily in compartmentalized actions such as

▪ Hiring more people of color and women

▪ Implementing onetime diversity and anti-bias training sessions

▪ Acknowledging differences (though rarely through a lens of systemic privilege, power, and oppression)

Today in the nonprofit sector, the terms *multiculturalism* and *diversity* are giving way to the terms *cultural competency, cultural fluency, cultural humility,* and the term that most resonates with me, *critical cultural competency.*

Diversity describes one aspect of cultural competency: the extent to which an organization has people from diverse backgrounds or communities involved as board members, staff, and volunteers. Differentiating between the terms *diversity* and *critical cultural competency* emphasizes that representing diverse communities within an organization does not always lead to deeper respect for and incorporation of the needs, assets, and viewpoints of diverse communities.

This newer and still evolving thinking about critical cultural competency is more holistic. It analyzes systemic issues of privilege, power, and oppression and asks the question "Toward what end?" Critical culturally competent practitioners use a variety of tools such as system theory and action research to uncover root causes at the organizational cultural level. These tools become means to managing different social identities in ways that support people in functioning effectively in the context of cultural differences and in critically incorporating the sociopolitical history and realities into the organizational culture. The potential advantages of critical cultural competency for organizational or group performance are maximized, while the potential disadvantages of multiculturalism or diversity frameworks are minimized.

Look for Signs of Critical Cultural Competency in Organizations

Maurianne Adams and her co-authors offer a useful analytic tool in the simple question, "In whose interest is the prevailing organizational system operating?"[21] In broad terms, we can begin to say that an organization is culturally competent when

■ Every constituency group involved in the work of the organization understands how critical cultural competency is integrally linked to the mission—the very essence of the organization

■ The organization is seen to be "walking the talk"—that is, reflecting the attitudes, values, and behaviors described in the mission

■ Commitment to inclusion is demonstrated in behaviors, structures, publications, policies, plans, programs, and practices

■ This demonstration takes place at many levels—in board members, executive leaders, managers, staff members, volunteers, and members

■ The organization incorporates the needs, assets, and perspectives of a diverse workforce into inclusive decision making and delivery of programs and services

■ The organization recruits and retains diverse staff, board members, and volunteers to reflect the different composition of the communities they serve

■ The organization invests in group-process skills at the levels of board members and staff leaders

■ Nonprofit board and staff leadership develop group leadership skills that encourage constructive conflict and critical culturally competent communication

■ Beyond involving diverse individuals, there is the culture of a learning organization—one that encourages insights from communities of color; from lesbian, bisexual, and transgender people; from low income, differently abled, and young people; and more

Translate Theory into Powerful Practices

Kurt Lewin, a pioneer of organization development, once said, "There is nothing so practical as a good theory." A theoretical framework that helps us make sense of what we observe in our client systems, in communities, and in the nonprofit sector is a valuable resource. I have found as a White antiracist professional that it has been helpful for me to answer questions such as these:

■ How do I ensure that the body of knowledge, norms, and mental models associated with White culture are not simply accepted as the standard, rather than being understood in reference to other cultures?

■ How do I use our White social identity and the unearned advantages it gives us to interrupt and weaken systems of advantage and address White privilege and racism within the organizational systems I serve?

■ How do I create partnerships with people of color in the organizational systems I serve?

On the path toward critical cultural competency, organizations will encounter situations where their formerly successful ways of operating don't work anymore. If they take a good look, though, many organizations may be surprised to find that their people on all levels have many transferable skills and competencies that the organizations have never drawn upon. Qualities that have become important are often missed because the dominant culture in the organization shuts them out from the beginning.

Conversely, when people simultaneously examine the issues of dominance, power, and oppression—and when leaders model a commitment to build a critical culturally competent culture—energy is unleashed. People come forward and offer to help. They step up to the challenges because they believe that who they are, what they know, and what they do matters.

Case Study: Three Dimensions of Critical Cultural Competency

I saw this new set of possibilities firsthand while assisting a nonprofit client—a progressive, advocacy-based civil rights organization—to build the organization's critical cultural competency. In the process, the organization as a whole created new mental models that brought the performance of this nonprofit into alignment with its mission. This choice required members of the client organization to

- Reexamine their core values, vision, and mission
- Develop a new culture through a systemic lens of power, privilege, and oppression among and between the full board and staff
- Speak openly, knowledgeably, and compassionately about the intersection of systemic privilege, power, and oppression at play within the organization
- Speak in the same way about the different and overlapping individual cultural locations within that systemic framework
- Strive to build a community of inclusion throughout a thirty-two-month process

The combination of theory, tools, and exercises that we chose to support this client were adapted from a model created by John D. Adams, which he describes as six dimensions of a sustainable consciousness.[22] This well-established behavioral science model is based in systems theory and action research.

My work with this client produced insights in three key dimensions. First, *critical cultural competency is a way of being, a way of viewing the world and showing up in all aspects of your life.* This is more than possessing a skill set. To ensure that critical cultural competency becomes a way of life for organizations, it is essential to examine the organizational culture. We must see how this culture is shaped by individual mental models that filter all external information and unconsciously shape our understanding of how the world works.

In this organization, for example, there was a rich conversation about *safe space,* a construct used by many nonprofit organizations. When difficult issues were raised, members sometimes checked out of the discussion, claiming that they felt "unsafe." After authentic and difficult discussion, White board members and staff leaders determined that they evoked "safe space" as a way to avoid or devalue the emotions of dealing with racism. In fact, they felt vulnerable, scared, uncomfortable with conflict, or afraid of rejection, rather than truly being unsafe.

Members of the organization moved forward by aspiring to a new construct: building a respectful and critical culturally competent learning community. *Respectful* includes characteristics such as active listening without prejudging or becoming defensive, and not withholding, shutting down, or demonizing others when difficult issues are raised. *Learning* means "leaning" into individual issues—even when feeling discomfort—as a means to becoming an ally and obtaining feedback. Learning also means the willingness to make mistakes, own them, learn from them, and apply those lessons. In other words, people embraced their identities as lifelong learners.

A second dimension of critical cultural competency is *being able to hold and value multiple perspectives.* As French writer Marcel Proust observed so long ago, "The real voyage of discovery consists not of finding new lands but of seeing the territory with new eyes." Critical culturally competent organizations embrace the idea of "one mission, multiple perspectives."

Members of this organization struggled with a conflict between two major perspectives: short-term and long-term. The organization was operating without strategic or operational plans that were written and approved. With the ongoing pressure to fulfill the organization's short-term mandate, longer-term cultural aspirations remained undeveloped. Our goal was to close the gap between their short-term mandate and their long-term process of culture change.

We used an exercise based on the *Fifth Discipline Fieldbook* called "fixes that backfire."[23] The key point is that many decisions carry long-term *and* short-term consequences, and the two are often diametrically opposed. In broad terms, what happens is this: A symptom of a problem cries out ("squeaks") for resolution. A solution is quickly implemented (the "fix"), which alleviates the symptom. However, the unintended consequences of the fix actually worsen the conditions that you want to correct.

This model yields some powerful questions: What are the undesirable or unintended consequences of focusing only on what needs immediate attention? How can you minimize these? What are the deeper problems that the organization faces? And what is the implicit goal behind every fix that backfires?

Board members and staff leaders concluded that cultural competency is built over the long-term; it is not a "quick fix." Realizing that they faced an ongoing, iterative process, people began to think in three-year cycles. Our initial efforts were viewed as the launch, or first cycle, to be followed by another cycle of practice and institutionalizing, and a final cycle where genuine breakthroughs would occur.

Third, *critical cultural competency implies social change.* Although the organizations that I often serve are deeply rooted in racial equity and social justice, those ideals are not fully realized. White privilege and racism persist. This fact creates opportunities for the progressive, advocacy portion of the nonprofit sector to live out its espoused values by building critical cultural competency.

My client organization set a goal to move its leadership team beyond the polarization created by "either or" thinking about power, privilege, and oppression. Members instead wanted to develop "both and" thinking that embraced multiple realities.

Certain tools and exercises helped the organization move toward this goal. One of them involves a distinction between target and nontarget groups, as defined by Valerie Bates.[24] *Target group* describes people of color and other marginalized populations who have been viewed as different and inferior in comparison to a dominant population. *Nontarget groups*, in contrast, promote a mainstream viewpoint and receive unearned privilege in such forms as increased longevity, higher employment, easier access to credit, and higher incomes.

After explaining this distinction, I asked members of the organization—both White and people of color—the following questions:

■ When have you been a member of a target group?

■ When have you been a member of a nontarget group?

■ What strengths resulted from your experiences as a member of either group?

■ Can you describe a time when you were treated better than others as a result of membership in a nontarget group?

■ Can you describe a time when you found yourself treating a person in a target group as less than yourself?

This exercise covers many aspects of the organization's culture associated with the dynamics of power, privilege, and oppression. People of color expressed surprise at the number of times they had been members of a nontarget group. Lesbian and gay members of the staff and board observed that they can experience discrimination based on their sexual orientation *and* privilege due to being White. Further, White gay men and lesbians came to understand that people of color who are gay and lesbian experience additional oppression in distinctive ways because of their membership in a racialized group. All of these are examples of "both and" thinking based on a holistic, systems approach. This way of thinking honors the intersection of individual cultural locations, social group identities, and community-wide interests.

In relation to the issues of power and privilege playing out in the organization, we did other exercises that revealed an individualistic culture based on "looking out for number one." White members of the organization shifted their operating questions from *Is racism and White privilege showing up in our organization?* to *How is White privilege and racism showing up?* They also moved from, *How can I eliminate my privilege?* to *How can I use my awareness of racism, privilege, and power to be more effective as an antiracist and catalyst for change?* This "reframe" allowed White members of the client organization to more fully accept their humanity, including their racism, and change what was hurtful to others and themselves with forgiveness and compassion.

Acknowledgments

The following individuals contributed their thoughts and challenged me to dig deeper in my exploration, understanding, and thinking about White privilege and racism: Jim Henkelman-Bahn, Margery Freeman, Judith Katz, Achebe Powell, Trish Kerlé, Maggie Potapchuk, Brigette Rouson, and Edith Seashore.

VICKI ASAKURA

Chapter 2
Each Generation Is Different

I am a third-generation (*Sansei*) Japanese American whose grandparents emigrated from Japan in the 1890s. I was born after World War II and raised in the Central Area of Seattle. At that time, the neighborhood was largely African American and Asian (Japanese, Chinese, and Filipino), but it was also surrounded by icons indicating that it had once been home to the Jewish community.

My African American friends would go to the small Japanese family-owned stores or to Chinatown to buy salted ginger, sour balls, and dried squid to snack with Asian American friends. Likewise, our own culture—how we spoke and choices of music and dance—was influenced by our African American friends. Our experience provided a context for understanding race and privilege that would shape our lives through the years to come.

My paternal grandfather was an entrepreneur as well as an adventurer, coming to a new land to make his riches and ultimately to return home. His native Japan had just emerged from a feudal period, which closed it off from most of the world for 250 years. Opportunities there were limited for younger sons of a large family. Like many immigrants of his era, he ended up staying in America and later brought a bride to Seattle through an arranged marriage.

Despite anti-alien land laws, my grandpa owned several hotels and a barbershop. He organized the Japanese Barber's Association in pre-World War II Seattle. He was also active in the Yamaguchi Kenjinkai, one of many associations providing mutual support to people who came from the same prefecture in Japan. (These associations are similar to Chinese family associations and the ethnic mutual assistance associations established by refugee groups after their arrival in the United States.)

Unlike most Japanese American families, neither my father nor mother was among the 120,000 people of Japanese ancestry living on the West Coast who were incarcerated during World War II. My father was drafted and served in the 442nd Infantry, a segregated Japanese American unit that was most highly decorated during World War II. Ironically, many of these soldiers had been recruited from behind barbed wire, where they had been placed for looking like the enemy. My mother was able to leave for Detroit immediately before the forced evacuation, an option that was not available to most.

The war experience had a profound impact on our community. It resulted in parents pushing their children to be the model minority, proving to the rest of America that we were loyal and good citizens. We did this in a quiet, uncomplaining manner through achieving academically, working hard, and staying "inside the box" to avoid embarrassing our families and the community. More than thirty years later, the redress movement provided the venue for many *Issei* (first-generation or immigrant) and *Nisei* (second-generation Japanese Americans) to talk publicly about the hardships endured during their internment as well as the personal and financial loss resulting from it.

My family's history and values strongly influenced who I am and the work I do. My father was involved in numerous civic activities and local politics. For example, he worked on the repeal of the anti-alien land law and ran unsuccessfully for state representative in the 1950s. In contrast, my recollection is that the Japanese American community was not active politically at that time. Perhaps it was discouragement and disillusionment with the political system that had failed them as U.S. citizens. In addition, most Japanese families had just returned from being incarcerated during Word War II, having lost money and property and having suffered mentally and physically from the uncertainty of this horrendous injustice. They focused on rebuilding their lives and enduring hardship so their children could be a part of the American dream.

The lack of political clout for Asian and Pacific Islanders is still hurting us, and my siblings and I have been engaged in community change. Today I am executive director of the Nonprofit Assistance Center, a diverse multi-ethnic organization focused on racial equity and social change through community capacity building and policy change. I chair the United Way of King County Employment Impact Council and serve on their Public Policy Committee. In addition, I serve as chair of the Alliance for Nonprofit Management's Cultural Competency Initiative Advisory Group and board member of the Northwest Area Foundation-funded BuRSST for Prosperity Initiative. I am a member of the Asian Pacific Directors Coalition, Minority Executive Directors' Coalition of King County (based in Seattle), Japanese American Citizens League, and the Tri-County Refugee Planning Committee executive committee.

Asian and Pacific Islanders in America: A Demographic Overview

Asian Pacific Islander is a classification that includes diverse ethnic, cultural, religious, and language groups. The term masks complexities and differences based on gender, sexual orientation, class, privilege, and other subgroupings. Within the Asian American community are refugees, immigrants, political refugees, and undocumented individuals as well as families with two, three, four, or five generations of history in the United States. Each generation differs from earlier ones, their values and beliefs shaped by external influences that are new and constantly changing. Also included among Asian Pacific Islanders (API) are many people of mixed heritage. Keep in mind that Pacific Islanders from U.S. territories and states such as Guam, American Samoa, or Hawai'i are not immigrants, unlike their counterparts from islands that fall outside U.S. jurisdiction.

Asian Americans and Pacific Islanders are among the faster growing populations in the United States. The Census Bureau estimates that there were nearly 14 million Asian Americans (AA) and one million Pacific Islanders (PI) in the United States as of 2004. Chinese (24 percent) are the largest AA group, followed by Filipino (20 percent), Asian Indian, Korean, Vietnamese, and Japanese. Native Hawai'ians (46 percent) followed by Samoan are the largest of the Pacific Islander groups. More than half of the Asian American population lives on the West Coast.[25]

When working with Asian Pacific Islanders, look for several important demographic factors that affect community capacity. Based on census data, for example, the Asian Pacific Islander community has the highest rate of families with multiple members in the workforce. It is not uncommon for Asian Pacific Islander wage earners to hold more than one job. This leaves them with less time for community and civic activities, family and school involvement, and self-development. In addition

■ Asians have both the highest and lowest college completion rates among all racial and ethnic groups.

■ There is a similar pattern for not completing a high school education. Fifty-nine percent of Hmong fall into this category, as do 53 percent of Cambodians, 49 percent of Lao people, and 38 percent of Vietnamese. In contrast, 14 percent of Koreans have not completed high school, nor did 13 percent of Filipinos, 9 percent of Japanese people, and 8 percent of Indonesians.

■ Even though they have a slightly higher rate of workforce attachment, Asians and Pacific Islanders are more likely to live in poverty than their White counterparts.

■ Hmong and Cambodians have poverty rates higher than any of the major racial and ethnic groups in the United States. Asian Americans have the highest rates of multiple wage earners, followed by Latino and Pacific Islanders.

■ More than one-third of the Asian population (4 million people) can be labeled with the term Limited English Proficient (LEP). This is true for 61 percent of Vietnamese, 58 percent of Hmong, 53 percent of Cambodians, 52 percent of Lao, 52 percent of Bangladeshis, 51 percent of Taiwanese, 46 percent of Koreans, and 45 percent of Chinese people. Twelve percent of Pacific Islanders are LEP, as are more than one-fourth of Tongans and Fijians.[26]

Asian Pacific Islander communities continually struggle with the lack of good demographic information. Data are not always disaggregated (separated by subgroupings), which means that the diverse range of needs within the community is not adequately recognized. Within the API category, smaller ethnic communities that have high needs are often dismissed by researchers as "statistically insignificant." Disaggregated data that reflect the diversity within the Asian Pacific Islander community will make it easier for its members and community-based organizations to make their case to funders and policy makers.

The Historical Context— Waves of Immigration and Prejudice

Why is culturally competent capacity building so important? There is an old saying about the importance of understanding the past to know where we are going in the future. As capacity builders, we are agents of social change. To work in and with the Asian Pacific Islander community, capacity builders need a historical context that includes the impacts of race, power, class, and privilege. This means understanding the dominance of the mainstream culture over communities of color, including exclusionary practices and systems that create structural racism.

The history of immigrants has been closely linked to the economic and political climates of their countries of origin as well as of the United States. Poor economic conditions in their homelands attracted early Asian immigrants, primarily men, to come as laborers to work in agriculture, logging, and fishing. Some came to build the great railroad system that connected the West Coast with the East. Some also came as indentured servants. In this land of opportunity, they also faced anti-immigrant sentiment that was rooted in fear and racism—a story that unfortunately repeats throughout history.

Often missing from the pages in our history books are details of the history and contributions of Asian Pacific Islanders and people of color in general. Among the early immigrants were the Chinese who came as early as 1849 in search of the "Mountain of Gold." Despite doing backbreaking and often dangerous work, they were viewed as a threat—particularly when economic times worsened. Anti-Chinese riots led to deaths and expulsion of hundreds of Chinese workers. The Foreign Miners Tax, passed in California in 1850, originally targeted Mexicans and was amended in 1852 to also prevent Chinese from competing with White miners and business owners.[27]

Similarly, Japanese, Koreans, and Filipinos immigrated to Hawai'i, Alaska, and the U.S. West Coast. They came to work on plantations, farms, in lumber mills, and in canneries. In addition, a community of agricultural workers from India settled in California in the early 1900s. All of these groups fell victim to a series of anti-immigrant legislation beginning with the Chinese Exclusion Act of 1892. This was followed by miscegenation laws and anti-alien land laws. Until 1952, immigration laws restricted Asian immigrants from becoming naturalized citizens. In Washington State, the anti-alien land laws from the 1920s were not repealed until 1966.[28]

Shortly afterward came a wave of change. The Civil Rights Act of 1968 and local fair housing ordinances addressed housing discrimination. Other laws passed in 1965 and later in 1975 allowed immigrants to be admitted on the basis of skills and relationship to family members already here. This resulted in a new wave of Asian immigrants from Hong Kong, Korea, the Philippines, India, and other countries. Immigrants who arrived during the 1970s and 1980s included many skilled professionals, and later immigrants have brought current technology skills.

Following the fall of Saigon in April 1975 and the end of the war in Southeast Asia, the U.S. government opened its doors to thousands of refugees from Vietnam, Cambodia, and Laos. This first wave of Southeast Asians consisted largely of former military and government officials and other professionals who supported the United States. Also included were a number of ethnic groups such as the ethnic Chinese, Hmong, Mien, Khmu, and the Khmer Krom, as well as the Cham, a Muslim and religious minority group. By 1990, former political prisoners released from re-education camps were allowed to join family members in the United States.

The next wave included the "boat people" who escaped by sea. Among them were ethnic minorities and less-educated refugees from fishing and farming backgrounds. Many Cambodian refugees who came in the late 1970s and 1980s had lived under the Pol Pot regime in which they had suffered the loss of family members and other atrocities. They were deprived of educational opportunities, contributing to high poverty levels and low education rates.

World War II, the Korean War, and the Vietnam War brought American military men, their Asian wives, and their Amerasian families to the United States. The Amerasian Homecoming Act of 1987 allowed Amerasian children born of American fathers to come to the United States, an opportunity that did not previously exist.[29]

Though these developments opened the doors of the United States to many Asian Pacific Islanders, immigrants from other parts of the world still face prejudice and discrimination. For example, it was reported that youth in the Pacific Northwest's Sikh community refused to uphold cultural and religious practices because of harassment and ridicule at school. This created discord with Sikh parents, causing additional stress within families.[30] The Sikh and Punjabi communities in the United States were also victims of hate crimes following 9/11, including a November 2007 incident in which a Sikh cab driver in Seattle was injured in an attack by a passenger who accused him of being a terrorist.[31]

Community-Based Organizations Emerged

Asian and non-Asian ethnic communities formed mutual support organizations, often supported by membership dues and donations from the community. Many new Asian Pacific Islander community-based organizations emerged after the civil rights movement in the 1960s. This was a time when a lot of federal funding was available to fight the "war on poverty." Within the Asian Pacific Islander community, there came a growing need for culturally competent services, including bilingual and bicultural staff.

Like their immigrant counterparts, refugee groups formed ethnic mutual assistance associations (MAAs) to provide needed social services and support to their community members following the arrivals of Southeast Asian refugees in 1975. Unlike other immigrant ethnic associations, however, early refugee MAAs had access to set-aside funding from the federal Office of Refugee Resettlement (ORR) to build ethnic community capacity. These resources helped many large ethnic-specific refugee organizations grow and develop. National organizations such as the Cambodian American Network Council, Hmong National Development Organization, National Alliance of Vietnamese American Service Agencies (NAVASA), and Southeast Asian Resource Action Center (SEARAC) also emerged.

In areas such as Washington, there was a specific focus on supporting coalitions of refugee MAAs. This led to creation of multi-ethnic refugee organizations, including the Refugee Federation Service Center (formerly Southeast Asian Refugee Federation) and the Refugee Women's Alliance (formerly Southeast Asian Women's Alliance). Both are examples of Southeast Asian organizations expanding to include all refugee groups. Many of the Asian Pacific Islander community-based organizations and the larger refugee-led organizations in Seattle began as direct service organizations. Over time, these organizations engaged in advocacy at an individual agency level and at a broader community level. This organizing occurred because of inequities and disparities in health care, education, jobs, and other workforce issues and housing, along with the need to change policies and institutional practices.

Many other national Asian Pacific Islander organizations advocate for racial equity and civil rights. They include groups such as the Japanese American Citizens League (JACL), Organization of Chinese Americans (OCA), and the Asian American Justice Center.

Implications for Capacity Building

The more a technical assistance provider, consultant, or funder knows about our community, the more effective the process of capacity building. A culturally competent consultant from the same community or a similar one will pick up on small but often important nuances that signal different values and larger variations in decision making and leadership.

Building capacity is difficult for newer communities, where leaders struggle to support their families while facing language and cultural barriers. As noted earlier, Asian Pacific Islander communities have diverse needs and varying levels of capacity. Some Asian Pacific Islander groups face the barriers of poverty, lack of access to resources, gender and generational differences, difficult board-staff relations, and funding gaps. Groups with less capacity need more hands-on technical assistance, implementation support, and help with delivering services in sustainable ways. In addition, smaller grassroots organizations often lack experience working with consultants. This may translate to different expectations regarding the role of the consultant, issues of trust, a lower priority on formal (including paid) assistance, and fewer consultants who are prepared to address the issues.

Established Asian Pacific Islander communities have had more time to build community capacity, infrastructure, and an economic base. Nonprofits within these communities typically have more capacity and experience, including the ability to draw upon a wider range of skills and expertise within their respective communities. Such groups tend to value strategic planning and being mission driven.

Good intentions can backfire without cultural context and understanding. During the 1970s and 1980s, for example, some well-intentioned people working with immigrant and refugee women encouraged them to stand up for their equal rights. Having come from countries that were male dominant, following this advice often created cultural and marital conflicts, resulting in divorce and social isolation.[32] Bilingual and bicultural staff who understood these changing power dynamics helped to mitigate problems within families. Over time, Asian Pacific Islander women have taken leadership roles to organize and address related issues, such as domestic violence and human trafficking.

At the Nonprofit Assistance Center, where I work, cultural competency plays a crucial role in both service delivery and in capacity building for nonprofits based in or serving the Asian Pacific Islander community. While writing this chapter, I spoke to a few people about key factors in selecting a technical assistance provider or consultant. Having a trust relationship with the capacity builder or other consultant ranked high. Knowledge about the Asian Pacific Islander community and knowledge of specific ethnic groups within this community was cited, along with having the required technical skills. Also important is empowerment: allowing a group to plan jointly with the consultant rather than expecting the consultant to come up with all of the answers.

Following are general suggestions for providing culturally competent services to Asian Pacific Islanders (including some that apply more to immigrant generations):

■ Recognize the importance of family in the care of elders, children, and others who are unable to fully care for themselves.

- Understand the importance of respect and pride. This implies reverence for the past, for tradition, and for elders. It also means not showing weakness to others.

- Honor values of duty, obligation, and repayment of debts of gratitude in response to a favor or act of kindness.

- Remember that respect and reputation are often more important than financial or material success.

- Keep in mind the high values placed on harmony and balance, resulting in some individuals and groups preferring to avoid conflict situations.

- Remember that the importance of the collective rather than the individual remains a touchstone.

- Realize that strong oral traditions are still a fact of life among some Asian Pacific Islanders.

Other factors to consider are the following:

Look for multiple identities. Depending on circumstance, Asian Pacific Islanders may identify by race and ethnic heritage. There are a growing number of mixed-race Asian Pacific Islanders as well. Another relevant factor is diversity in sexual orientation (LGTBQ). Capacity builders also need to look for distinct generational differences between Asian Pacific Islander youth and their parents. There are nuances in personal identity that depend on how long families have lived in the United States and whether they live in a tight-knit ethnic community.

Look for norms that affect sharing of information. Trust and relationships are extremely important when working in Asian Pacific Islander communities. Culture has a strong influence on what information is shared and with whom. This is based on common values and insight.

In Asian Pacific Islander communities, people are often discouraged from sharing problems with outsiders. At work, they may behave in the same way. Problems, if discussed at all, may be shared openly with only a select few. This occurs more often with older or immigrant generations.

"Pacific Islanders may face language and cultural barriers, experience poor communication with mainstream institutions, and lack access to quality education, job training, employment opportunities, and social and health services. Families may also lack the opportunity, confidence, and understanding of the processes for becoming involved in a community or democratic process. The most effective method of reaching and disseminating information to these families is through Pacific Islander local churches, community organizing, and culturally relevant family services and programs."
—*Sili Savusa, trusted advocate*

Look for indirect communication styles. In many Asian cultures, communication is often indirect and possibly more circular than linear. Because of a traditional focus on the team or collective, people often speak more in terms of "we" rather than "I."

Styles of communication are also influenced by values such as humility and the practice of downplaying one's own skills. This can lead to not taking full credit for accomplishments and struggles with "selling" personal strengths during an interview.

Expect body language to communicate different messages depending on whether you are from Eastern or Western culture. For example, in many Asian cultures, direct eye contact is viewed as disrespectful, while in Western culture lack of eye contact has negative connotations.

Learn about protocols tied to respect and position. Cultural competency includes understanding norms about who speaks, when they speak, and in what order. At the Nonprofit Assistance Center, we experienced a relevant example. An executive director and his staff from a refugee organization were in a meeting. A person who was neither refugee nor Asian Pacific Islander thought the executive director's presence prevented his staff from speaking. Out of respect and deference, however, staff members were waiting for their leader to speak first. In turn, the executive director felt reluctant to speak because he had an opinion that may not have been supported by people outside of his organization.

Many immigrants and refugees come from cultures where dissenting opinions are not valued. Members of these cultures may not be comfortable with group input during meetings about controversial topics. A Cambodian leader who had lived under the Pol Pot regime reminded us that people who gave opinions or dissented often disappeared in the middle of night and were killed.

> "Cultural competency is extremely important to organizations working in fields such as health or domestic violence. Service providers need to understand South Asian culture, including gender issues, relationships between men and women, and how issues such as HIV and birth control are addressed and received by the community."
> —*Pradeepta Upadhyay, executive director of Chaya*

Listen and observe carefully. A consultant with poor observation and listening skills will often miss key information. Some consultants approach work with the assumption that they have all of the answers. At the Nonprofit Assistance Center, we experienced a few situations where some technical assistance providers or consultants with high skills were unable to work effectively with certain groups because they took on a "missionary approach." They believed that they, not the groups, had all of the answers.

In contrast, consultants who listen to community members are more effective, particularly when they honor empowerment—an approach that engages the group to identify and work through their own solutions.

Notice the importance of consensus. Mainstream consultants often get frustrated with Asian Pacific Islanders and other communities of color because they use a slower, consensus-based process for making decisions. Using Robert's Rules of Order often creates conflict for new immigrant groups when a vote is called and the decision is made by a majority rather than the entire group. The lack of full agreement could create dissent and conflict.

Provide a role for community elders. In many refugee and immigrant communities, elders play a key role, even though they may not be as fluent in English or recognized by mainstream consultants as leaders. When it is difficult for elders to serve on nonprofit boards, we have suggested a policy of inviting them to serve in advisory groups instead.

Support leaders based in the community. A few years ago, the Nonprofit Assistance Center (NAC) that I lead was responsible for organizing a large community meeting that included focus groups with members of nine ethnic or language groups. NAC staff proposed that we train bilingual bicultural community leaders ("Trusted Advocates") to facilitate focus groups with members of their respective communities in their native language.

After overcoming some strong resistance, our approach succeeded. It allowed community members to participate directly in the process without interpreters. This was an example of our early efforts to create paid consultant opportunities for refugee and immigrant leaders, and it was empowering for them. This form of leadership is a key factor in building strong organizations. The success of many communities is tied to the success of grassroots organizations and their leaders, particularly as it relates to civic engagement, social justice, and human services.

There are different definitions and values around leadership. Some communities have leaders who are acknowledged by the community with this title, given as a result of earned respect and trust. There are also self-appointed leaders who often can bridge with the mainstream but are not viewed by their community as representatives. This often occurs among immigrants where leaders might be elders or others without a good command of English.

Asian Pacific Islanders and other communities of color often do not have representation or access. Their voices are marginalized and their work often unrecognized. These communities use nonprofits as a vehicle for social change and racial justice. We will need strong leaders and strong organizations to create lasting impact. J. D. Hokoyama, president and CEO of Leadership Education for Asian Pacifics (LEAP), founded that organization on the premise that leaders are made and not born, that they must know community issues, and that they must give back to the community. Leaders change communities. Strong leaders can retain their own culture while developing skills appropriate for success in diverse environments.

Understand customs related to giving. Asians are often taught to decline more than once before accepting a gift or offer of food or help. This is true regardless of need. Likewise, the person offering is also expected to ask more than once. The extent of such cultural practices may vary by ethnic group and generation. Yet understanding these customs is important when offering services to a person of Asian background.

Giving gifts and money are also tied to customs. Money is often given without "an ask." As a result, making a direct request for money or other help is difficult for many Asian Pacific Islanders.

Charitable giving is not foreign to Asian Pacific Islanders, however. Many immigrant families live with and support extended family members. They send money back home to support other family members through formal remittance services and informally through friends and family. Janet Gow Pettey in her book *Cultivating Diversity in Fundraising* describes numerous customs in Asian Pacific Islander traditions involving gifts of money.[33]

Remember the diversity within Asian Pacific Islander communities. It is also important to understand the history of Asian Pacific Islander communities and dynamics that exist *between* these groups, particularly for Pan-Asian or multi-ethnic organizations. The Asian Pacific Islander community itself is quite diverse. Values, communication styles, and practices vary significantly among individuals and organizations. There is no "one-size-fits-all" approach. Creating a strong and sustainable organization calls for legal and fiscal compliance while integrating flexible, culturally competent practices.

Look for issues related to race, power, and privilege. Funders have an enormous amount of power and privilege. They, too, have their circles of influence, which capacity builders (including intermediary organizations) have the opportunity to influence. The report *Mapping the Immigrant Infrastructure* notes that organizations found it difficult to get sufficient funding to develop their multicultural infrastructure and that funders did not always understand the complexities of the work.[34]

In addition, capacity builders of color have been passed over by some organizations due to the perception that their White colleagues have better access to resources. After living with years of internalized oppression and racism, some communities of color themselves feel the answers and knowledge exist outside of their communities rather than within.

An effective capacity builder, however, is one who supports solutions that originate within the affected community and who can guide this process to bring about community change. As capacity builders, we help organizations build their infrastructure and navigate multiple systems to carry out their mission and sustain their work. We often facilitate processes that allow answers and solutions to emerge from within a group rather than outside it.

Take time to build trust. Why do I do this work? What are the implications of my experiences for capacity building? My personal life experiences and values intertwined with my professional experience of providing capacity building have been the key to my success as a capacity builder. In my work with the refugee community, I have been told that that they see me as a fellow refugee, meaning that there is a special relationship of trust, respect, and understanding.

The rationale for building trust is that it offers a chance to influence individuals and groups, each with their own "circles of influence." Those who are in the inner circle have greater potential for influencing change than persons on the outer cores. Those in the inner circle also receive more detailed information, allowing for a better analysis and recommendation.

Funders are generally focused on results. They want to know how their investments increase organizational effectiveness and sustainability. For many communities, relationships rank high. To get results, first create trust.

Note: Source material for this chapter includes an interview with J. D. Hokoyama, president and CEO of Leadership Education for Asian Pacifics (LEAP) on April 3, 2006, Van Sar's dialogues with selected nonprofit leaders within the Cambodian Community during March 2006, and an April 4, 2006, interview with Pradeepta Upadhyay, current executive director of Chaya in Seattle and formerly with South Asian Network in Southern California.

Ike's Principles

Tsuguo "Ike" Ikeda was the executive director of Atlantic Street Center in Seattle for thirty-three years. Now in retirement, Ike continues to mentor leaders. He takes pride in sharing his principles with community members, including multi-ethnic participants in both grant writing and leadership classes at the Nonprofit Assistance Center.

Ike's eleven principles are Japanese inspired. He notes that they "will help each of us with tools for stress management, *kaizen* (continuous growth), new perspectives in problem-solving, and mental discipline." Here are the principles:

1. *Bonsai:* I imagine myself as someone of significance with clarity of who I want to be and can be. I regularly prune the unwanted growth in my life so my dreams become reality.

2. *Gambaru:* I persist and I have a choice of deciding what information I believe as "fact" as I overcome hardships at home and work.

3. *Ikebana:* I see limited resources as an opportunity to accomplish powerful action with focus. Limitations can promote creativity.

4. *Judo:* I use leverage to attain desired results when confronted with a situation in which it appears that I am at a disadvantage.

5. *Ukemi:* I accept failing as a normal process and am not intimidated by difficulties. I set long-range goals that may require ten to twenty years to attain. I will tolerate, without flinching, a couple of hundred failures along the way.

6. *Bamboo:* I will develop flexibility as well as a broad root system of knowledge as both a specialist and a generalist so major "winds" of change will not topple me.

7. *Seito/Sensei:* I will become a lifetime student "driven" by a continual desire to learn. I will share my knowledge and be a teacher who helps to create the direction we need in our society.

8. *Daruma:* Through self-discipline, I will rebound quickly, learning from my mistakes, and successfully move forward in a much shorter period of time.

9. *Tofu:* I will establish my quality base of service or product. I will practice the strategy of continuous small improvements daily.

10. *Mizu:* I will observe the power of water. I will learn to push and when to go around big problems, forming a natural landscape, as I persist and fight to develop a long-range plan for my life.

11. *Karate:* I will practice facing problems and be determined to complete tasks without fear and procrastination. I will learn to focus beyond the barrier.[35]

MONIKA K. MOSS

Chapter 3
Meaning Making Is the Challenge of Cultural Competency

African American, Black, Negro, Afro-American. What to call people of African descent is still a controversial topic. Its complexities only begin to illustrate the diversity of thought, heritage, values, and philosophy, and the impact of slavery and oppression that informs any individual, group, or community that might bear the label *African American* or *Black* in the United States.

One of the most important aspects of cultural competency is understanding the historical ground and cultural contexts of a particular group of people and how they intersect with your own cultural, racial, gender, class, and sexual identity. In this chapter, my intention is to offer you a perspective that frames these complex impacts.

I can only share what I know, what I have experienced, and what I have observed. My own life experiences, values, and worldview frame this approach. My hope is that you will view these words as one way of making meaning of a world described by one young woman of African heritage, who shall remain anonymous here. Describing her current daily experience as oppressive, she simply writes, "I am constantly being forced to live a life that is unaccommodating to me in many ways."

My Personal Journey

I am a smart, six-foot-one-inch-tall, educated, powerful, African American woman. I am of the fourth generation that was emancipated from slavery, and the second generation college educated. I am the daughter of a civil rights worker. I am Southern, which brings its own unique culture, customs, perspectives, and awareness of oppression.

I have the mixed heritage of most Black people whose ancestry is connected to slavery in the Americas. Our family on the slave owner side was Irish and French; on the Black side, African and Choctaw. It is the heritage of many people in Louisiana.

My religion is that of my oppressors, Catholic. My spirituality connects me to my ancestors—my African and Native roots and traditions, dances and music—in ways that sustain me and scare others because they do not remember.

My grandfather Frank Moss was the product of a plantation owner and his African Choctaw mother, who was free at some point but still lived in the shack behind the big house and cared for the master and his children (some of which were her own). Frank was a strong man, a railroad man who built the first Black school in Winnfield, Louisiana, and sent all of his children to college.

My father, Donald T. Moss, was the youngest of twelve and destined to be the first lawyer in a family of teachers—well, until he was arrested for leading a sit-in and expelled from Southern University in Baton Rouge along with other students who later became known as the Southern 16. This incident launched his career as a civil rights worker and public servant of the Black community through empowerment and community development programs, both public and private, from the 1970s to the year 2004, when he retired.

My memories of race and integration are images from my childhood. I remember being in the car with my mother in Washington, D.C., during riots in the late 1960s. A man in the next car told my mother to turn her headlights on so they wouldn't turn over our car.

I am a mother and a sister to many siblings—some biological, others chosen family. I am a play daughter, play niece, play cousin, and auntie to countless Black people with whom my relationship was too impactful and too love-filled not to be considered family.

My mother, May Haugstad, was the first Black woman to be hired—and the first Black and first woman to become department chair—at the University of New Hampshire, where I spent much of my early childhood. We were one of two Black families in the school district, which encompassed about three or four small towns. Upon moving to Louisiana as a teen, I was truly foreign as a Black hippie in the South. I felt a huge sense of deprivation at not having had the experience of growing up in the Black community and the Black church.

I entered Howard University and Columbia University seeking truth and ways to make a difference through theater and the performing arts as an artist, manager, and producer. This desire shaped my career paths and current work.

I moved into consulting as a strategy to supplement my burgeoning theater career and then later to be at home and parent my children while supporting my family. In addition, I had a deep desire and intention to do my part in making the world a better place. By working as a consultant with multiple organizations and communities, I could have a greater impact than working for one organization.

I am a practitioner. I am privileged in many ways, one of which is that I am able to be a capacity builder and entrepreneur—a healer of sorts. I offer support and permission to individuals, groups, organizations, and communities to do things differently and to envision a different way of being.

My gift for process design and facilitation has helped people to not only create a roadmap to their vision but to find ways of hearing and seeing others—and of being heard and being seen. These gifts of witness, support, and challenge have brought tremendous healing to individuals, groups, and organizations as they experienced new ways of communicating and interacting with themselves and others. The results will affect people in ways beyond what I will ever know.

The Impact of White Supremacy

There are as many views on the historical and cultural lay of the land for the Black community as there are Black people to speak them. In this overview, I want to bring fresh attention to the impact of White supremacy and American slavery as a way of making meaning of our current situation in this country as it relates to Black people. I chose this topic because it is the most pervasive issue in our history and culture. It crosses class, educational, and religious boundaries. And it is the piece that is least discussed when it comes to cultural competency.

In his book *The Racial Contract,* Charles Mills describes race as an artificial construct that divides the world into White and non-White, a strategy for perpetuating White supremacy, and the continued justification of the conquest of the world's land, people, and natural resources by a small minority of the population. Relevant events include the Treaty of Tordesillas (1494) in which Spain and Portugal divided up the world; the Valladolid Conference (Spain, 1550–1551) to decide whether Native Americans were really human; the later debates over American slavery and abolitionism; the Berlin Conference (1884–1885) to partition off Africa; and various inter-European pacts, treaties, and informal arrangements on policing their colonies. According to Mills

> . . . [T]he legacy of this world is, of course, still with us today, in the economic, political, and cultural domination of the planet by Europeans and their descendants. Globally, the racial contract creates Europe as a continent that dominates the world—locally, within Europe and the other continents which designates Europeans as the privileged race.[36]

This historical context is central to seeing connections between many events in the cultural history of Black people, from the Romans' smashing and pillaging of Egyptian pyramids to the rape of natural resources in Africa today. It is equally critical to understand how the inventions and ideas contributed by Black people to every aspect of our modern life have been systematically suppressed in order to justify and maintain White supremacy. These developments are part of the reason that addressing institutional racism is so elusive. Doing this would require that we dismantle the entire global economic system and the paradigms upon which it was built. Since capitalism has almost become synonymous with democracy, it is politically dangerous to even discuss alternatives let alone to make widespread, fundamental changes.

This explains why the contributions of Black people and other people of color are missing from the history books and thus the consciousness of most human beings. This information does *not* support the maintenance of the status quo—that is, White supremacy. We live in a world where there are more than enough resources for every human being to have enough food, clothing, and shelter. Yet 20 percent of our planet's population controls nearly 80 percent of its wealth.[37]

The Continuing Legacy of Slavery

The great suffering or *Maafa* (African holocaust) forcibly took more than two-thirds of the African population into slavery in the Americas over a 400-year period. This began in 1619 when the first slave ship arrived in Jamestown, Virginia, and continued until the practices of breeding and the domestic slave trade had become more efficient and cost effective. At that point, the importation of enslaved men, women, and children from Africa into the United States ceased. We must be clear that breeding was more cost effective than importing new enslaved people who needed to be broken in order to be useful on the plantation. Understanding the horrors of slavery in America for Black people—its generational impact and the current manifestation of that system in today's world—is key to connecting with, understanding, and valuing Black people.

According to one theory, overcoming a family trauma such as incest, violent death, or abuse takes seven generations. Based on this principle, my conclusion is that there has not been a single generation of Black people in the United States that has been free of societal trauma perpetrated against them by White society. First it was slavery; then Reconstruction, voter disenfranchisement, land displacement, Jim Crow, and segregation; then Vietnam, integration, the war on drugs, and the prison-industrial complex. This is not to speak of welfare reform and the dismantling of civil rights in the name of the war on terrorism. In addition to all of these are the individual and family traumas caused by lynchings, rape, false arrest and imprisonment, sharecropping, Black Codes, and other forms of bondage.

The result is what Joy DeGruy-Leary calls post-traumatic slave syndrome, described in depth in her book *Post-Traumatic Slave Syndrome: America's Legacy of Enduring Injury and Healing.*[38] Grounded in firmly established psychiatric research on post-traumatic stress disorder (PTSD) in combination with collective group trauma theory, this syndrome refers to attitudes and behaviors resulting from trauma passed down from generation to generation. Survival techniques developed during slavery have been carried into the present even when they are no longer needed, to the detriment of the Black community. "There was never a period of time when Africans in this nation were given the permission or the wherewithal to heal from our injury, so the trauma has continued," DeGruy-Leary notes.

We may not be able to document the impact of these modern traumas through empirical research for many years. Most researchers still look at issues in the Black community as phenomena due to some defect in this group or in individuals. Few investigators look at current community issues from a systemic approach that takes into account the impact of White racist oppression on Black people.

Many of the modern-day social ills and challenges in the Black community can be directly traced to the trauma of and behavioral responses to slavery. For example, consider the modern-day concept of "the sprayer" in Black communities—a term made popular in the 1980s by social workers to describe the phenomenon of Black men who have babies by multiple women in the same community or neighborhood. This is currently judged as dysfunctional and irresponsible behavior. Looking through this lens of slavery, however, we see the perpetuation of a behavior created by the breeding of slaves. The common practice was as follows: A male slave who was deemed valuable was forced to breed (impregnate) other female slaves on the plantation, just as a farmer might breed cows or horses. The breeding process did not allow Black men to form bonds with their offspring or the women who bore the children. The slave owner was responsible for the care and feeding of the child until the time he might decide to sell the child to a neighboring farm. This is another way that racist oppression destroyed and continues to destroy the Black family. The phenomenon is further evidenced by the number of Black men and women who wandered the country looking for lost family members after the Civil War and the cultural pattern of informal adoption of loved ones through becoming "play sisters" or "play cousins."

The current child welfare system mirrors and perpetuates these family traumas of loss. Current statistics show the over-representation of Black children in the child welfare and foster care system. In fact, more than two-thirds of all children in foster care are African American, not including children who have been removed from their parents and are in the care of relatives. Regardless of the circumstances of right and wrong, these systems re-create the slave trauma of child loss when they forcibly remove children from their biological parents as punishment. The children are then given to strangers who are paid to care for them. In all too many incidences the children experience further abuse that is often more severe than the neglect that poverty brings.

Thus the trauma of loss from the era of slavery is perpetuated each day on a new generation of children and parents. Because of the child welfare and foster care systems and their practices, we now have three and four generations of children who have few if any family ties or connections. These children grow up without any felt experience of mattering to anyone, often not even to themselves. In the cultural context of people of African descent, where the principle of "I am because we are" is the underlying identity development process, these children have little or no identity other than the labels that government systems have placed on them.

The rhetoric of the foster care system is all too similar to that of the slave trade. "There are four siblings in this family; we hope to place them together, but we know we might have to split them up to find suitable placement," says the social worker. Compare these words to those included in an advertisement for the "Public Sale of Negro by Richard Clagett, March 5, 1833," in Potters Mart, Charleston, South Carolina: "A valuable negro woman, accustomed to all kinds of housework. She has four children . . . two of the children will be sold with the mother, the others separately, if it best suits the purchaser."[39]

As mentioned earlier, the new slavery is the criminalization of Black people, especially men, that feeds the prison industrial complex. A 2008 report from the Pew Charitable Trusts titled *One in 100: Behind Bars in America* states the following:

> For some groups, the incarceration numbers are especially startling. While one in thirty men between the ages of twenty and thirty-four is behind bars, for black males in that age group the figure is one in nine. Gender adds another dimension to the picture. Men still are roughly 10 times more likely to be in jail or prison, but the female population is burgeoning at a far brisker pace. For black women in their mid- to late 30s, the incarceration rate also has hit the 1-in-100 mark.[40]

The Pew report also notes that one in thirty-six adult Hispanic men are behind bars, compared to one out of every ninety-nine people in the general population.

Many factors contribute to these trends, including get-tough policies such as "three strikes you're out." These, along with the swelling ranks of high school dropouts, feed a system that puts prisoners to work at wages so low that they might embarrass other "third world" nations who accept corporate outsourcing.

When you talk to Black people, you discover that every Black family and community has been directly affected by trauma in each phase of a horrific history. It amazes me that Black people are able to get up in the morning, much less find a "way out of no way" in a hostile environment. We educate ourselves, raise families, support our institutions, start businesses, invent things, create brilliant art, perform extraordinary feats on any playing field that has been open to us, and raise our oppressors' offspring with the love and care that we would our own. It is in this very context of trauma that our ability and capacity to love and overcome adversity makes me so proud to be Black.

Learning from Clients

For me, so much of cultural competency is about being nonjudgmental as you understand the ground or context of the group of people with whom you work.

Cultural competency is also acknowledging that I will never know enough to be able to say what should be done. I trust the wisdom of the group to map their own future. My contribution as an outsider is to humbly suggest additional options, to share excitement about clients' visions for themselves, and to encourage them to be bolder than their cultural mores or oppression would normally permit.

The impact of racism and oppression in America shows up as a context in my work in many ways. One of the most profound lessons in this regard came as I entered a strategic planning process with a group of Black leaders in rural Georgia. Their first battle was getting their regional funder to let them hire me. I was not on the approved consultants list, nor was any other person of color.

Then came the work. It took three sessions for the group members to create their vision. During the first session, people could not get past their current reality and crisis response to the oppression from "White folks" that they were experiencing in their communities—in school systems, the courts, and all other realms. Essentially, my work became giving them permission and supporting them in remembering how to dream about the future. For some, it was about learning to dream for the first time.

During the second session, group members dreamed so big and so wide that they basically envisioned solving the world's racial problems and all of the issues that racism had created for Blacks and other oppressed people. They needed to do this and be validated for it. It would have been oppressive and culturally insensitive to tell them—after they had finally allowed themselves to dream— that something was wrong with what they'd done.

In the third session, we translated their big dream into concrete steps. The focus question became: Given the dream you have about the change you want to create, what can be accomplished in the next three to five years that moves your bigger dream forward?

Recently we have been working with a group focused on domestic violence. Members are looking at how to move their empowerment philosophy into the infrastructure of their organization. The first aim is to empower the staff. Through this lens, they ask: Do our current policies or practices perpetuate the abuse cycle from which women have managed to escape? This means evaluating the impact of locked cabinets and the doling out of supplies and food by staff to residents of their shelter. The larger context is that many of these women often had to go to their abusers for permission to do everything—

even to get food or clothing within their own homes. The group's challenge is how to manage their limited resources in ways that don't perpetuate this form of abusive control. This is an example of using the lens of culture to do organizational development work. This group would not describe their work as diversity work nor did they hire our firm for that skill.

Beyond the "Right Way"—Making Meaning

The challenge of cultural competency and cultural immersion is to make meaning. The meaning that outsiders make of actions and events is usually very different from the meaning that insiders make. The idea of a *right* way—a *normal* way—must be placed in the golden box of illusion.

We need to embrace each way of being as one that is chosen from the history and current experiences of each person or group of people. Looking to these contexts allows us to see the creativity in the adjustments that any people—especially Black people—have made for their mutual survival in a hostile world.

Speaking dialects and slang, for instance, was a creative way for slaves to talk in front of their masters without being understood. It is still a useful strategy for people as they make meaning in a hostile environment. This is not an isolated example. "Corporate speak," the language of the boardroom, serves a similar purpose: It ensures that people without a certain type of education and positional status cannot engage in the conversation. To judge either way of speaking and being as right or wrong, proper or ignorant, is to minimize the value that each has for its users.

Every organization and group has its own way of speaking and its own unique set of values. It is the capacity builder's work as a guest in any system to find value in the differences between groups and to raise awareness about the impact of such differences. We must do this without judging it as bad or good. It is simply "what is."

Building Cultural Competency

In our capacity building we must be clear about our own issues relating to race and prejudice. We need to understand the lay of the land—White supremacy along with its flip side of internalized racist oppression and its impact on each of us as capacity builders, whatever our background. We must educate ourselves about our own heritage as well as the privilege, backlash, and barriers to well-being created by White racist oppression. As we learn about other groups of people, we can also learn about our own triggers, biases, and prejudices.

Black people are the most studied race in the world. We are the subject of literally thousands and thousands of studies, articles, and books—many of which were written to justify our second-class citizenry. And there are also many books, articles, and studies written by Black authors, scientists, and scholars that provide a non-Eurocentric view of the world and Black people's history and place in it.

If you are an experiential learner, just begin to integrate yourself in the communities. Know that each community will have different values, different definitions of Blackness, and different use of language. But if you are open and pay attention, the experience of just "hanging out" in this context will teach you a lot about yourself. Through working in low-income Black communities, I have learned much about my own privilege of being a Black educated female. It is a humbling experience that has been priceless in my own development. It nurtures my ability to show up more fully as who I am and to allow others to show up more fully as who they are.

Beyond Individual Relationships: The Systemic Level

To bring thinking and practice together, consider identity and its relationship to larger systems. Many indigenous cultures give priority to the group or community over the needs and wants of the individual. The Eurocentric perspective, however, puts individual concerns or wants higher than those of the group. In interracial discussions, this difference causes people to overlook the perspectives of each other.

Many people of color focus first on the *systemic* level. This is due to culture and to recognizing the racism built into many organizations' policies and procedures. For people of color, this form of racism greatly affects group survival, regardless of any individual's ability to navigate those systems safely. Yet most White folk want to engage Black folk at an *individual* level. It is this framing that causes them to say, *I am not racist* and then wonder why someone wants to hold them responsible for what others in their group and their ancestors have done.

The response to Hurricane Katrina taught us what happens at the level of systems when race tops the list of criteria. Scenes from this event are embedded in my memory and the memory of many others. Images of White citizens wading through water with bags of groceries and clothing were interpreted as "survival," while the sight of Black people wading through water with bags of groceries and clothing was seen as "looting." The reality of racial bias in America came out of the closet. To believe that such bias stops at the doors of nonprofits, even those founded with a vision of racial justice, is to ignore reality.

Recently I was engaged by a wonderful White, female executive. We continued to miss each other until I heard myself say, "I can't go to the individual level with you until you understand and acknowledge the impact of systemic racism on me and mine." Finally, we were able to get unstuck and I obliged her by connecting with her person-to-person, at the individual level. She left the conversation recognizing my humanity in a new and deeper way, finding a way to join her struggle with mine and feeling satisfied in the interaction. For me it was excruciatingly painful. I found myself weeping spontaneously for several days. This brought new understanding of why I do not often go to the individual level where race and racism are concerned. Being left in a hopeless place is not helpful for me in my stand against oppression and my quest for freedom and choice for all.

Capacity builders must pay attention to the individual, the relational, and the systemic issues involved in racism and White supremacy. For me to really make a difference in the world, I must support organizations addressing both sides of the equation as we examine the impact of unspoken intentions. The critical question echoes the one framed by the domestic violence organization mentioned earlier: Does this policy, procedure, or practice perpetuate racism or White supremacy?

It is my role as a capacity builder to support organizations and their leaders in looking at such impacts. I point out choices that organizations can make to solve or prevent problems with promoting oppression. This pushes the envelope of trust as well as the paradigm that says workers are inherently dishonest and will abuse the system. It requires that I as a capacity builder hold the complexity of race, class, gender, religion, sexual orientation, and culture side by side along with management dilemmas, service mandates, economic realities, and organizational mission even when my clients cannot do so. The implications of this role for cultural competency in capacity building are as vast as you can envision.

Expanding the Vision

Seeing through the lenses of culture, racism, and other "isms" that affect our internal and external environment can only create stronger, more strategic, and more informed leaders, organizations, and communities. Honoring culture and valuing the wisdom of communities of color go a long way toward healing the wounds of oppression. Validating the experiences of these individuals and their communities helps in finding sustainable solutions to complex organizational and community challenges.

The goal is not to make race and culture a non-issue. The goal is to manage the dilemmas of the organizations while valuing the impact that race and culture have on all of us and finding solutions that reduce the repercussions of White supremacy and racism.

The brilliance of Malcolm X and Martin Luther King Jr. at the end of their lives was their great appreciation for the value of moving this discussion beyond the Black-White boundary to the boundary of human rights. Doing this successfully involves a highly complex set of skills. It requires us to honor and value individual identity and group context. It requires us to value different ways of seeing and to discover how those perspectives can all "come to the table" to improve our world. In this perspective, we find energy to create, to innovate, to solve complex problems, and to create peace on earth and goodwill to all women and men.

Thank you for all that you do to contribute to our moving, as a species, toward peace and enlightenment.

Chapter 4

I Can Hear the Heartbeat of the Drum under the Surface of the Words We Speak

The familiar lilt in the voice—a bit nasal, but warm and endearing, like a blanket tenderly thrown over your shoulders to keep out the wind—tells me I am at a gathering of American Indian women. We are talking about what it means to support tribes, communities, and organizations in a culturally appropriate way.[41] There are a few scattered baritone voices in the room, deeper versions of their sisters' warm tones. I can hear the heartbeat of the drum under the surface of the words we speak.

The question we're asking ourselves is what does it mean to provide capacity building in a good way, in a way that engages through the lens of culture? Some of the answers include

- We work with honor and respect in a multigenerational way.
- We include whole family systems and network with other tribes, agencies, and communities.
- We keep "weeding," keeping the things that work for us and throwing out those things that are irrelevant.
- We remember that we are born with inherent capacity. Our work is about recapturing it, trusting ourselves, and trusting our history.
- We see each other in our complexity; we know we aren't the stereotypes.
- We respect spiritual practices of different tribes.
- We understand a key element is our internalized oppression; we deal with that too.

I am Patricia St.Onge, Haudenosaune and Quebecois in ancestry. I grew up in New Hampshire, in a homogenous (Quebecois, Catholic) community and a large extended family. I am the second of five children. I did not speak English until I started school. I have a sister who has been in a wheelchair as paraplegic amputee for more than twenty-five years. More than half of my family are born-again Christians, many of them Republicans.

Currently, I am a life partner, mother, grandmother, and progressive political activist in my community of Oakland, California, where I have lived for nearly twenty years. My journey from childhood to where I am now is marked by a series of life choices and circumstances that have widened my most intimate circles to include a wonderful array of loved ones. My partner is African and Native American; between us we have six daughters and five grandchildren. Two of our daughters are lesbians, partnered with African American women. One daughter is partner to a Mexican American, another to a Caucasian. The father of our second youngest grandchild is Puerto Rican. Our youngest granddaughter is the child of a White couple who are adopting her and want her to have an extended family that is multiracial. She is African American. She's adopting us as her grandparents.

I'm introducing myself in this way for two reasons: First, because it is often the tradition in Native circles for people to say who our people are. Second, I believe that one of the ways that we increase our capacity to work and live effectively across differences is by creating intimacy with people who are different from us. We do this by, not necessarily marrying or living with people whose life experiences are very different from our own, but by intentionally creating our lives in such a way that we have intimate relationships with a wide array of perspectives and life experiences. We are enriched by expanding the circle of our interactions. I feel very rich and equally grateful.

The Historical Landscape of Native America

One important point to keep in mind when thinking about Native America is that the notion of "a Native culture" is a bit of a misnomer. In fact, in the United States alone, there are 562 federally recognized tribes and an additional 172 nonrecognized tribes. That's more than 730 separate indigenous nations.[42] Native American nations are different from other communities of color in that they have a nation-to-nation relationship with the U.S. government. They have their own laws, law enforcement practices, and tribal government structures. There are dozens of language groups with varying life ways. They are very different in terms of economic structure, degree of self-sufficiency, land base, and size, ranging from a few dozen people to tens of thousands. Their historical and cultural landscapes vary widely.

Much of the cultural and spiritual practice of most Native American communities was outlawed by the United States for more than a century. During that time, it was maintained by elders who passed it on in secret or at least in resistance to federal policies of assimilation. Today, languages are disappearing as elder speakers are dying. There is a renewed commitment to teaching and recording the languages before they are gone forever. The same is true for cultural practices. In addition, there has emerged a "pan-Indian" culture that is a mix of multiple traditions.

There are, even among members of the same nation or tribe, different experiences depending on several key factors. Communities on the reservation have a much stronger sense of their own particular tribal culture and traditions. Urban Indian communities are more pan-Indian, in that most of their work and the communities they serve are intertribal. Many urban Indians have close ties to their home reservations, and it is not unusual for people to move back and forth from the "rez" to the city. This energizes urban communities and keeps traditions alive.

Several other phenomena influence the landscape of "Indian Country." There are untold numbers of indigenous people who were "adopted out" as babies, essentially stolen from their families and given to White families to raise. As adults, they struggle to find their place in the larger Indian community. The rise of the American Indian Movement (AIM) in the 1960s politicized many. There are increasing numbers of "Black Indians," people who identify equally with both racial and cultural groups.

There is also a growing number of people who come into their Native identity as adults; they find out one way or another that they have some Indian blood. They take on the identity of "Indian." This "newcomer" phenomenon is challenging for the whole community for a couple of significant reasons. Often they romanticize what it means to be Indian; they don't know enough or are not willing to make an investment in the community. They sometimes take cultural treasures and exploit them in order to make money, trading in that romanticized notion of being Indian. It works best when newcomers make a full commitment to the community and invest their time and resources, as well as their cultural interest, when they give to the community and not just exploit it for its art and culture. Those "wannabe" Indians are people who hang around the fringes of the community, taking the cultural and life ways, and then use them to make money for themselves. They also romanticize Native identity, *and* they exploit others who also romanticize it by leading seminars and workshops on Native culture, often calling themselves "shamans."

Depending on the tribe, LGTBQ people are more or less integrated. In some communities, they are called "two spirits," acknowledging a more comprehensive integration of their male and female spirits. Often they are spiritual leaders. In other communities, the influence of the broader U.S. religious right culture and the results of religious colonization have influenced the tribes toward increasing homophobia, leading to the banning of same-sex marriage.

More about the Historical Framework

The European communities that encountered indigenous peoples had different reactions to them. Each story is complex, but there are themes that emerge when you look at the historical data.[43] The interactions were informed by those who came from other countries. The British settlers' strategy was to annihilate the tribes they came in contact with, after using them as allies in their various wars with other Europeans. The Spanish and Portuguese, largely looking for gold and other bounty, enslaved the indigenous communities they encountered, providing a labor force for their conquests. The Russians who settled in the Pacific Northwest essentially ignored indigenous people, and the French, who were mostly priests and trappers, married the Indian women.

In every case, and in varying degrees, indigenous people were perceived as less than the Europeans. Native communities perceived the Europeans as equals for the most part. Overwhelmingly in Indian Country, a core value is reciprocity. The European core value was manifest destiny. It is not hard to see how these would collide. This is one of the fundamental differences that led to the overwhelming decrease in indigenous populations during the seventeenth through nineteenth centuries. Today, it is still one of the defining issues in the tensions that exist between Indian and non-Indian communities.

Indigenous nations are sovereign nations with a supposedly peer-to-peer relationship with the U.S. government. Yet the United States has *never* honored a treaty that it made with any Native tribe or confederacy. During the Andrew Jackson administration, there was a total removal policy. Blankets, the vehicle for honoring and trade among many tribes, were deliberately infested with small pox by the department of the army. The Trail of Tears, which forced Natives to relocate to what is now Oklahoma, was the largest, but not the only forced removal of Natives from already downsized land, finally taken over completely by the ever-growing number of settlers. Estimates are that there were more than fifty million indigenous people living across the Americas when Columbus arrived. By the end of the nineteenth century there were fewer than five million, some nations having been wiped out completely![44]

As the U.S. population moved West, the pattern repeated itself. Nations were removed from their land by treaty and laws prohibiting them from maintaining their traditions of sustenance. Hunting was outlawed or regulated, for example. The nations were pushed toward agriculture, but on the least farmable land. Eventually, most indigenous nations were forced onto reservations and given government commodities as a way of keeping them dependent on the U.S. government.

In the mid-twentieth century, U.S. public policy continued to focus on the elimination of the Native population. Reservation land was re-granted to families rather than to the tribes. Then, the United States waged a campaign to relocate many of those families to urban centers with promises of housing and jobs in exchange for their land. Of course, when they arrived in the urban centers, there were no resources for them. Relentless oppression has led to a level of despair that increases numbers of suicide, substance abuse, and fracturing of families and communities. Re-introducing cultural practices is a key element to the healing of our communities. That cannot be done by outsiders; it is a healing that must come from within.

Under the pressure of such relentless oppression, most communities and individuals develop internalized oppression; they believe the messages of the oppressor. In their paper on grant writing with tribes, Alisha Drabek and Carrie Rothburd state

> Tribes are in the process of coming to terms with and recovering from the scars of historical and ongoing oppression. This oppression has given rise to high rates of unemployment, alcoholism, drug abuse, disease, domestic violence, and suicide among Native Americans. From outside the tribe, the trend has been to approach these issues as individual or tribally-enabled problems. This has perpetuated the perception of tribal members in need of outside assistance, and in turn, has the negative effect of disempowering the individual even further.

Today, more tribes are asserting their right to seek solutions on their own through community building and cultural revitalization. They are applying traditional wisdom to address issues in a way that makes sense within a tribal worldview. The common thread to these solutions is self-determination. Through empowering tribal courts, tribal social service advocates and tribal schools that teach a curriculum based in Native ways, tribes are taking back their right to care for and govern their communities in their own ways.[45]

I would add that as tribes develop economic self-sufficiency through gaming and other economic development practices, their power for self-determination increases as well. For some tribes, gaming is a pathway to economic self-sufficiency that is seeding other economic development strategies.

The approach to self-determination that is critical to acknowledge and affirm is the intergenerational nature of the work. Elders are realizing more and more that young people need to be rooted in their own traditions before and while they are learning how to engage successfully in the dominant culture. It is not enough to carry on the traditions alone, and it is deadly to our communities if we only learn the coping skills needed to succeed in the larger society. Indigenous communities, organizations, and individuals, like all people of color, need to dance in a way that holds both.

My Process

My space in the landscape of Native America is that of a newcomer. Growing up, we all knew that my father was Iroquois, but that was the extent of our engagement. It was an interesting piece of information about our family, but we did not live culturally as indigenous people. When I was fifteen and my mother's father was dying, he told everyone that he was Canadian Mohawk. This intrigued many of my family members, but still it had little impact on our day-to-day lives.

Several years later, I married a man of African and Native descent. For his family, too, the indigenous ancestry was interesting but not informing their daily lives. Having grown up in a homogenous community, I was not prepared for the intensity of the racism that we encountered. Neighbors petitioned our landlord to evict us. A neighbor put up a fence between our house and his; he did not want to look at my children playing in the backyard. After several years in New England, we moved to Oakland, California, where we were not so much of an issue. In fact, my children were in a school that had nineteen mixed-race families, something we just did not see much of in New Hampshire. Partly in response to the relentless racism that my children experienced and my increasing alienation from my French-Canadian identity, I really began to explore my Native identity. In that process, I became engaged in the local Native community. It was in the intimacy of those relationships that I found my cultural home.

After serving as executive director of several agencies, helping to found two Habitat for Humanity affiliates and being regional director of West Habitat for Humanity, I saw how people organized themselves very differently to accomplish the same mission. I soon recognized that one key element to those differences was their cultural perspective. One consequence was that I became more aware of my own cultural identity as a mother and later a grandmother of mixed-race children. This, coupled with my fascination with organizational systems and our capacity for individual transformation, led me to open a consulting firm. I chose the name Seven Generations Consulting because I want to keep in the front of my mind the hard work and sacrifice of the generations who came before me *and* to hold in my heart the faces of those generations who will come after me.

In addition to the convening in San Diego that I shared at the beginning of this book, I had several conversations with people who helped me with the landscape and historical elements. A good percentage of my work is done with Native communities, both on reservations and in urban centers.

In one community, I was interviewed to work with a Native coalition; the first part of the interview was a conversation with the co-chairs that felt like a very linear, typical interview. They concluded by saying that I would have to meet with one of the tribal elders before the final decision was made. When I met him, he took my hand, held it for a few minutes, and said: "You'll do." I was hired!

Implications for Capacity Building

Another core value in most indigenous communities is the notion of "giveaway." It is a key element to our social interactions. In some communities, a family's status is determined by the extent of their practice of giveaway. For example, when anyone dances publicly for the first time in their regalia, it is called a "coming out ceremony." A core element of the ceremony is to acknowledge and thank those who are important in your life and in your community with a giveaway. To those who have most influenced your life, a blanket is usually the most appropriate gift. When my grandson "came out" we gave blankets to his godparents, his day-care provider, and the "grandmother" who had made his regalia. Other gifts are given as well to extended family and community members. I once received a waffle iron in a giveaway! At the end, there is usually something for everyone, including candy and toys strewn around the circle for the flurry of children who run to gather them up.

Why I Am Telling You about Giveaway

It feels like this narrative is a giveaway of sorts. By sharing the stories and sharing implications for the field, I recognize there is a possibility that someone might take the gift and use it as the basis for the illusion of their newly found expertise in doing capacity building with Indian communities. I am trusting that as a reader, you will honor the spirit of the giveaway and see the story as informative to your practice without being tempted to enter into a relationship with any indigenous communities as an "expert."

I offer my understanding of the implications for the field as a giveaway to the capacity-building community.

In working with Native communities, it is important to recognize that there is no such thing as Native American culture. There are Native American cultures. Depending on the setting—reservation or urban center—the identity of the Native community is different. Working in different settings, with different nations, is also a different experience.

There can be no capacity building without acknowledging the existing capacities. We start from a position of strengths, not needs. We honor those who have come before us, and we make all of our decisions based on their impact on seven generations to come. The richness of Native cultures and the deep connection with and pride we feel in our ancestors, often collides with the exclusion from or invisibility in the larger American culture. Our view of ourselves, experience, and history is held in contrast to the larger culture where we are either romanticized to the point of dehumanization or ignored to the point where we don't matter or don't exist.

The relentlessness of the discrimination, annihilation, and exploitation has led to significant levels of internalized oppression. It manifests differently for different communities, from rage to despondency. In contrast, it is often absent for some newcomers and "wannabes." This makes the latter more likely to be "easy" or "comfortable" for capacity builders from outside the community to work with. What often happens, as a result, is that the people who are least connected to a community are also the ones most comfortable with the ways of a dominant culture. In this case, it may be a funder, intermediary, or whoever is driving a capacity-building initiative. On the other hand, those who are perceived and acknowledged to be leaders by the community may or may not be fully bicultural and often get overlooked by outsider capacity builders. You can imagine the results when the least connected to a community become the leaders in a capacity-building process, and those most deeply connected to the community cannot or don't want to relate to it at all.

The role of a culturally competent capacity builder is to translate interests of a funder in ways the community can relate to and to translate to the funder the community's traditions, practices, and commitment to self-determination. This is a tall order, but when it is not done, we run the great risk of violating the first law of engagement: At least, do no harm!

When working with tribes in Montana,[46] I realized that while all the Native tobacco policy contractors were competent, they were struggling with their relationship with the state tobacco use prevention program, through which funds were funneled to the tribal contractors. A roadblock was an assumption, imposed from outside the community, that "just say no" was the only approach. Over a series of meetings, the Native contractors developed an agenda for articulating the more complex message of "keep tobacco sacred."[47] They had a series of retreats where they formed a coalition and designed an action plan for addressing the state in solidarity, thus minimizing the level of "divide and conquer" strategy the state could employ. One key element of the discussions was to look at how internalized oppression was holding the Native contractors back. By looking at their pasts and sharing their stories, they were able to feel more strongly connected to each other. They launched a campaign that led to real change at the state level and opened the door for them to not only engage the sacred use strategy, but to educate county contractors who had Native youth in the off-reservation schools.

Finally, I would invite you to ask yourself some questions before engaging in capacity building within Native communities:

- Am I aware of my own cultural location?
- Have I talked with the community's leaders, or just those who present as leaders who I can recognize?

■ Do I understand the landscape of this particular indigenous community?

■ Is there a community leader or someone who knows this particular community that I can partner with?

■ Have I asked enough questions to know that there is much that I don't know about this community?

■ Am I open to learning from this experience, as well as bringing my knowledge and experience?

■ Am I prepared to honor the community's ways of engaging in social change? This can include prayer before each meeting, the offering of tobacco or smudging with sage, consensus decision making, varying relationship with time and place, and defining change itself.

Again, I quote Drabek and Rothburd on consensus decision making in a planning process:

> The Native way of looking at the world reveres the connections among generations, people and place, the past, present, and future. In respect for diverse perspective and unity among its members, tribes value the importance of consensus decision-making in formulating plans. Indigenous peoples recognized the complex interrelatedness among what initially appear to be unconnected ideas and approaches. Discussion and planning spirals through many layers in order to arrive at the best solution or truth. This is an organizational style in which the opinions of all matter equally and where elders are viewed as the experts in life. It is only when everyone has internalized and agreed to a shared choice that action is taken. This reasoning reflects the emphasis on community and the need to include traditions and varying points of view. It is impossible to separate and look at aspects of a problem or situation; the whole must be considered and a solution or next step sought that takes into account all aspects of that whole at once.[48]

There is much work to be done if we are going to create justice in the world. Indigenous communities have a significant role to play in that work. Our capacity building can support that role and further the whole community's movement toward peace and justice in the world.

Note: I am grateful for feedback from and conversations with Janeen Antoine, executive director of American Indian Contemporary Arts, and Mary Trimble Norris, executive director of American Indian Child Resource Center.

Chapter 5
Changing the Conditions that Made Me Feel Unwelcome

I'm a nonprofit capacity builder in the United States. I did not know I was "Latino" until I went to college in the United States. Before that, I was Salvadoran, migrating from war-torn Central America in the early 1980s with my mother and brothers. We were looking for safety, peace, and work. The United States was our destination because we had family there. The United States had committed to aiding El Salvador's government in its fight against what the United States labeled "communism." In our minds, the United States felt like our protector, our rescuer. In coming here, we anticipated being welcomed and feeling safer than in our own homeland.

Growing up in a family of teachers and other professionals, I knew that I wanted to pursue a profession and that I had to catch up with my English to make that happen. So, with my high school diploma and one semester of Salvadoran college under my belt, I enrolled in adult school to learn English. Since one could register only to either the morning or the evening programs in the local school, I enrolled in the morning one as myself and in the evening one under a different name. Documentation was not required. This gave me a total of nine hours a day of English language instruction from Monday through Friday. Then, as if that weren't enough, I enrolled in the local library's reading program on Saturday mornings, where seniors came to teach people like me how to read English.

The pain and trauma of having to leave my home, my friends, and my country appeared to be easier to take as I learned more and more English with an aim at "having my life back." As much as I will always love my country and its culture and people, it appeared I had to acculturate into American culture and language before I could be respected by anyone in the United States. My strategy for navigating a new culture while keeping my Salvadoran identity intact was to learn the ins and outs of the second culture while rejecting the assimilationist forces that comprise much of U.S. culture.

Nine months after starting adult school, I was speaking English fluently enough to venture into the world of work. My first job in the United States was at a gas station in San Francisco. These were the days when gas pumps could not be programmed to stop at a specific amount. Customers would say, "Five dollars unleaded, please," and I would pump the exact amount and collect the money. I used to pride myself in being a good gas attendant. I definitely tried harder than my colleagues Joe and Mark, who were White males, one of whom had not finished high school. I tried to do a better job by figuring out how to pump gas for three to four cars at a time, briskly walking around them while pumping and keeping a mental rhythm in my head as to which one I should click off first, second, and so on. My colleagues did not find this amusing; my customers did and always appreciated my getting them out of there as quickly as I could.

One Saturday afternoon, a car pulled up while I was pumping gas for a customer. Out of this "muscle car" came a long-haired White man. I approached him, asking, "Good afternoon, how much, sir?" He replied, "Five bucks." I immediately began pumping, then went back to my first customer to click the pump off just as it was reaching the five-dollar mark she had ordered. I collected from her and went right back to the "muscle car" customer to finish pumping his order. When I clicked off and took the nozzle out, he grabbed it from me, spit on my face, threw the five dollar bill on the ground in front of me, threw the nozzle on my back as I reached for it, and slowly turned and walked away saying, "F—ing beaners!"

This entire sequence confused me, humiliated me, and made me feel like I had done something wrong because I did not know what a "beaner" was, and this had been done by someone who was a citizen of my host country. The United States began to feel like a different place from one where everyone can experience safety, peace, and freedom.

I held several other service jobs, including dishwasher at an expensive French restaurant on Nob Hill, delivery truck driver for a local bagel store, and day laborer for a shipyard in Oakland. Though I met and worked with some good, respectful people through these experiences, the message many kept giving me—especially American bosses and other Latinos—was that I was there as an object of servitude, that "my kind" was less than Whites and other Americans, that I should not work harder than anyone else because that makes others look bad, and that I was not worthy of the rights and privileges that "true Americans" enjoyed. I felt these things not because I did not have all my "documents" in order, but because I was different, had a different work ethic, spoke with an accent, did not understand American football, had olive skin, and was too short.

This change in the way I perceived my new home made me rethink what I wanted to do with my life. At first I wasn't sure what that meant. Shortly after, I began to realize that my personal history in the United States would be about changing the very conditions that made me feel humiliated and unwelcome.

Fast forward to 2004, after a couple of college degrees. I would proudly walk to work every day to challenge and change the United States' paradigm of assimilation and oppression through building the capacity of people in the nonprofit sector. Some of my most rewarding professional experiences have included consulting for and training social justice organizations, teaching undergraduate students about diversity issues at U.C. Berkeley, leading discussions about U.S. foreign policy with very bright graduate students at San Francisco State University, and organizing young people in a major urban area to better balance local government decision making between the will and needs of adults and those of youth, especially youth of color, who are so often "left behind."

Hispanic and Latino people in the United States make up an estimated 44.3 million people as of July 1, 2006, making it the largest ethnic or minority group in the country. In fact, almost half of the people added to the nation's population between July 1, 2005, and July 1, 2006, were Hispanic. By 2050, according to Census Bureau projections, Hispanic people will number 102.6 million—24 percent of the U.S. population.[49]

Instead of analyzing statistics that are widely accessible, I would rather focus this chapter on how I work to build the capacity of Hispanic or Latino organizations and on culturally based differences that call for unique consulting strategies.

The Reality of Colorism, Racism, and Classism

If I were to emphasize three aspects of culturally competent consulting in Hispanic or Latino communities and organizations, they would be *personalismo* (defined later in this chapter), true (not superficial) understanding of the differences among Hispanic and Latinos, and the pervasive role that classism plays within the community and in its members' interactions with the mainstream.

Often mistaken as a race, when in fact we are an ethnicity, Hispanics or Latinos throughout the planet span many groups. Because of numbers, population size, and visible characteristics, many assume that all Hispanics or Latinos belong to the racial blend known as *mestizo,* a mix of White Spaniard and indigenous populations of the Americas. Mestizo skin complexion in Latin America varies from European-looking Latinos to darker brown-skinned, more indigenous Aztec, Mayan, and Inca populations, to name a few.

In reality, the shades of "brown" throughout the continent and in the United States actually originate from various other races throughout the world. Some of the enslaved Africans who came to the "New World" actually ended up in the Caribbean Islands and Atlantic coasts of Mexico and Central and South America.[50] There are millions of Latinos of African descent who have inhabited these areas for longer than many other later arrivals. In Peru and other South American countries, there are regions populated by Latinos of Asian descent, specifically Japanese and Chinese communities, who have populated such regions for generations. Yet to American readers, they might appear to be recent "transplants" from Asia.

In Latin America and in the United States, colorism—claims for some inherent superiority of lighter-skinned people—has major implications for the democratic process. Colorism plays out most visibly with wealth and power distribution and classism, not only in Latin America but also in Hispanic or Latino communities in the United States. It is not uncommon to find that lighter, more European complexions in Latin America correlate with more wealth and power, while darker, more indigenous populations are significantly more represented in lower socioeconomic strata.

In summary, two dynamics are at work. One is that being Hispanic or Latino does not imply membership in one racial or ethnic group. Second, many people whose first language is not English or who actively identify with Hispanic or Latino cultures face racist practices and structures.

Key Differences to Remember

For ease of reference (and, perhaps, ease of control), American mainstream society has a disconcerting tendency to lump people together in groups, using categories that ignore differences. Capacity builders need to look beyond these categories when working with people of Latino or Hispanic origins. Following are some important distinctions.

Migration and upbringing experiences: Many Hispanic or Latino people are not recent immigrants. Yet migration experiences influence how they participate in this experiment we call "democracy" and in the nonprofit sector. People who migrated to the United States mainly for economic reasons might have different priorities than those who migrated here with political reasons at the fore. I have found that it is not uncommon for Mexican American-led groups to identify more with economic development or business development issues, while Central American-led groups focus on issues of human or civil rights. If such priorities do not exist at an organizational level, individuals within such organizations may hold such priorities.

Length of time in the United States: Differing from more recent arrivals from Latin America, many Mexican communities in the Southwest have inhabited these regions from times that pre-date the arrival of Europeans to the continent. The issues that appeal to a fourth-generation Mexican American or Chicano group may differ from those appealing to a community of mostly recent arrivals from Oaxaca in East Los Angeles. The issues that are important to middle-class Cuban Americans in Miami will usually differ from those appealing to inner-city, working-class Puerto Rican Americans in a New York City borough.

Country and region of origin: If you work with a mostly Mexican- or Mexican American-based nonprofit organization with strategic planning and are making "small talk" with the executive director, don't tell that executive that "one of my neighbors is Latino from Ecuador." Your intent in doing this might be to appear to know something or someone from Latin America. Yet, in my experience, most executive directors of Mexican or Mexican American background do not identify with much of what's going on in Ecuador or Ecuadorian immigrant groups in the United States.

People from different countries with Hispanic or Latino populations, and even from different regions within a country, are different. Their needs are different, their food is different, and their experience of the United States is different. Don't lump us together. Respect our differences.

Religious affiliations: While various religious affiliations exist in Latin America, Catholicism is the norm by far. In some regions, indigenous traditions are observed and practiced. For Mexican and Mexican American Catholics, La Virgen de Guadalupe remains a popular icon, and civic engagement agendas often take on *mutualista* (mutual aid society) overtones. For some Central American Catholic communities, liberation theology and popular education models are common.

Language abilities and geopolitical differences: As a bilingual and bicultural Latino in the United States, I'd like to share with the reader that I continue to experience a difference in the way I am treated in hotels and restaurants based simply on whether I speak Spanish or English in conversation. In California, the Southwest, and in the Northeast, I am treated with less respect and less hospitality if I speak Spanish. In localities like Miami, it is the opposite: I receive better attention and service when I speak Spanish.

Without getting into the appropriate level of discussion about why this happens, I can say that simply speaking Spanish or even being fluent in it does not necessarily increase one's odds of effectively building capacity for Hispanic or Latino nonprofits. The value of speaking Spanish in the United States varies with geography, race, ethnicity, and the socioeconomic status of the client and of the capacity builder.

Political affiliations: Political views found in the United States differ from what is found in Latin America. And political views differ within distinct parts of the United States. For example, it is common to find large segments of society in Latin American countries who identify simultaneously as politically liberal, environmentally conscious, and "pro-life."[51] So for capacity builders in the United States, it is important to realize that the U.S. political framework is but one framework. We cannot and should not expect such a framework to successfully explain how other countries define their political affiliations.

Celebrations: Cinco de Mayo, May 5, is an important date in Mexican military and political history and is celebrated mostly in Puebla, Mexico. Ask the average student in Mexico what they know about "Cinco de Mayo," however, and you'll find that few outside of Puebla know it well or regard it as a national festivity.

In the United States, on the other hand, this day is a major festivity for many in Mexican communities and has been co-opted by American mainstream culture and commerce as the day when Hispanics or Latinos throughout the nation celebrate their heritage. The assumptions involved here are not only inaccurate but utterly frustrating. Many Hispanics or Latinos not only do *not* celebrate Cinco de Mayo, they know little about it. As a result, it means little to nothing in their lives. Many Hispanics or Latinos living in the United States participate in Cinco de Mayo festivities out of a sense of community but, oddly enough, in the context of it being an *American* creation.

Don't mistake "American" with the real thing! An American phenomenon similar to Cinco de Mayo involves salsa dancing and Mexican American food items like "burritos." Yet, you can drive for days on end throughout the Mexican territory and not find a place that sells burritos or plays salsa music, even in many major urban areas. Even so, a capacity builder in the United States working with a Mexican American group might arrange for the delivery of "burritos" and for salsa music to play in the background during lunch at a board retreat. If people in the group are of Mexican background, they may easily experience such food and music to be as foreign as eating Brazilian "churrasco" or dancing Argentinean tango. Salsa dancing as it is done in the United States with all the choreography and contests, burritos, and Cinco de Mayo as pan-Latino are largely American inventions. As capacity builders, we have to be careful and not assume what is appropriate.

The elderly: For the most part, Hispanics or Latinos value older community members in ways that differ from their American mainstream counterparts. Elderly people are community leaders and are involved in the day-to-day experiences of their own family. While growing old, one continues to be actively engaged with one's children. We look forward to remaining engaged with family and community throughout our "third age."

Additional Factors in the Consulting Engagement

In addition to the above considerations, consultants who want to provide technical assistance to nonprofit organizations in a respectful, client-centered way can also remember the following about working with Hispanic or Latino groups.

Personalismo: Hispanic or Latino nonprofit leaders with whom I have worked place a premium on *personalismo*. This is a Latino cultural *more* that values personal connection. My consulting work benefits from sharing such cultural value with many of my clients. Often this has meant that clients become more like acquaintances or friends in the initial stages of consulting before we broach any business or contractual terms (such as asking early on how much an organization has budgeted for the work). However, I don't do this just to be politically correct; I do it when there is a genuine affinity based on background and philosophy, mutual connection, or both. I have had Latino clients with whom this *personalismo* step never materialized.

Cost: In my experience, whether or not that initial personal connection happens, most of my Hispanic or Latino clients usually proceed to discuss cost of services as an important "second" item. Talking about cost right after trying to establish a personal connection is not the easiest transition. However, it is one that I try to make happen because of the way in which Hispanic or Latino cultures view the cost of capacity building.

For many, the idea of spending $10,000 on consultation leading to a strategic plan will seem excessive, even if the funds have already been secured. This may result from previous experiences when the same service led to a failed process or product, or it may be related to a lack of experience with such service. In any case, my clients will often express how it is a dilemma for them to spend so much money on this instead of on program services. In such situations, I have assisted clients by sharing with them how funding and assistance like this are commonplace in American philanthropy and by explaining how it is beginning to go in the same direction in countries like Mexico, where there is a growing number of fully operational grantmaking foundations.[52]

However, there is an important caveat I make whenever I refer to American *anything* as a model worth imitating. One aspect of U.S. society that is worth considering as a model, especially for Latin America, is institutional philanthropy in the form of foundations. Yet this is not to say that the foundation world in the United States does not have its challenges. Most judicial frameworks that set forth the nonprofit sector in Latin America are similar to those in the United States, yet there are almost infinitely more nonprofits in Latin America than there are foundations to fund them.

Hispanic or Latino executive directors are more than "EDs": In my experience, Hispanic or Latino nonprofit leaders, especially executives, often play roles beyond those in their job descriptions. Their roots in the communities they serve often run deeper than those of mainstream executives. Why is this an important cultural competency point when discussing work agreements? Because, depending on the type of capacity building, the project will require participation by that executive, and it is crucial to make sure that he or she makes the time to be available. I have worked with Latino executives who underestimated the amount of time the project would require out of their existing work week, which also includes community-related activities outside of their job description. In these circumstances, I have offered assistance with time-management tools.

Data collection and presentation: Depending on one's cultural background, some data may be more easily shared than other data. Because of classism in Latin America, there is a sense of "face-saving" (*el que diran*) that plays out in people wanting to look like they have more money and resources than they may actually have. While this is true in other cultures, in Latin America this is related to perceptions of character, level of education, and overall sense of worth. Here in the United States it is known as "keeping up with the Joneses." In Latino organizational environments, it can manifest in a reluctance to disclose, at least initially, one's organizational financial position or one's salary range. Such data and information can be more accessible during initial consulting interactions in American mainstream organizations. As a Latino consultant, I pace my clients. Such information can be discussed when the client is ready, not when I think it should happen.

Decision making: Interpreting data and attempting to make decisions can be a challenging exercise for any nonprofit leader. In my experience of consulting to Latino nonprofit leaders, often the most effective interventions are those that honor cultural practice:

- If the data points to staff reductions or the necessary removal of board members, I remain mindful of *personalismo* and "face-saving" to prevent public humiliation.

- If the data points to a need for immediate program expansion and funding appears to be available, I take extra measures to advocate for balance and measured risk taking. Many Latino nonprofit leaders carry intense schedules because they are expected "to be many things to many people." As a result, it becomes even more important for me to alert them to potential burnout and to remind them that the organization cannot be, and should not be expected to be, all things to all people.

- If the data point to strategic planning, I engage the client in additional discussion to understand the differences between strategic planning, operational planning, and long-range planning. My experience working with many nonprofits, not only Latino-based, is that this difference is not well understood. Many go into these efforts with unrealistic expectations.

I have worked with Latino organizations where I became a part of their team and process. This means that, at some point, I was not seen as an outsider anymore and became more of an ally to the organization. Evidence of this is that some of them contact me regularly now, not only for repeat business but to check with me as to whether I know anything about a prospective consultant they might be considering to hire. Referrals (*recomendaciones*) are big in the Latino community, in my view even more than in other contexts. You are less likely to be hired because of your professional attributes and more likely to be hired because someone you know also knows the client and this person has recommended you.

Conversation as a tool for transformation: *Platicar* (to talk) is more than a verb in Spanish and Spanish-speaking countries. We talk with people, business partners, friends, and relatives at different levels, depending on the topic, the context, and the relationship between those conversing. The art of *platicar* is definitely not unique to Hispanic or Latino cultures. However, in my experience, values clarification happens when we talk, a deepening of relationships happens when we talk, and transformation takes place for the parties conversing.

In my culture, it is common for people to spend hours visiting. I describe this as *strengthening* each other. We share not only how we're doing, how we're working, and how we're entertaining but also how we are surviving, how we're navigating a world blinded by White hegemony, and how we are using our strengths to ameliorate the trauma of racism and discrimination. In Latino environments, *platicar* increases each others' capacity to achieve goals.

I teach beginning consultants the importance of talking with clients at every step of the consulting engagement as a way to transform the consultant-client relationship into an empowering experience for everyone involved. In this vein, I suggest that clients take as long as they need to talk about whatever the client is interested in, particularly at the entry stage. Every word at the entry stage is information that a consultant needs in assessing the client's situation.

One consequence of years of colonization is that many Latinos are used to and expect consultants who are styled as experts to "fix" problems for them. It's built on the assumption that the technician knows best, a mind-set that did not stop with Spanish colonization and continues with American economic colonization (or, shall we say, globalization). People throughout Latin America continue to fall prey to consumerism, environmental degradation, institutional oppression, and so many other ills sold and smartly packaged with the sorry pictures of American pop culture on the gift wrapping.

Truly helpful capacity building cannot happen without meaningful conversation between client and consultant. In such conversation, the consultant must practice client-centered consulting—the practice of genuinely seeing a problem or issue through the client's eyes. Rather than defaulting to being the expert, consultants can help the client discover how solutions to problems already exist within the client's own system.

The Primacy of Process: Creating San Francisco's Youth Commission

CompassPoint Nonprofit Services is a consulting, research, and training organization with offices in San Francisco and the Silicon Valley. The Institute for Nonprofit Consulting (INC), CompassPoint's training consultant, demonstrates that the process of capacity building with community-based nonprofits is as important as any product. Clients are, by definition, the experts in the consulting relationship and can benefit most from a process consultation approach like that first described by Edgar Schein.[53] The role of someone from CompassPoint is to create a safe, nurturing, and efficient working relationship through which we can assist our clients in discovering solutions that are already a part of their organization. Without our help, these ideas may fall by the wayside or may be applied in ways that produce unintended results.

In 1996, a colleague and I in the youth development movement carried out most of the organizing that resulted in today's San Francisco's Youth Commission. This meant visiting youth programs and convincing people of two things: first, that a youth commission could pass in the upcoming election; and second, that adult help was needed to influence public and private decision makers since most young people could not vote.

The process we designed and followed centered on the unique ways that young people see the world. In convening more than sixty youth groups throughout the city, our meeting ground rules were few:

■ Show up.

■ Respect others' opinions.

■ Wait for your turn.

■ Share the floor with others.

■ Speak from the heart, not from the head.

■ When making any decision, think about how it will affect young people in the future.

These simple ideas contrast with the practices of adults who speak from the head and omit important facts from their platforms to manipulate the electoral process.

The sixty-plus youth groups came up with their own voting systems and identified eleven candidates citywide who could serve as first-term youth commissioners. Organizers then used those young people's names and connections to generate enthusiasm for this first-ever cohort of commissioners. The process was something like a mayoral candidate approaching the head of every city department prior to an election and asking for permission to use their endorsements to generate public support.

It worked. In a city known for its unique catering to a mostly adult citizenry, the proposition that created San Francisco's Youth Commission passed with flying colors and became the first such commission in the country to be written into a city charter. This charter gives the commission "teeth" by declaring that, prior to final referral to the board of supervisors or other commission, all initiatives affecting young people in San Francisco must first be discussed and reviewed in light of recommendations made by the San Francisco Youth Commission.

PATRICIA ST.ONGE

Part Two
Key Aspects of Cultural Competency

Power

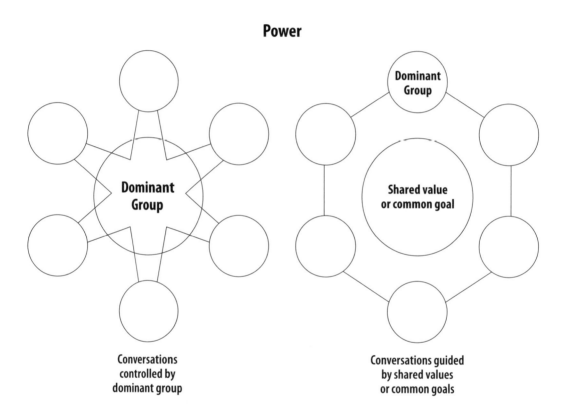

Conversations
controlled by
dominant group

Conversations guided
by shared values
or common goals

Chapter 6
Cultural Competency as Discovering Context

In your mind, picture a group of circles, with one circle in the middle and the others orbiting around it, as illustrated on the opposite page. The circle in the middle represents the dominant group in any dynamic. In the United States, this middle circle is filled with White, heterosexual, Christian, middle-aged, able-bodied men. The circles that orbit the dominant group represent people who are marginalized to varying degrees. These orbiting circles include women, people of color, LGTBQ people, old people, young people, Jews, Muslims—you get the picture. Each of those circles represents a different context, with the middle circle functioning as the dominant one. All of the conversations are brokered through the circle in the center. Most players don't even realize it's happening, not even the group in the center. In the second set of circles, the group that was in the center has moved and is now orbiting like the others, realizing that they, too, are one of many different lenses through which the world is interpreted. They are no longer "the norm"; they are a cultural group. The space in the middle is now free to be occupied by a shared value, a goal, anything that applies to all the cultural groups that are orbiting around it. The conversations aren't necessarily brokered by one party. Every circle can communicate with any other circle in the orbit. When issues arise between two circles, any other circle can serve as mediator or broker.

Capacity building rooted in culture is complex. It happens simultaneously at individual, organizational, and community levels. Even when we work at one primary level—for example, as a coach with individuals—we have to remember that people are located in context. Context informs who they are, how they fulfill their roles, and how they engage with others. We do no one a service if we support a belief in their own isolation.

Suppose you come from a culture that celebrates individuality and competition. Then one day you find yourself working with a community that values cooperation and a collective identity. You could experience immediate disso-nance that, left unaddressed, can undermine your ability to succeed in working effectively with that group.

Working in marginalized communities requires attention to the whole of their cultural perspectives—and to your own. In addition, this work calls for affirm-ing *all* perspectives as legitimate. It's a matter of conscious choice to behave in a culturally competent way.

Omisade Burney Scott, a consultant from the South, invited us to think about the "ecology" of the nonprofit sector. Her analogy draws from the fact that regions of the earth are connected to each other, and within these regions are elements that cooperate and compete with each other. Ecologists, for example, must have an understanding of how insects, soil, and weather interact in ways that affect food production. Likewise, if the fruit we're trying to bear in the nonprofit sector is a more just and equitable society, then what are the elements that support this mission, and what are opposing elements?

"Being culturally aware in capacity building means to me that you acknowl-edge that there are different characteristics at play based on people's work and life experiences," says Omisade. "I'm African American, Southern, a woman, and about to be 40. So if I come to the table as an individual in a larger movement-building strategy and disregard these characteristics, it can destabilize movement building."

This chapter examines nine ways to discover key contexts in the ecology of cultural competency:

1. See differences as always present.

2. Locate your own cultures.

3. Develop intimacy with the "other."

4. See the dominant culture as one of many.

5. Discover the influence of geography.

6. Look for conflicting cultural norms.

7. Look for intersecting identities.

8. See race as the major fault line in the U.S. context.

9. Look for historical roots of institutions.

See Differences as Always Present

Culturally competent capacity builders see the presence of differences as a powerful way to travel on our journey toward justice. Everyone is already at the table!

Imagine yourself in this situation: You've just entered a room filled with people from many backgrounds. They come in all shapes and sizes. They speak different languages. They are young, old, straight, gay, disabled. They descend from the first nations of the continent or from immigrants of another generation.

How do you feel at this moment? Frightened, anxious, exhilarated, joyful, intimidated, delighted? Whatever you feel, you are likely to experience such a scenario. This is the world we are becoming.

Even when you walk into a roomful of people who all look alike, cultural differences are still at play. Every individual is a multicultural being. Each of us has layers of personal identity based on a whole range of characteristics—race, language, religion, gender, sexual identity, physical ability, and more.

As capacity builders, we need to recognize that few organizations or communities are monolithic in culture. This has been true on the East and West Coasts of the United States for some time and is becoming increasingly true throughout the rest of the country. There are few places anymore where people look alike and share the same cultural norms. Differences are always present.

I was giving a talk at a student conference about the importance of cross-cultural effectiveness in an increasingly diverse world. A young White man stated that he was likely to go to a state where diversity was not an issue. He asked what relevance this topic of diversity had for him. I replied that diversity is now a fact almost everywhere in the United States.

After that meeting, I looked up census data for Wyoming—a state widely assumed to be monocultural.[54] Even in this state, people of color make up 8 percent of the population, and 1.8 percent are "mixed race." These figures only skim the surface; they don't speak to other elements of any state's diversity, such as differences in sexual identity. In short, the issue of cross-cultural effectiveness is not one that many of us can avoid. If we are committed to social change, then this is a critical issue, no matter the census data.

One of my friends, a former director of the World Institute on Disability and now a consultant, recalled someone who described himself as "temporarily able-bodied." These words brought tears to her eyes. Here was an affirmation—an acknowledgment that people with disabilities may have been able-bodied at one time, and that any of us can become disabled in the future. If we live long enough, in fact, most of us probably will experience some type of disability. This man's skillful choice of words brought everyone in the room to common ground, even as he acknowledged a key difference in personal context.

Discovering Differences

I was invited to facilitate part of a weekend training for a Unitarian Universalist youth group. The people in the room looked homogenous—middle-class, White, suburban kids. They wanted to know how to engage in a healthy way with teens who were different from them.

We started by playing a game. I had cut shapes of different colors out of construction paper: squares, hearts, diamonds, circles, and more. I put these out for the kids to use and then posted the following grid up on the wall:

	Birth order	Generation	Religious tradition	Sexual identity	Class	Ethnicity/ race	Geographic origin
	Square	*Triangle*	*Rectangle*	*Oval*	*Heart*	*Circle*	*Octagon*
Blue	Oldest	'80s	Christian	Gay	Poor	Native American	Outside the U.S.
Pink	Youngest	'70s	UU	Bisexual	Working	Caucasian	Northeast
Orange	Second	'60s	Muslim	Straight	Wealthy	Asian	Deep South
Red	Middle	'50s	Hindu	Trans- gendered	Middle class	African	Midwest
Purple	Only	'40s	Jewish	???	Upper middle class	Middle Eastern	Southwest
Yellow	Third	'30s	Buddhist			Australian	West Coast
Brown	Fourth	'20s	Earth- centered or Pagan			Pacific Islander	Northwest
Green	Fifth +	Teens	Indigenous				East Coast

I asked the kids to pick the shapes that best described themselves. Each of them ended up with a handful of shapes. Then they went around the room to find someone who had the same hand. The results were surprising. Only two kids found someone who had exactly the same handful of shapes.

Next, I asked them to go around the room again. This time each kid looked for someone with a handful of shapes completely different from his or her own. No one succeeded at this task.

Afterward we talked about differences as a source of strength. This set the tone for the conversation about engaging with people who are more visibly different from us.

Locate Your Own Cultures

What is most important to finding a good fit with the nonprofit you're supporting? Locate yourself first. *If you want to work in a culturally competent way, then develop a strong awareness of your own cultural identity.* That sentence gets to the heart of this book's message. I cannot emphasize it enough.

I can gather reams of information about a community—census data, who the leaders are, how community members interact during meetings, and more. But if I don't understand the cultural perspectives I bring to the encounter, then I risk the assumption that my way of thinking and my way of doing things is the norm. This is the first step to cross-cultural misunderstanding.

Once I am clear about my own cultural location, I can more authentically understand my relationship to the cultural identity of those with whom I work. Understanding my own cultural location and its influence on me is the first critical step. This allows me to see that my cultural location is one of many—not the only one, and not the best.

Understanding My Own Cultures

Culture includes many attributes, including the behaviors, norms, attitudes, and assumptions that inform a group of people who are joined by common values, myths, and worldviews. Culture serves as a roadmap for the members of the group as they deal with issues related to race, ethnicity, language, gender, sexual identity, socioeconomic status, age, and religion.

Recall the "iceberg" metaphor used in the introduction to describe the dual nature of culture. The visible, outward attributes of culture include food, dress, music, art, dance, literature, language, and celebrations. Below the surface, however, are the more subtle and invisible attributes. Examples of the latter are attitudes, values, competitive or cooperative ways of engaging with people, patterns of emotional response, relationships to time and space, and styles of nonverbal communication.

With this metaphor in mind, name three cultures to which you belong. Then, describe three attributes of each culture.

■ Culture _____

■ Attributes _____

_____

_____

■ Culture _____

■ Attributes _____

_____

_____

■ Culture _____

■ Attributes _____

_____

Develop Intimacy with the "Other"

I once heard a preacher say that our communities will always be as integrated as our dinner tables. In addition to being clear about our own cultural location, we can create intimate relationships with the "other"—people whose culture differs significantly from our own. This is essential to building culturally based skills for capacity building.

The word *intimacy* is critical. It means going beyond superficial acquaintance. Knowing a community only in theory and trying to work with its members is a recipe for disaster. The only way I know how to develop intimacy is "walking the talk" based on mutual respect.

My sister Debbie was in a motorcycle accident when she was twenty-two. She lost a leg and is paralyzed. When my daughter Breonna was about six years old, she asked her aunt what it felt like to be in a wheelchair all the time. Debbie had an extra wheelchair, so she invited Breonna to see for herself. For twenty-four hours, they were both in wheelchairs. Breonna learned how challenging it is to transfer from the chair to a toilet and to a bed. We went to a restaurant that didn't have accessible bathrooms. The two of them rolled out and found an accessible bathroom down the street.

After twenty-four hours, Breonna was ready to give up the chair. Yet in those twenty-four hours, she developed intimacy with something that was wholly "other" to her. She walked away with a deep appreciation for the complex life of a person with a disability—knowledge that she carries to this day, twenty-five years later.

I am not suggesting we must literally live in someone else's situation for twenty-four hours, powerful as that experience might be. Rather, we need to take the time to deeply understand what life is like for those who are not like us. There are moving examples of this level of intimacy, including victims of crimes who reach out to the families of the perpetrators or families who lose children to murder and then adopt the children who did the murdering. Stories of such incidents exist in almost every culture.

There is a cost to this work. In a peer dialogue conducted in Atlanta during the researching of this book, a White participant put it this way: "As a White person, to avoid racism, you have to cut yourself off from some other White people. You want to build ally relationships with POC [People of Color], and there are some White people who don't understand that." I was moved by her comment.

Being an ally still does not give us the most profound levels of access to any group. *Intimacy is as close as we get.* It is critical, but it doesn't give us the complete experience. Breonna could have put the wheelchair away at any point. Debbie cannot. Yet, without some measure of intimacy, we cannot know the experience of others enough to assist them in building capacity.

See the Dominant Culture as One of Many

I have done the Understanding My Own Cultures exercise (see page 85) dozens of times with different groups—some relatively homogenous and others quite diverse. It is my experience that, overwhelmingly, White people don't identify *White* as a culture and that people of color do. Men don't view being male as a cultural location but women do. Heterosexuals don't view their sexual orientation as a cultural location, but LGTBQ people do. Middle-aged people don't view their age as a cultural location, but young people and elders do.

This is an illustration of the orbiting circles that were mentioned earlier (see page 80). When any aspect of our identity dominates a group, we tend not to think of it as a culture. Actually, we often don't think about it at all; it is "normalized."

Something similar happens as people of color engage with an "other" in their work as capacity builders. The perceptions that each group takes to the process is largely informed, if not determined, by the beliefs and attitudes of a dominant group. These perceptions are communicated via mass media and a whole range of human interactions.

When I did tobacco policy work, the middle circle was occupied by the American Cancer Society, American Lung Association, and American Heart Association. The orbiting circles included grassroots organizations working to change tobacco policy and serve communities targeted by tobacco companies. Because the "big three" had the dominant infrastructure, they received the lion's share of the funding for tobacco policy work. In some states, they re-granted funding to the grassroots groups, but only marginally. After nine years, the initiative evaluation showed that the only group for whom tobacco addiction had significantly decreased was middle-class, highly educated White people.

As long as the dominant group sees itself as the norm—and the marginalized groups comply—it is difficult to energize any conversation that does not go through the middle circle. This is true whenever a "mainstream/margin" dynamic plays out in group relationships.

Dismantling assumptions about which culture defines the norm can bring a major dividend by granting full value to all cultural perspectives. Members of the dominant, mainstream group can see themselves as carriers of one perspective or worldview among many. When this happens, the group moves out of the center and joins the orbiting circles. Conversations can happen across all the lines between circles, and there is no need for a single group to act as a "broker" or "gatekeeper." Then, through a collective conversation, members of all circles can determine what belongs in the center circle. What's placed there is usually a core value instead of the norms that belong to one particular group. When we make such a shift, we begin to change more than behaviors; we begin to create more culturally based worldviews and systems.

I recall a speech by Manuel Pastor, professor of geography and American studies and ethnicity at the University of Southern California and director of the Program for Environmental and Regional Equity (PERE). He invited us to re-examine the framework for leadership that we bring to the field. He emphasized that our current political leaders tend to think of leadership as a chess game. Different perspectives are represented by only two colors, and only two parties can play. The game pieces have different values, and it's a good thing to knock an opponent's pieces out of play. Above all, the object is to win. A new metaphor for twenty-first-century leadership encourages us to think instead in terms of a jigsaw puzzle. When we're making a puzzle, anyone can contribute. The more colors there are, the more interesting the result. Every piece is valuable and the object is to create a beautiful picture. At the end of his talk, Pastor invited us all to become partners in creating new narratives. I want to make puzzles!

Discover the Influence of Geography

During the peer dialogues and interviews that preceded this book, we discovered geographic and regional sensibilities. Conversations about race, class, culture, and power shifted as we moved around the country.

In the San Francisco Bay Area, where I live, the world is at our doorstep. Students in Oakland's public schools speak 157 languages. This differs from Chicago, where the focus of many discussions about race is on building "Black-Brown" coalitions, reflecting the lingering influence of neighborhood politics. In Atlanta, however, the debate is still overwhelmingly about Black and White, although that is beginning to shift.[55]

In the Southeastern United States, distinctive elements of culture include religious identity and family background, often coming to the fore in nonprofit and community settings. "I don't know any other part of the country that has to deal with organized religion as much as in the Deep South," said a participant in one of our peer dialogues in Atlanta. While acknowledging the primacy of the Black and White paradigm in this part of the country, this person noted the force of the religious context: "You're living in a community where when you're introduced, they say, 'Are you churched or not?'"

In their contributions to Part One of this book, Alfredo Vergara-Lobo and Vicki Asakura point to the variations of experience based on the geography and geo-political events in immigrants' home countries. These can't be separated.

I once worked with a church of first-generation Korean immigrants, and they referred to themselves as American Koreans. It was a signal to me that seeing them as part of the great melting pot would likely be culturally incompetent.

As a capacity builder—especially if you travel a lot—you need to take the time to understand factors that matter in the area where you work. Ask about history, politics, personalities, and other cultural markers that shape the conversation between cultures. Though these may not be apparent at first, they will help you understand the attitudes and actions of the people you are serving. I often try to find out which indigenous nation lived in the space where I'm doing the work. Honoring them and honoring the earth is an element I have incorporated into my practice.

Look for Conflicting Cultural Norms

Communities have different norms relating to age, gender, and sexual identity, as well as to whom they define as outsiders. What happens when the norms of a particular group offend you?

This question came up in a workshop in Louisiana. One of the participants asked, "What if you come across a group of people who are doing female genital mutilation, and they say it's part of their culture. Do I have to support that?"

My response was threefold:

▪ If there is a subgroup within the group itself that is working to eliminate a particular cultural practice, I can support them in that. But as an outsider, I can't make it my mission to "fix" another culture.

▓ Our Judeo-Christian tradition is to do male genital mutilation, but we don't call it that; we call it circumcision. Someone who doesn't share that practice might consider it offensive too.

▓ If something is offensive to us, it is a good opportunity to recognize that we are not a good match for this particular project. It is fine to choose *not* to affirm certain aspects of culture that conflict with your core values.

From Frank J. Omowale Satterwhite, founder of the National Community Development Institute, I learned to avoid this level of challenge. The key is, on each project I work with a planning team from the community or agency. I ask for as wide a range of perspectives as they can provide. The planning team then gives us a preview of what is likely to come up with the larger group. In a small group, I find it much easier to untangle challenges. The small team then provides support to the members of the larger organization or community who share their view. It is much more likely that the whole group can move forward if the planning team has worked out the challenges ahead of time.

Challenging cultural practices and dynamics can be as important as honoring traditions. To be of greatest service, a capacity builder does not simply accept cultural ideas or practices because they represent the status quo. Cultural competency means being centered on the client or grantee by seeking common good through social change—not simply reinforcing a nonprofit's practice when it could be against the best interests of the community.

For instance, an immigrant community needed to reconsider ingrained gender roles limiting the power of women to certain traditional activities. In one case, a consultant took on the role of creating change by negotiating a process with an immigrant community group. By replacing the culturally based, authoritarian approach taken by a male leader—a business executive serving as board chair—the group adopted a participatory process.

In a related situation, an immigrant group was unwilling to rethink the gender roles involved in its programmatic approach. A consultant declined to take the engagement.

In the end, it is important that a capacity builder be a good fit for a group. It is better to say no to a potential engagement—or to partner with others, especially in the case of grant making—than to pose as a messiah who can solve all problems.

Look for Intersecting Identities

Identity development in individuals, organizations, and communities has a cultural component. A growing field of practice called *intersectionality* looks at how different aspects of identity relate to each other. For example, a person of color with a disability may face a double whammy in terms of his or her levels of opportunity. When we pay attention to intersectionality, we create more possibilities for change.

With intersectionality, we recognize that focusing on race, ethnicity, and particular communities—African American, Asian American, European American, First Nations People, and Latino/Latina—limits us to a small piece of the cultural territory. There are many people in the United States whose cultural identity doesn't fit neatly into one of these boxes (Arab Americans, for example). Within each category, moreover, there are people who are *bi*— biracial, bilingual, bicultural, bisexual. Add to this the new cultural formations that will be created by young people.

The point is that we have many ways of connecting one to another, and the various cultural formations are increasing exponentially. In addition, the cultural markers are ephemeral and temporary. All of this increases the complexity of our work and makes it richer at the same time.

It is interesting to note that race is a foreign concept to many immigrants. They identify primarily as nationals from their home countries—Irish, Portuguese, Venezuelan, Ghanaian, Japanese, and so on. It is in the United States that they learn to sort themselves in a racial pecking order. Many immigrants are not initially interested in racial distinctions. However, the pressure from U.S. culture is so strong that within a short time they absorb the attitudes of the larger society. Many of them resent the imposition.

It takes mighty intent and deliberate practice to swim against the current of our dominant culture when it comes to the context of race. Alfredo's story about being called a "f—ing beaner" (see chapter 5) was intense on multiple levels, including his inexperience with the notion of race as a categorizing agent.

Intersectionality is also revealed in differing notions of race and identity among immigrants and people raised in the United States. There is a tension in this country between people of African descent born in the United States and African immigrants. I was shocked, though I'm not sure why, to learn about the experience of some friends of ours from South Africa. Before immigrating to the U.S., they saw videos that portrayed African Americans as lazy, criminal predators. They were told not to associate with African Americans. They came filled with propaganda about their cousins. Before long, however, my friends realized that no matter how much they disassociated with their cousins, our culture lumped them all together. Within a few months of being here, the police stopped one of my friends and harassed him. They said his seat belt was not fastened properly. At that point, he had an experience in common with many African Americans that informed his views.

Tensions such as those between Americans of African ancestry did not come up overnight. They will take time—and shared experience—to address. There is cause for hope, however. Every time I work with young folks, especially folks of color, I am encouraged to see how little of the propaganda they are buying. They work better in coalitions, and many of them have multiple identities themselves. They understand in fundamental ways that social change doesn't happen at the expense of others. Movement building is the framework that incorporates and goes beyond the needs of specific organizations and communities while holding the vision for a just society.

See Race as the Major Fault Line in the U.S. Context

By our own definition, culture applies to a broad range of human groupings. Yet even as we acknowledge the reality of intersecting identities, our focus is on cultural competency in the context of race and ethnicity.

The rationale for that decision is embedded in United States history. Within our power structures, race is still the major fault line. As revealed throughout Part One of this book, race has been at the heart of the taking and growing of this country. From the first landing of Europeans, through conquest, slavery, exclusion laws, internment, ongoing disparities, and internalized oppression, the largest crack in the fabric of our life as a society is located in race. Even within groups that have been denied privileges and protections, racism, and colorism are prominent.

So while we acknowledge the oppression manifest in all of the "isms," we see racial and ethnic differences as the most significant in the United States today.

While researching this book, we scanned published literature dealing with cultural competency in the nonprofit field. (For more details, see the Resource C near the end of this book.) There are few examples of nonprofit organizations successfully tackling issues of race and power. Instead, we found documentation for

- Racial inequity in nonprofit management and leadership
- Structural and institutional racism in community building
- Lack of inclusiveness in nonprofits and in access to paid capacity-building work
- Disparities in outcomes for people of color and communities of color

Compared to other topics in nonprofit management literature, little information is available about the knowledge, skills, and strategies that capacity builders need to address racism, inequity, and disparity. These issues do surface in recent work related to generational identity, immigrant and refugee status, and the identities of gay, lesbian, bisexual, and transgendered people. We also have anecdotal evidence of other important work in culturally based capacity building.

Not enough is documented, however, and rarely is the writing by people of color documented. The world of publishing is, like most elements of our society, dominated by the voices of the mainstream. Fortunately, more recent publications are starting to provide a corrective. We hope that this book offers one more contribution to this growing body of work.

The nonprofit sector could benefit tremendously from further research and documentation of capacity-building approaches. What role does the race and ethnicity of a capacity builder play in supporting culturally competent leadership? What additional knowledge, skills, strategies, and approaches are needed for a culturally competent practice? These are urgent questions. Our research points to answers, and, although not definitive, they represent major progress. Capacity builders, as change agents in the nonprofit sector, are key players in addressing these issues.

Of course, race is not the *only* fault line. Even within nonprofit organizations, rifts may develop between support staff and professional staff, between constituencies with different sets of needs or between staff groups that have undergone a merger, with one side having the perceived upper hand.

Challenges are often exacerbated when organizations take on the cultural identity central to their mission or constituents. For example, I have seen social-change organizations whose approach is confrontational. They take on community leaders and hold them accountable for policy making. They argue, yell, and find other ways to harass public officials, and they are often effective in realizing short-term external aims.

The difficulty is that when such organizations engage with each other, they often use the same tactics and strategies. It is not surprising to see people engage colleagues in the ways that they engage with their "targets." This is true for many organizations that serve "victims" of one kind or another. In fact, organizations may take on a victim identity. When they lose their funding, for instance, they automatically look for a "perpetrator" who inflicted this problem. This, too, can create challenges for the capacity builder who wants to support an organization through change.[56]

Look for Historical Roots of Institutions

As we try to minimize power differentials and increase equity, it is important to remember that we can't do this in a vacuum. We have to pay attention to historical factors, constantly seeing the impact of history on today's systems and structures. There is no separating them.

When we understand the historical context, we can begin to understand how deeply rooted the experiences of racism and oppression are in our country's psyche. They are part of the fabric of our identity. Broken treaties are the primary legacy of the United States government to First Nations people. And the thread from slavery to Jim Crow laws to segregation and nominal desegregation leads us to heightened racial profiling in post-Katrina New Orleans.[57] Here are the words of a 2005 report from the Center for Social Inclusion:

> One question regularly posed when over one hundred thousand, mostly Black, people were stranded and abandoned in appalling conditions in New Orleans was whether the faces of the abandoned exposed racism. The short answer is yes, but not in the way we typically think about racism. The way we have structured society—suburbanization, concentrated poverty and the fragmentation of and incapacitation of government—left people of color vulnerable before and after the levees failed. . . . Our national policies created isolated communities of color in the first place. National policies disinvested in them and choked them off from opportunities. Then we began to starve the federal government of resources to invest in communities, which hurts communities of color more, but harms opportunity for all communities.[58]

As you read the historical narratives of the contributors to Part One of this book, imagine a thread that pulls each historical event into today. It is easy to see the mark that it leaves on our country, its people, and its soul. For example, Vicki Asakura notes that U.S. law has excluded people of Asian descent from immigrating to the United States and sent more than 100,000 of our sisters and brothers to internment camps. These groups fell victim to a series of anti-immigrant legislative actions, beginning with the Chinese Exclusion Act of 1892. Anti-immigration laws were followed by miscegenation laws and anti-alien land laws. Until 1952, immigration laws restricted Asian immigrants from becoming naturalized citizens. New immigration laws in 1965 and later in 1975 allowed immigrants to be admitted on the basis of skills and relationship to family members already here.[59]

In her contribution to Part One of this book, Monika K. Moss puts the African American experience in a historical context:

> It is equally critical to understand how the inventions and ideas contributed by Black people to every aspect of our modern life have been systematically suppressed in order to justify and maintain White supremacy. These developments are part of the reason that addressing institutional racism is so elusive. Doing this would require that we dismantle the entire global economic system and the paradigms upon which it was built. Since capitalism has almost become synonymous with democracy, it is politically dangerous to even discuss alternatives let alone to make widespread, fundamental changes.

Monika also points out that our prison-industrial complex has become the new slavery. As an institution, it learned well from its predecessor. If you look at the prison population, you will find it reflects—disproportionately—the communities of color surrounding it.

There are many reasons for this outcome. One is well-documented racial profiling by police. On one small section of the New Jersey turnpike alone, black drivers accounted for 17 to 19 percent of the traffic between Exits 1 and 7A in August and September 2005—but nearly 31 percent of traffic stops.[60] Many more examples of racial profiling are detailed in *Race and Ethnicity in America: Turning a Blind Eye to Racial Injustice,* a report from the American Civil Liberties Union.[61] Other factors include prosecutorial decisions that put more people of color into the system in the first place. White and affluent defendants are significantly more likely to be represented by a private attorney. Public defenders have much larger caseloads and might meet their "clients" for the first time in court.

History also reveals a deafening silence about the contributions made by *all* communities of color to our country. Even so, those contributions are countless. For example, consider the contributions by indigenous communities just since the arrival of Europeans. In his book *Indian Givers: How the Indians of the Americas Transformed the World,*[62] Jack Weatherford chronicles some examples. Of note is the fact that most earlier European immigrants came from monarchies and were not familiar with democratic forms of government. They knew what they didn't want as they examined options for creating a political system. It was Canassatego, chief of the Haudenosaune (called Iroquois by the French colonists) Confederacy, who suggested the colonies unite into a confederacy and shared the Haudenosaune model with them. Similar contributions were made ranging from food and medicine to transportation and trade.

Today our legislatures and courts use their power to extend old racist systems and to invent new ones as new "enemies" have emerged. If you do some analysis of many laws, you find there are racial implications. Even the Fourteenth Amendment to the Constitution, which was designed to mitigate the consequences of slavery, has been used far more often by corporations to assert their rights as individual persons to carry on, much to the devastation of our social infrastructure. And the Constitution's plain language is that enslavement remains legal for people convicted of crimes (see the Thirteenth Amendment).

I have often heard people of color say, "I could let it go if it were over, if it weren't still happening." Our country still in large part reflects the systems and structures established by the wealth and power gained by the "landed fathers." This line of thinking punctures the "I didn't have slaves, so it's not my problem" argument. The legacy of conquest and slavery lives in the fabric of our society. It is the foundation on which we stand. It will take deep commitment to create justice and equity for everyone.

Chapter 7
Cultural Competency as a Community Process

How is *cultural competency* more than just good *capacity building*? This question has come up more than once, and it's a fair one.

One of our interviewees, Jan Masaoka, is known for phenomenal leadership in the nonprofit field as an executive, author, and researcher. "I don't agree with the premise of cultural competency," she said. "I don't like it to be pulled out as a separate element. I think it's about technical excellence. Often, what passes as a case of cultural incompetency is just bad practice. Communities of color need different strategies, not parlor tricks."

We agree that cultural competency is a way of life, not a skill set. Healthy, productive working relationships do not depend only on passing through a set of practices or exercises. They also depend on organizational processes that continually clarify and work through the tensions that arise in modern-day, multi-ethnic organizations.

Peggy Saika, executive director of Asian Americans/Pacific Islanders in Philanthropy, notes that the nonprofit sector is best poised to lead this process for the United States. "We make the road by walking," she says. In other words, this is not a sprint; it's a marathon.

Ultimately this book is about good capacity building, and paying attention to culture is good capacity building. This is not something that happens on the side. It is part of everything we do. Culturally competent capacity building requires a long-term investment. It is rooted in values of equity and justice. It recognizes the value of "soft skills" and becomes part of the "hard skills" work as well.

Going beyond parlor tricks into actually "walking the road" means that the cultural competency process is as important as any outcome produced. *How* we do our work is as critical to success as *what* we accomplish. If we get to a great place but we've destroyed each other along the way, is the traveling worth it?

Start with Nonharming

In *Epidemics,* a classical text on medical treatment, the Greek physician Hippocrates suggests a basis for starting this process: "First, do no harm."[63] This is a powerful idea, one that can still guide health care providers—and nonprofit capacity builders.

There are many ways in which harm is done to marginalized communities by well-meaning (and sometimes *not* well-meaning) grantmakers, consultants, intermediaries, and other "helpers." Fortunately, as Masaoka points out, "People of color can and always have survived culturally incompetent 'help.'"

Even so, as a principle of nonharming, culturally based capacity building still holds. This process calls for paying attention to relationships, both internal and external. It means being deliberate about bringing a full range of stakeholders into the room. This process also calls on capacity builders to reflect on themselves, including their own cultural location and its influence. In addition, it calls for genuine collaboration rather than brain picking and exploitation. These are practices suggested or implied by Alliance for Nonprofit Management.

Look for Signs of a Sustainable Process

How do I know a culturally based process when I see it? I look for visible evidence, such as the following:

- Everyone who needs to be at the table is present and all voices are honored equitably.
- There is space in the room for multiple leadership styles.
- The community, organization, or individual I am working with controls the agenda and guides the process.
- If there is a historically dominant group in the room or process, they locate themselves not at the center of power but in one of the orbiting circles.
- There are sufficient resources to take the extra time required to build trust and clear communication.
- Strategies are consistent with shared values and guiding principles, all of which the community determines.

In addition, capacity builders bring their whole self to the engagement and expect to meet the whole self of everyone in the room. Everyone has space for authentic, candid speaking. At the same time, capacity builders maintain some measure of objectivity. We recognize that measuring success may be difficult by common evaluation practices. So we use additional resources for participatory evaluation, where communities determine their own benchmarks for success.

Using a culturally competent approach in all aspects of our work—including fund-raising, financial management, and governance—generates a unique process and set of outcomes for any organization. In this chapter, we explore several aspects of cultural competency as a process that creates, transforms, and sustains community. The following chapter expands on this idea, presenting institutional change and social justice as the key outcome.

Base Cultural Competency on Intention and Values

The process of becoming culturally based is an intentional one. It is not the property of any particular community. Just being part of a community does not automatically make anyone culturally competent. One of the people we interviewed, a capacity-building funder, put it this way: "There is a big gap between diversity and cultural competency. It's one thing to have a board that's diverse; it's another to have a board where diverse people feel welcome."

In addition to recognizing our own cultural lens and appreciating those of others, we can become more intentional by grounding our work in shared values. Every conversation that we had in the process of researching this book identified values as critical.

I worked with an organization located in the middle of a neighborhood that was changing demographically. The staff members wanted to continue serving the local neighborhood residents rather than becoming a commuter agency where their clients drove in for services. As they got to know the newcomers to the neighborhood, they learned that people weren't coming in for services designed to support individuals. Instead, families were a high priority. In a short time, the agency expanded its services for whole families and provided child care in every situation. The intention to ground their work in community values created an enduring change in outcomes.

Notice Who Is in the Room—and Who Is Not

One hallmark of a culturally competent process is constant attention to who is "in the room." Remember that people have varying resources. Get an idea of who is in the room and what they bring.

You can do this by asking questions. For example, do we have the resources needed for everyone's participation to start on an equal footing? The answer might include translation equipment or translators. Have we paid attention to the real needs of the community for participation? If the meeting is early evening, this can mean providing food. If there are parents in the group, we may need to have child care available. We can also use multiple approaches in presentations to accommodate different learning styles.

Core Values for Capacity Building

During a workshop on race, class, and power in capacity building, participants listed some of the values that guide their work. They are summarized below.

Values focused on myself as a capacity builder

■ Being honest with myself, modeling honesty with others, being authentic, joining my honesty with curiosity

■ Understanding and appreciating my own complexity

■ Building awareness of my power and privilege, working to level it, and building real equity in the group

■ Building awareness of my assumptions

■ Maintaining sensitivity to the fact that "I don't know what I don't know"

■ Walking the talk, being the change I want to be in the world, believing and acting in possibility

■ Being open to learning from others, continual learning, knowing that every day is a learning opportunity

Values focused on the processes—how we work

■ Uncovering strength-based attributes, qualities, and core values embodied in group work

■ Understanding where others are coming from; not jumping to conclusions

■ Recognizing that we are all different; celebrating and embracing those differences rather than seeing them as an obstacle

■ Promoting participatory democracy and the involvement of each individual in the life and direction of the organization

■ Acknowledging power imbalances and creating space for voices to be heard across different levels

■ Looking for the love, caring, and connections that unite us

■ Recognizing the complex picture of "what is"—the complexity of multiple realities in a group that allows them to find and create what they need

■ Serving with excellence and integrity; leading by example and being a person of my word

■ Listening with openness and compassion

■ Maintaining my humanity in this work; ensuring that when folks leave the room, their humanity is intact

While who is in the room influences how the work gets done, who is *not* in the room can have equal influence. It is a good practice to ask participants who is not in the room but should be. In my experience, simply posing this question raises awareness and brings attention to the missing elements of the community. This can be a critical role of the capacity builder.

"I am conscious of what's going on in the room," says Sojeila Silva, manager of the Fiscal Fitness Program for the Northern California Community Loan Fund. "It usually has cultural elements. I find tools that help the group work through power imbalance, and I make an effort to use different tools that work in this culture. I watch for the group's 'aha!'"

Self-Assessment in Three Parts

My capacity to pay attention to the whole constellation of issues at play in a given situation increases my capacity to address it in a culturally competent way. It's particularly important to assess three areas: what's going on with me, what's going on in the room, and the historical context in which we are operating. You can ask questions to build your awareness of each area:

What's going on with me?

■ What am I wearing? How am I talking? Where am I looking?

■ What cultural lenses do I bring with me?

■ What language do I use? (code switching)

■ What are my first impressions of people?

■ What assumptions do my first impressions spark?

What's going on in the room?

■ How are the seats arranged?

■ Who is sitting where?

■ Is there a plan for movement that stretches people beyond the usual practice—and typical power relations?

■ Who speaks more or with a greater sense of confidence?

■ Who speaks less or more tentatively?

■ Who likely feels welcome? Who might not?

■ How am I working to bring equity into the room?

■ Where is the privilege in the room?

What historical issues are at play?

■ What are the practices of this organization or community as they relate to power and privilege based on the following:

Race and ethnicity
Education
Class and socioeconomic status
Language
Immigration status and national origin
Gender, gender identity, and sexual identity
Physical ability
Age and generation
Religion
Family constellation

■ Who has had to overcome what to be included [sitting] here?

■ Where are there likely points of internalized oppression?

Note: An expanded version of this tool is included in the Resource Section. See Self-Assessment in Three Parts on page 207.

I like to imagine I'm building a structure. I first see which tools and materials are at hand. Then, I make a plan for getting what's missing. If that is not possible, I re-imagine the structure that we can build with the materials at hand. In every case, we start where people are and focus on the assets they bring.

See Everyone as a Learner

Culturally based capacity building implies that everyone who needs to be in the room is present—and that everyone present is willing to learn. This is another theme that arose over and over in the conversations that generated this book. People said, "I have to remember that I'm not the expert." "It's about learning every time I walk into a room." "I put on my learning hat in every interaction."

The opposite of this is entering a relationship *wanting* to be the expert, always being the teacher, and having little appreciation for the treasures we receive when we are open to learning. This just doesn't work. We can never know everything about every culture. We cannot see a situation through every lens in the room.

When cultural competency is part of our practice, we love learning. We create a space where everyone learns from each other. We model being a learner, which supports learning organizations and learning communities.

As a student of life coaching, I learned that another key factor in supporting someone in their change process is curiosity. I find this particularly holds true when someone says something that hurts or offends us. For most of us, the initial reaction to a hurtful or inappropriate statement is to become angry, hurt, or defensive. That is often followed by a judgment about the person who made the statement. If we're fast enough on our feet, it can culminate in a sharp or clever response. Imagine if we could come to the point where instead of anger, hurt, or defensiveness, what got triggered was our curiosity. "I wonder what life experience that person has had that would lead him or her to that conclusion." Or "I wonder where that idea about this group of people comes from." Or even, "I wonder how someone could get to be that age, living in such a diverse community, and still come to that conclusion." Curiosity suggests a gesture of openness. Judgment implies a gesture of shutting down. Which do you think promotes dialogue more thoroughly? In my experience, if I get curious, I'm more open to thinking about what I want to share with the person that will move the larger, more global conversation forward. If I get judgmental, I shut down, and more often than not, so does the conversation.

In addition to curiosity, the skill most necessary to being a good learner is being a good listener. And the only way to listen well is to make sure we're not the only one talking!

We interviewed Julie Simpson, whose professional and voluntary leadership experiences span grantmaking, consulting, and board service. She has crafted efforts to improve capacity related to generational issues, arts, and national membership organizations. She touched on an openness of mind that promotes learning:

> I'm not sure it's different approaches so much as it is paying a lot of attention to listening and not coming in with any sort of pre-ordained [view]—the amount of customizing and tailoring that needs to take place, and starting from an asset-based approach where you look at what somebody has, not necessarily in terms of a traditional lens that equals assets. . . . What are the things that an organization is already doing? What are the things that they have at their fingertips that really make them strong and serve them, as opposed to coming in with some sort of a notion [of uniformity]?

Honor Transparency and Trust

As people get to know each other, they build trust among themselves. That's a good beginning. The next step is a strong sense that everyone knows what is going on. If there are tiers of access to information, trust is destroyed. This form of holding power leaves some members powerless.

Transparency is a key practice that the capacity builder can model for the group. This idea has emerged repeatedly

The Power of Sitting

I've been asked to do work with AmeriCorps programs about community entry. I talk about the power of sitting. If I get sent to Kenya, where my Peace Corps volunteer work was, the first two years I'm there, I listen. I sit and I listen.

How does this feel familiar to me? Culturally in the South, the front porch is a place of meeting. It is the town square. If I go home to Newborn and see my Aunt Carrie who's eighty-two, I'm going to go to her home and sit. We're sitting on the front porch and she's telling me everybody's business—who's got sugar [diabetes], whose blood pressure is high. And she is waving to the people who are walking by. It's a way to stay connected to the community.

So I talk about the power of sitting, and the front porch, as distinct cultural characteristics of the South. Thus, when people from elsewhere are wanting to come and partner, if they can't sit still, it creates such dynamic tension. There's a rhythm to organizing, to relating; it is about your ability to set your ass down. That is so significant to how I engage in relationship building that it has become a part of my pedagogy as a consultant.

—*Omisade Burney Scott*

in peer dialogues, interviews, and our own practice. When any of us know what is happening, we feel more invested. When we have a part in determining what is happening, we are even more engaged. We can more readily take ownership of a process or outcome. The more we disclose, the more inviting we are to others who are affected by our work. A workshop participant said, "Disclosure is a power tool!"

There are related practices that surfaced in our conversations, including

- Surrounding ourselves with people who don't let us live in the delusion of our power
- Having a daily practice that locates us in a larger picture of life
- Seeing ourselves as a vehicle for the gifts, talents, and skills that we have
- Remembering that information is power

Barbara Meyer, a funder who has focused on the rural South, listened to grantees who put a premium on trust building:

> In terms of impact, if I had to say in one sentence . . . of course money counts, but what we heard over and over is that it was the affirmation they got from us. It was the trust. It was the confidence. People trust us and they know we trust them. It's a huge impact; it's huge because of what it enables them to go and do around their community organizing. The most vivid example was from our meeting a year ago December. . . . We had a former board member who was chief of the Houma nation in New Orleans, which was almost destroyed. He said, "You believed in us, and I went out and told the Catholic bishops that our children weren't going to school" because of the lack of support for their own cultural base.

Be Willing to Wear Many Hats

When we work across cultures, we can be prepared to unlock leadership potential in many forms. As long as we have just one idea of what a leader looks like, we cripple ourselves and our process.

Once, in a group of indigenous people, I introduced myself as a consultant. Someone replied, "That's a fancy way of saying you're unemployed, eh?" Whether in response to a joke or an inquiry, I often say the same thing. There is a deeper meaning to this response. It means that we need to know when to wear which of the multiple hats that are at our disposal as capacity builders. If we know ways to be an "expert," a "learner," a "facilitator," a "trainer," a "planner," and a "mediator," we will be more responsive to what is going on in our landscape.

We found some good examples of organizations doing this successfully. A regional foundation acts on its core belief in the leadership of its grassroots base—the board members, who make major decisions. This funder makes grants to efforts led by and for the very community residents whose conditions must change. The reasoning is this: We focus on grassroots communities, supporting community organizing from a progressive perspective. The communities define the issue. We look at the work, and if it's an effective model, we give a general support grant. We believe that is how you achieve diversity, by watering the grassroots base, giving leaders the resources with which to do their work.

My appreciation for the different and creative ways that people organize to get things done is one of the reasons I became a consultant. I was regional director for Habitat for Humanity with seventy affiliates in California, Nevada, Arizona, Hawai'i, and Guam. All of them had the same mission of helping low-income families build their own homes. I was delighted and amazed at how seventy groups could see that mission in such different ways. They paid attention to what was going on in their communities, what their capacity was, and what they valued as process for achieving the mission. Houses got built throughout the region. Some affiliates built alternative houses, like those made of straw bale, while many designed and built other forms of "green" houses. Some had multiple staff members and built fifty houses a year. Others were all volunteer and built a house every two years. My role was to help them do the best they could in their own contexts.

So it is with all cross-cultural engagements. The more open we are to what leadership and assets communities bring, the more ownership of both process and outcome they have.

Our responsiveness starts with seeking input from the nonprofits we are supporting and allowing them some choice about which roles we will play. Then we can engage in a mutually agreed upon process, which increases the likelihood that people, organizations, and communities will own the process and the outcomes. This is more likely to lead to real transformation—not just a Band-Aid solution.

Paying Attention to Culture: In My Coaching Context

As often happens, the call for coaching came when the organization's leader was at her wit's end.

Alice was the director of a housing and community development agency with a staff of twenty-eight. A Japanese American, she had more than twenty years experience in a different jurisdiction.

Her staff was made up largely of two groups. One was an older "civil servant" crowd, mostly White, many within three or four years of retirement. The other group was a cluster of young "activists," including many people of color recruited from social-change organizations. They all worked in a poor community with high unemployment and many undocumented residents.

The community had changed dramatically since the older staff started working there. Some of the staff "problematized" the community, but Alice came in with a different perspective. She had grown up in a similar neighborhood and had firsthand experience creating a sense of "home" in communities that bureaucrats had written off. Her agenda was to create an environment where families could thrive.

After three days on the job, the "old-timers" gave her a list of their demands. They didn't want to have to do extra work, be responsive to the concerns of the community, or engage the community in decision making. Alice began to identify people on her staff who grew up in the neighborhoods where they now worked. She decided to work with them and to let the old-timers wait for their retirement. It didn't work. They felt threatened and called for her resignation.

A few weeks after starting coaching, Alice got a pink slip from the county. She felt blind-sided.

I invited Alice to consider the cultural assumptions about what kind of leader she should be. Her staff was looking for a charismatic, take-charge "big" leader. As a Japanese American woman, this was not the leader-self that Alice had cultivated.

In one coaching session, Alice wrote down all the leadership qualities that she considered important and that she embodied. Her list consisted of words like *honoring, consensus building, humble, competent,* and *empathetic.* As a coaching assignment, Alice wrote a letter outlining these leadership skills.

After sharing this letter with her bosses, they rescinded the pink slip. Alice is now in her fourth year, and she's seeing the results of staking her claim to her culture-based leadership style. She is not trying to remake herself according to the expectations of the dominant culture. Her leadership style is transforming the culture of the department.

How was coaching helpful in this situation? It helped Alice identify the cultural elements contributing to the dynamic. She worked to articulate them so that they became visible to her supervisors and her staff. Coaching gave her permission to explore her strengths and to engage in a dialogue with those who might not initially recognize them as strengths. She increased her sense of being an effective leader.

To be an effective coach, put culture on the radar screen. Understand that culture is alive on multiple layers, including racial, ethnic, and historical dimensions. A culturally competent coach understands how each layer influences the capacity of the organization to heal and change. Paying attention to culture is a key piece of making the space safe and respectful for everyone, including leaders.

Name the Elephants in the Room

Have you ever shared space with an elephant? There is an old expression about how the biggest issue in the room—the "elephant"—is avoided, talked around, or ignored. This happens in groups that resist talking about difficult issues.

Sometimes cultural competency is about naming elephants—bringing up difficult issues that have been left unspoken or unresolved. One practitioner described this dynamic: "I might do SWOT [strengths, weaknesses, opportunities, threats] analysis. But if I know that an organization in its various aspects—program, staff, board—is in denial around something and skating around a topic, I'll use the process to get at that. We don't lecture. We ask and reflect [on] what we're doing."

These comments continued with a specific example: A Latino-run organization got a grant to bring Latino and African American residents together. A person from the organization said the following: "They portrayed that they had significant African American input in the grant writing, planning process, and people on the steering committee, but it wasn't true. They were asking us to facilitate the process and make sure we have enough African Americans in the room."

I said, "Let's look at what's here, talk about who's done what. Let's paint the picture." They came to the realization that if we wanted this to be real, we were going to have to do something differently. We were going to have communication with other community groups, and we were going to make this happen. But this is a fearful thing, because nobody knows how the dynamics are going to change in the process of bringing new folks in.

The biggest fear is loss of control of the process. We have to nudge folks to face the reality. We get things on the table. Where does it take you? What does it inhibit in terms of real progress if it is left unaddressed?

It is interesting to note that the elephant often surfaces about fifteen minutes before a meeting is supposed to end. We can experience a genuine fear of dealing with difficult issues. At the same time, there is an authentic yearning to be our fullest selves. As a result, groups (and individuals) often dance around the deep issues, holding both the fear and the yearning. Just before it's time to go, the yearning often trumps, and someone surfaces the challenging concern.

When this happens, it is our responsibility to acknowledge it and to decide with the group how to respond. In my experience, people will often agree to stay later to deal with the issue or at least to map out a plan for dealing with it later. Once it's out in the open, the elephant is far less scary.

I worked with a "self-help" mental health coalition on strategic planning. During the first meeting, I thought everything was going nicely. Then, about ten minutes before the scheduled ending time, one of the co-chairs started calling the other one names and stating why she thought he wasn't fit for the position. I invited everyone to take a deep breath. I asked if we could postpone the next strategic planning meeting and asked for a meeting with the co-chairs. We ended up meeting three times as they did some work on co-leading and communications. One month later, the co-chairs felt more competent in dealing with each other and focusing on the planning process itself. With the elephant thus addressed, the group could move forward.

Create a Shared Vocabulary

There is something to be said for an orchestra of musicians when all of them play from the same sheet music. Likewise, one critical step to full engagement with communities is creating a shared vocabulary. When key terms are either new or have different meanings for people, start your work together with definitions.

Here are some key words to consider:

■ Culture
■ Capacity
■ Community
■ Success
■ Change
■ Justice

Some might object that there already *are* definitions to each of these. Why not just use those?

I answer that cultural competency calls us back over and over to the notion of context. *Webster's* dictionary may not be sufficient for a community that is diverse in age and race and struggling with including homosexuals (or heterosexuals) as equal partners in community planning. The definitions that make meaning for that community will arise from the shared stories of the community members themselves. I might define success differently depending on whether I've ever been allowed to the table before and whether the community is making space for me now.

I worked with a large child care provider serving more than five hundred children in multiple sites with a staff of more than fifty people. We met every Thursday evening for several months to develop a more culturally based approach to the work. The students were diverse; they came from cultures of many languages, though many of their parents were monolingual speakers. The staff reflected much of the student diversity.

We went around and around trying to create agreements about how to do the work. When someone spoke, the response often was, "That isn't how I would do it." So, we reframed the discussion. I gave people an opportunity to talk about each element. What was the norm for their own community?

After all participants got to tell their story in small groups, we came back together as a whole. This time, I said, "Given the varied ways that each of you engages, based on your cultural practices and experiences, what can we say will be the common agreements for us, here at the Stone Street Day Care Center?" The combination of validating their own experience and creating a specific set of agreements for their workplace allowed us to move along.

When we moved to Oakland from New Hampshire, my kids had friends from every background imaginable. This was new to all of us; we were used to bringing diversity to a community. In order to honor all the different practices from different households, we always prefaced our remarks about behavior with the words "In this house, we . . . " This allowed my kids and their friends to live with a plurality of perspectives while still being clear about what would be acceptable and not acceptable in our house.

Fully Engage People in Processes that Affect Them

The field of organizational development places a high value on full participation in decision making by the people those decisions will affect. Excellence in building nonprofit capacity requires the same.

Paying attention to culture in full engagement requires more than just asking people to participate. Our research—interviews, peer dialogues, literature reviews—repeatedly raised the importance of involving *all* stakeholders. By taking the time to truly understand the cultural perspectives of all participants, we can practice organizational development on a much deeper and more meaningful level.

For example, ensuring diversity among participants in a meeting often takes extra time and effort. It is not enough to say, "Half of the people I invited are people of color, so they had an opportunity to participate—whether or not they actually did." Achieving diversity for a meeting often means getting on the phone or asking others who are more connected to certain people to reach out on your behalf.

We must hold ourselves responsible for the outcome (achieving a diverse group) as well as the process (sending invitations to a diverse group). Often people of color, low-income people, or otherwise marginalized groups may not find time to participate if their input has not been sought or valued in the past. People will need to know that you are serious about their being present *and* that their ideas and suggestions will be heard. They may need options for public transportation or child care. How you reach out will set the stage for their full participation.

"In my world, it's often been around democratic—small 'd'—participation and decision making," says Sojeila Silva of the Northern California Community Loan Fund. If a consultant or funder (and likewise, a researcher, educator, or other professional) did not understand how important full participation is, that person could not be effective.

Practice Authentic Collaboration

During the original team process for creating this book, we learned that *doing* cross-cultural collaboration is more complicated than talking about it—even for people who pay attention to culture as a central part of our work. Inequities between mainstream institutions and ethnically identified cultural institutions can translate into unintentional (or intentional) disregard.

One theme in our research is a tendency for mainstream organizations to use the connections and intellectual property of others for their exclusive or disproportionate gain. Many capacity builders of color talk about White colleagues who want to "collaborate" with us. They pick our brains, take our ideas, and then sell them as their own.

We heard numerous stories about people of color who shared their experience and expertise. Their ideas about delivering programs or services in a culturally competent way were then taken forward by the mainstream institutions to gain funding. In the process, people of color were left out or received only token compensation.

This happens, too, in much-touted "partnering and collaboration" arrangements. Large mainstream organizations receive major grants for community economic development. Generally, such groups do not have ties to the communities they need to reach and must partner with grassroots organizations. Too often these organizations are brought in to help, with uncompensated time and minimal percentages of the original grant.

Here is a related issue that surfaced in several contexts (including Atlanta and Chicago dialogues): the practice of nonprofits hiring an "outreach worker" whose job is to bring non-English-speaking folks to the table. While their language skills are recognized as valuable to a nonprofit organization, the outreach workers are often paid far less than their coworkers. In addition, they are rarely considered for advancement opportunities and seldom have the ear of managers. One group of organizations in Florida actually gathered to resist such policies. They set out terms of engagement that included having a voice in how resources are used and an agreement to receive fair compensation.

A participant in a peer dialogue also lamented the affinity of individual donors and foundations alike for White-led mainstream institutions that already have enormous resources. Many of these successful nonprofits avoid collaboration if it involves sharing power and funding, and they typically devote little attention to programs reflecting the culture of historically marginalized communities.

These findings have two implications. One is that the capacity of organizations led by people of color needs to be developed before a true partnership can unfold. Second, the capacity of organizations needs to be developed, so that they can hold multiple leadership styles represented by different leaders. This takes us beyond hiring people from historically marginalized communities that are fully bicultural and can navigate fully the dominant culture or can be "developed" to do so. Finally, authentic collaboration means building relationships that make sense to the organizations and communities with whom we work. Many agencies consider that once they've hired people of color their work is done. However, this is the first step—not the last. It is important to move well beyond the mind-set of getting "one of each" in the room.

Consider Creating an Identity Match

Dime con quien andas y te dire quien eres is a Mexican saying that means "Tell me who you walk with, and I will tell you who you are." These words point to one shortcut to cultural competency that we sometimes try—achieving an "identity match" between the capacity builder and the nonprofit being supported. For instance, we might sense that an African American consultant would be a better fit for an African American-led organization, or that a young consultant would be more successful with a youth-led organization, a lesbian with an LGTBQ organization, and so on.

Identity matching can open doors and create a rapport that may not be present with an "outsider." In his contribution to Part One of this book, Alfredo Vergara-Lobo writes about the importance of *personalismo*. He describes how developing a strong relationship up front is essential with some Latino-led groups. Creating trust is key to building capacity in many communities and organizations, and this can be easier when people feel that they share similar cultures.

Clearly, language ability is critical to involving groups that are often left out. I recently partnered with a consultant to do training on policy advocacy. The audience was largely Latino, as was the other consultant. It was delightful to watch her pepper her conversations with Spanish words. It created an intimacy that I couldn't provide. It reminded me of my aunts sitting around the table speaking a sweet blend of English and French, which often made for funny grammatical formations.

During our interviews, some capacity builders related insider/outsider dynamics more to who is local and who comes from another region. With a cultural competency lens comes a recognition that "You actually have local capacity to carry out organizational development work; you're not bringing in people from outside," says Thomas Watson of the Southern Organizational Development Initiative, which deals with rural communities. "That doesn't mean you don't have someone with expertise or you don't broker bringing someone from the outside, but you really start out with local capacity."

The matchmaking process happens at multiple levels. The deepest is one of self-reflection, where we determine if we share core values with a person, organization, or community. If they are not shared, then do we *appreciate* their values? Intuition lets us know when a particular gig is not a good match for us. The key is making the time to listen. I find that paying attention to what is going on inside me relating to a particular project adds to my effectiveness as a capacity builder.

Matchmaking also has to do with style. Mine is to be responsive. As a consultant, I don't have any cookie cutters, and I use few templates. I work only with groups that are willing to invest time in a planning team that co-designs the project with me. I also work mostly with groups that are actively and intentionally in it for social justice. It is better to do this analysis at the beginning than to jump in without analysis and "discover" the mismatch later.

In addition, I'm usually not directive. On several occasions, it was clear during the interview that a group wanted someone to come in with lots of their own ideas and tell people how to proceed. We quickly decided that I would not be a good match for those particular groups. By looking at it in terms of a match, I don't have to feel bad when we decide not to work together.

Another level of identity matching is about knowing the history of a community and understanding its current issues. This allows us to pick up on subtle cues that can help or hinder progress with a group.

Investing Time in Identity Matching: Three Lessons

It is true that a little bit of information can be dangerous. Working in communities that we are not connected to and thinking that we know them when we don't can bring disastrous results.

After experiencing a family emergency, a colleague asked me to take her place in facilitating a meeting. She checked this out with the organization's coordinating committee. (I suspect she said good things about my facilitation skills.) They agreed.

I showed up thirty minutes before the meeting time and introduced myself. The planning committee welcomed me. As participants began to arrive, I introduced myself to them as well. This was the fifth in a series of meetings. All of us—the planning team, my colleague, and I—assumed the group would continue with the planned agenda.

A large group of people showed up just as we were scheduled to begin. The chair of the planning committee introduced me and we jumped right in.

It quickly became clear that I hadn't asked enough questions beforehand. Historical, class-based animosities that had stayed below the surface during the first four meetings now surfaced. Most people were ready to deal with the agenda, which involved a community planning process. But a small, vocal group wanted to resolve the historical tensions first.

I was in a quandary. People were clearly uncomfortable. I asked for a fifteen-minute break and invited those who felt the tensions were more pressing to meet with me. At that time I asked whether it made more sense for their "insider" facilitator to work with them on the more challenging issues; everyone already trusted her. They agreed, and after the break, one of them explained our suggestion to the whole group.

The lessons learned for me were as follows: ●

- When I come into a community that isn't my own, I need to take extra time to let people get to know me and for me to know them.

- If a situation comes up, I need to trust the group raising it and work with them to solve the problem.

- I need to know when I'm not the right person to handle a challenging situation. I can have suggestions, but ultimately the group has to come up with its own solutions.

While it is often helpful, identity matching is not just about whether we have the same racial or ethnic identity, come from the same neighborhood, or share other particular characteristics. It is about what we make of our life experiences and how we bring it in to professional encounters.

One member of the Standards Committee for the Alliance for Nonprofit Management told about working with a nonprofit that advances gay and lesbian issues. She believed that her personal support of diversity and gay rights would allow her to fully engage with the project. However, she soon realized that coming from a heterosexual culture created a host of complex issues. She did not feel she could speak as credibly to these issues as someone immersed in the life experience of a gay person and gay organizations. As a result, she withdrew from the assignment.

See the Pitfalls of Being an "Insider"

Identity matching also has some pitfalls, which in our research related to gender and generation. When consulting with more traditional cultures, for example, young female capacity builders sometimes have difficulty breaking through barriers.

Another pitfall arises when a perceived match is not genuine. Tawara Goode of the National Center for Cultural Competence, based at Georgetown University, candidly shared a story about this. She had a White colleague who had been working for decades in a predominantly African American community and was highly trusted in that community. For years she had wanted Tawara, who is African American, to come in and do some work with this community. Tawara feared it may not be a good fit but agreed to try it out. Despite the fact that she shared the same racial and ethnic identity as the community, Tawara came from an upper middle-class background. Highly educated, she grew up in a different part of town. There was significant mistrust of her within the group that she could not overcome in the one-day workshop. Her White colleague had achieved trust over time in that community. The lesson is that superficial "matching" between capacity builder and client may be meaningless or even detrimental.

Also, there can be an excellent match between people of different identities.[64] Sometimes a capacity builder (or member of a team) from outside a cultural group can listen and work across the enormous diversity *within* that group. One colleague, an African American, recalls that she was recruited to facilitate a group by and for women of Asian ancestry. They wanted someone who shared the experiences of women of color, but someone not perceived as favoring a particular group within that Pan-Asian spectrum.

Another group based in a particular community of color needed to move beyond their usual practice of avoiding disagreement. This valuable role was played by a skilled consultant from a different community who encouraged honest conversation, listened well, and respectfully played back to the group a sense of what people were saying. Her skills allowed group members to reconsider and clarify their direction. She was able to surface issues as a caring outsider, which helped tremendously to move the group forward.

Juan Cruz's experience with being an outsider is informative. "California passed a law earmarking funds for special mental health funding—part for underserved or unserved communities," he recalls. "There was a whole elaborate planning process outlined before [the] actual rollout of funds and programs." Elbowed out of the process, Native American communities weren't involved and didn't even know about it. Cruz adds the following:

> I was asked by a coalition of social service agencies to come in because of my background in mental health and program development. We developed a tight two-day, stick-your-toe-in-this-water kind of thing, because we also had to build capacity of Native American groups and state and local health officials to understand each others' issues. We had to do a dual thing. I helped them figure out what mental health people needed to know about Native Americans and how to bring them up to speed. Simultaneously, the Native Americans (tribes, agencies, providers) were able to learn about the mental health act and what that meant in terms of programming and funding for their communities.

Cruz did not bring any obvious match by ethnicity. Yet his combination of expertise and commitment to increased understanding on all sides made the difference.

The bottom line is that capacity builders need to be aware of their own cultural location and that of their clients and grantees. Partnering with someone who has experience in that community can be a way for us to learn and contribute when working with an unfamiliar community. There are no shortcuts, and even people with the most skills in cultural competency run into painful difficulties.

To overcome the sense of being overwhelmed and exhausted that often occurs in this work, stay close with a diverse group of colleagues. Be willing to listen deeply and learn from every step on the journey. Aspire to do your work with the confidence that your goals are based on a set of just principles.

Make a Long-Term Commitment to Build Relationships

Paying attention to culture requires a long-term investment. It takes time to build relationships.

Most of us have probably had at least one experience of "parachute consulting." A funder or a small group from the community hires a consultant who makes a simple intervention and moves on. Or a funder or evaluator enters for a quick change attempt. In my experience this is unsatisfying. In fact, the intervention may be done simply to appease people or patch things up, which may forestall real change.

I belong to a circle of women who piloted a curriculum that explores the intersection between peacemaking and spirituality. This particular group is diverse—racially, politically, spiritually, and by class and age. We are farmworkers' and professors' daughters; we are immigrants and indigenous; we have roots in communism and the Reagan years. Some of us are deeply spiritual with little history of political activism and peacemaking. Others are deep activists who have not explored spirituality. Some have a rich combination of both, each informed by the other.

It became clear early on that if we were going to build the level of trust it would take to have deep, difficult conversations, we needed to know each other better. The curriculum called for a twelve-week program with thirty minutes of introductions during the first session. We decided to take the first five weeks to tell our stories. Two women each had an hour to share their peacemaking and spiritual journey.

It was amazing. Not only were the stories different, we each told them in different ways. One woman used pictures. Another used a series of shadow boxes that depicted key moments in her life. One used a global map with pins to locate all the places she'd lived. As she spoke, she strung a thread around each pin. When she finished, she had a beautiful web of her life. We learned at least as much about each other by the *how* of our storytelling as by the stories themselves.

Because we'd taken time to get to know each other, we started exploring spirituality and peacemaking in a much deeper way. By session ten (actually our sixteenth session), we were able to have a challenging conversation about race and its impact on peacemaking. The White women in the group held each other accountable; the women of color shared our perspectives. It was among the most profound conversations on race that I've engaged in, and there have been many.

By contrast, an organization contacted me because they wanted to do cross-cultural sensitivity training. They'd set aside two hours for it Thursday next. I met with the planning team and posed a question: Suppose your financial systems were out of whack. Can you imagine calling in a consultant to fix the problem by teaching financial literacy to the whole staff in a two-hour session? They laughed. After some discussion, we decided that we would use the Thursday meeting to launch a larger process. They expanded the initial meeting to a half day, and we began the conversation. Afterward they established a working group charged with carrying the conversation forward and embedding it into the culture of the organization.

As a capacity builder, I may not be part of an organization's ongoing process, but my responsibility is to move the focus of cultural competency from an afternoon of parlor tricks (including some diversity "exercises") to an ongoing part of organizational development.

Bring Capacity Building to Executive Transitions

Executive transitions is a growing area of practice in the capacity-building field. Major advances have been made in understanding some of the key methods to help organizations through transitions. However, practitioners recognize that recruiting diverse talent is a major challenge in the field.

One consultant's experience was that women's organizations had no qualms about stating specifically that they want a woman leader. With "Black" and "Brown" organizations, however, it was different. They typically insisted that all they wanted was the "best qualified" executive director; ethnic identity did not matter.

This is a phenomenon related to power and privilege, and it includes several factors: whether funders are likely to extend support to a leader of color, the specter of reverse discrimination accusations, and whether people see the advantages of a shared cultural background with constituents. One capacity builder expressed the dilemma and his response to it:

> You look at leadership and the constituency the organization might deal with, and if it is an African American or Latino organization, they'll pay lip service: *It would be really great if we had a person who represented the community, but we want the most qualified.* They don't do the deep dive: What would it take to have someone who reflects them and who looks like them?

I've dealt with women's organizations—let's say, shelter-driven, with a mission [against] abuse. There's an inherent belief that a man can't lead that organization if they serve women who've been through abuse. I'm not saying that's not valid, but [other] people don't want to have that conversation; it's easier to find a lesbian or gay person to lead a gay or lesbian organization than to find a Latino to lead a Latino children's organization—or that's the way people think. People treat [ethnic identity] as an anomaly. I go back to dealing with the truth. Where one organization says, "Just give me the best person," I push back.

Another option is to consider transitional leadership. During our research, a young White woman, Lisa, recalled her experience with an organization that serves (and is also led by) people of color on its board of directors. When the nonprofit was looking for an interim executive director, a respected colleague of color with many years of experience and leadership in capacity building highly advised the board to hire Lisa in the role.

On meeting Lisa, the board was surprised and initially resistant, probably a response to her youthfulness as well as matcher race/ethnicity. Even so, they held an executive session and agreed to give her the job. She turned out to be a perfect transition leader, partnering with an executive of color already on staff who successfully stepped into the role as permanent executive director.

Leave Knowledge on the Ground, Supporting Sustainability

We all know the adage about the fish: If we give hungry people a fish, then they eat for a day. If we teach them to fish, then they eat for a lifetime. The familiarity of this proverb can blind us to its wisdom.

Some of us who are drawn to the helping fields can be overly caregiving. We tend to be rescuers and fixers. The important learning that needs to happen within a group often gets usurped by well-meaning consultants or other community helpers who take on the work of creating change themselves. As a result, the group misses the learning needed for the next level in its development.

I liken this situation to parenting adult children. It's only when I really let go that they are able to fly on their own. Resolving the tension between their struggles and my passion requires discernment on my part. I need to keep my own agenda in check, and self-awareness is key.

I worked for many years with Habitat for Humanity. Often, I heard people say that our work was about more than teaching to fish; it was about making the bank of the river accessible to people who couldn't otherwise own it. As I reflect on that, it is compelling to think that we can share information in a way that allows people to own it. This shifts the balance of power. When individuals, organizations, or communities access their own power, their relationships with "helpers" change. It gets closer to equal, and some of us who like having power over others can get uncomfortable.

I once served a troubled organization as interim executive director. People were exhausted, and when I showed up they were largely relieved. They essentially turned their power over to me, and I realized how easy it would be to exploit this situation. I could see them asking me to stay on as permanent executive director, and I knew I didn't want to do that. So, early on we talked about power. We also talked about their historical lack of commitment to administrative responsibilities. The organization had moved through several leaders in a few years. They just wanted to do programs and not worry about raising money or managing it—or even respecting those who did those tasks. Administration was an annoying bother, and that is how the program staff treated administrative staff—the most recent batch of whom had left en masse. Thus, the call to me.

The first thing we did was to make a list of all the administrative functions. Then we explored my role as interim. It turned out there were a lot of administrative functions that would be left undone until we could hire new staff. We doled out remaining jobs, and everyone had administrative functions to manage for three months. Their appreciation for the role of administrative staff grew significantly. As part of the operational plan for moving forward, they wanted to institute financial literacy and fundraising skills development for the whole staff. They decided that it was important for every staff person to carry some administrative responsibilities and for the new administrative staff to access program work.

This was an experiment, but the organization was fully engaged in it. It changed the way they do business, and people are modeling a new, less hierarchical structure for the groups with which they work. If I had accepted their invitation to manage administration, this capacity might never have been generated.

Each of us is deeply informed by our own cultural lens, and articulating its influences on our lives allows us to be more effective. Yet this is not enough. Our work is to leave every interaction ensuring that the client or organization is more adept at addressing their own cultural perspectives. We take seriously the notion of working ourselves out of a job. The transfer of knowledge in intentional ways is a hallmark of culturally based work. Given the deep divides that characterize our society today, this task is more important than ever.

Chapter 8
Cultural Competency as Changing Institutions

If you've read this far, you most likely share our interest in disrupting historical patterns of inequity. This goes beyond changing personal beliefs and habits. It goes beyond being more inclusive in a nominal sense. Cultural competency tackles institutional practices to achieve social change.

Race and class differentiation have deep roots in human history. Thousands of years of "civilization" concentrated large population groups, refined work categories, cemented social hierarchies, and allocated privilege to certain groups.

There are many theories as to why the story played out in this way. Jared Diamond's book *Guns, Germs, and Steel: The Fates of Human Societies* (later a public television series) offered one theory: Technology, sophisticated weapons, and immunity from certain diseases gave the conquerors an edge. This triple advantage allowed them to move across the globe while taking other peoples' land.[65] *Gold, Greed, and Genocide*, a report from Project Underground, tells the story from an indigenous perspective. It posits a different theory—that the domination of one group over others is motivated simply by a desire to have more.[66]

It is often assumed that almost all humans want to rise as high as they can in a hierarchy. Yet in our multiethnic modern culture, the cues to what it takes to rise in the "pecking order" are sometimes confused, hidden, and—all too often—tied to heredity.

A great deal of emotional energy and personal resources are expended in the effort to advance in status. Most of us are willing to get education or skills training in preparation for working in privileged career categories. Failure to advance can lead to personal crisis. Often individuals will partner with others to work together to achieve group advancement. Failure or frustration of this group effort can lead to debilitating or organization-destroying conflict, vicious political battles, or even wars.

Capacity building is advanced human skills work that continually raises questions: Will we only be the product of our biology and the suspicion of the outsider? Or will we resist that cultural training and become celebrants and artists directing our own lives and creating equity? Our answers to these questions must involve the issues of privilege, power, oppression, and systemic change. These are the main topics of this chapter.

Wake Up to Privilege

It would be a mistake to assume that exclusionary behavior is conscious. Often, neither the recipients of bias or privilege nor the targets of such biases are aware of the discrimination inherent in cultural structures. The evolution and integration of these cultural structures into everyday life proceeds at a glacial but steady pace. Generations are taught to accept and live with discriminations.

Privileged groups can have difficulty accepting that they have privilege because they never have to think about it. They find it difficult to even *comprehend* the concept of privilege since they have never experienced an alternative to it. Privilege is invisible and ubiquitous—the cultural sea in which they swim. Explaining privilege to these groups can feel like trying to explain the concept of dry land to a fish.

In her groundbreaking article of 1988, "White Privilege: Unpacking the Invisible Knapsack," Peggy McIntosh documented twenty-six examples of privilege that most White people enjoy without realizing it.[67] For example, "I can do well in a challenging situation without being called a credit to my race." And, "I can be sure that if I need medical help, my race will not work against me."

Privilege is manifest in many areas besides race. One can be privileged as a result of class, place of origin, language, body shape, and many other ways. Everyone has some point of privilege, even if we are targets of discrimination in other areas.

We were reminded of this during a Professional Development for Consultants training session.[68] One of the peer teams led us in an exercise to identify those places where we were privileged and those where we were not. Almost everyone in the room was a person of color. When we looked at categories other than race and ethnicity (such as religion, education level, and economic status), people were able to identify many points of privilege.

One of our workshop participants gave an example: "I am a person of color of East Indian descent, and I have felt disadvantaged at times because of that. At the same time, today I am celebrating my ten-year wedding anniversary. I am keenly aware that being married is a privilege my LGTBQ friends and colleagues cannot access."

Pursuing this line of thought reveals more examples of how we fall asleep to privilege, even with progressive programs. For example, providing veterans with access to educational, health, and financial benefits sounds like a just idea at first. After all, veterans risked their lives for our country. However, these benefits are distributed in ways that privilege White men: The GI bill was accompanied by admission denials at many schools for men of color, and women historically were not allowed to serve in combat. Yet veterans' benefits have become institutional privilege; they are not granted as the conscious act of a biased power broker.

A related concept is aversive racism, where people hold unconscious or subtle biases that are more detrimental to team performance than overt racism.[69]

When different cultural norms are brought together in a work or organizational situation, cultural conflicts can rise to the surface and shine a spotlight on differences in privilege. "Oftentimes in these environments there are people who have the burden of explanation," says Makani Themba-Nixon, a seasoned activist, writer, and executive director of an organization that provides funding and technical assistance. "White folks don't have to explain themselves because almost every book or movie that you have to view explains them."

One reaction to awareness of one's own racial privilege is to equate being White with being an oppressor. In our research, "appropriate Whiteness" emerged as a way to shift the quality of relationships among nonprofit leaders and capacity builders and promote mutual respect. This point came up in the Southern United States among people who realize that cultural competency efforts exist within a larger backdrop of explicit White supremacy. In this environment, good intentions are met by simmering resentments over the need to continually address racism. A Southern capacity builder of color, who is active and well known in national circles, framed the dilemma in blunt terms:

> One of the things that's going to hamper the project of cultural competency as it's done in a transracial or interracial way is that there's really

too little embryonic work done around appropriate Whiteness. There is a lot of work around the rejection of White supremacy, but not enough on constructing an appropriate European identity in a cultural way. People [are] not appreciating the positive aspects. Some people join the Klan because it is a group that talks about Whiteness in a positive way and affirms who they are rather than the group that's always talking about what's wrong with who they are.

The Privilege Continuum

While working with groups, I sometimes use a tool called the privilege continuum. I place a banner at one end of the room with the words *highly privileged* on it. At the other end of the room, I put another banner that says *underprivileged*. People place themselves along the continuum based on their sense of their own privilege in different situations.

For example, I asked employees of a university to spread themselves along the continuum as it related to their racial identity. As usually happened, skin color largely determined where people stood: people of African descent stood mostly at the lowest end of the spectrum, and European Americans stood at the higher ends.

However, one young African American man stood under the highly privileged banner. When I asked people to share, he said, "I'm very privileged as a Black man to be in graduate school." His point of reference was the larger African American community, not the institution.

We went through more categories, such as age, gender, and sexual identity. Some people moved back and forth a lot. A few hovered near one end or the other.

Finally, I asked people to place themselves based on their relationship to the university. The faculty stayed at the high end, while the staff almost ran each other down heading for the low end of the continuum. Students placed themselves all along the room. This was an enlightening moment. It was particularly important for the faculty to see how universally the staff felt marginalized.

During a conversation after the exercise, many people said that they felt uncomfortable while standing at the highly privileged end of the continuum. Generally, they didn't feel awkward *having* privilege. Yet it was challenging to acknowledge this fact openly and to have that act witnessed.

I invited the university community to explore where the greatest power rests within a community or organization. They decided that the people at the higher end of the privilege continuum—those with more power—are in a better position to change things.

Then the elephant came out! During a discussion, participants discovered that they are reluctant to extend privilege because they assume that they will lose something in the exchange. We ran straight into the notion of privilege and power as a zero-sum proposition: Your gain is my loss.

We followed up with role plays where people imagined extending privilege to everyone instead of shifting it from one segment of the group to another. To their surprise and delight, they discovered that, when they thought hard enough about it, they could always create strategies that allowed everyone to feel valued, empowered, and fully engaged.

During a workshop following the Alliance for Nonprofit Management conference in Los Angeles, I presented the privilege continuum exercise again. At the last minute, I added another category, asking people to place themselves along the continuum based on body size. The men had little trouble placing themselves. But it was stunning to watch a group of competent, beautiful women scramble while figuring out where to place themselves. They acted confused and off balance. It reminded me that sometimes we don't know what is at play in a room. What happens on the surface doesn't tell the whole story; more of the iceberg is underwater and invisible.

Recognize and Extend Privilege

It is essential that we recognize the points of privilege in our own life and work. Then we can better pay attention to how we engage with others who differ from us in these arenas. Further, we must remind ourselves that privilege has nothing to do with the inherent worth and dignity of a person. Privilege is not earned. Rather, it is usually artificially granted based on external circumstances.

The objective of this work is to extend privilege to everyone. Bringing historical processes into the light of understanding and choice allows capacity builders, executive directors, boards of directors, and nonprofit staff members—the next generation of leaders—to fully engage in creating a just society. Yet this is not easy to do. This confrontation can be disconcerting and uncomfortable for everyone, raising those instinctually xenophobic hairs on the backs of our neck. Target groups may adapt to the status quo and may not wish to confront deficits in privilege.

Our unconsciousness of privilege, and a resistance to recognize it, contribute to a "revolving door" phenomenon that makes it hard for nonprofit organizations to retain people of color. Interviewee Barbara Meyer, an innovator in the funding world who brings a progressive orientation, asked, "How many organizations have not been able to deal with race and class issues and [have] dissolved?" She goes on to say, "For me, there were painful times. I was the White woman with money in the room, and there were times when folks would want to go out to dinner and I didn't get invited. It was because people had stuff they needed to talk about. To me, it's about helping people of different race and class backgrounds to be in the room together; to make space for them to be able to say to each other, 'Hey,' rather than walk away. I had to learn and relearn how to *be present* and how to be an ally to people of color, even when it is personally difficult."

When privilege is not extended equally to all parties, it often falls to those with less privilege to go the extra mile to create a measure of equilibrium. This is a necessary step along the journey. But I am always relieved when those with the most privilege in a situation take responsibility for managing their own discomfort and doing the hard work of engaging their own privilege. (Beth Applegate's contribution to Part One of this book is a good example of that ownership.)

This process brings many challenges. If we see the whole enterprise of race and class analysis as a zero-sum game, where someone has to give up something so that others can have it, then it's a losing proposition. There is also the common trap of the mainstream media that seeps into nonprofit programs: trying to understand what is "wrong" with certain communities and paternalistically trying to solve their problems.

For capacity builders, helping the privileged understand the work they need to do may mean working separately with such groups. Many people of color become exhausted by having to "teach" White people, year after year, to unlearn their biases. Yet, when the focus shifts to privileged groups taking responsibility, the process can be rewarding for all. Paul Kivel's book *Uprooting Racism: How White People Can Work for Social Justice* offers strategies and approaches to bring the focus to White people's institutions and actions and how these can be changed.[70]

As capacity builders from any cultural background, we have a lot of power. Our position in relationship to our clients comes with a degree of privilege. We get to enter people's lives through an organizational or community setting where they share with us their most pressing concerns. All of us have different ways to remind ourselves that we are part of a larger system and that whatever privilege we have is there to support and benefit the whole.

Understand the Types of Power

Power is a word with many connotations, such as

- ▪ *Power over* something or someone: This includes power that comes with a job title or position, referred power that comes from connections to others, and expert power that comes from wisdom, knowledge, experience, and skills.

- ▪ *Institutional power* and *obstructive power* stems from the ability to coerce or block.

- ▪ *Personal power* stems from the charismatic personality of someone who gets things done.

- ▪ Power that generates action, much as an engine powers a machine: This involves *ideological power* coming from a compelling idea, vision, or analysis; *cultural power* resulting from the feeling of belonging; and *transcendent power* that comes from connection to a spiritual, natural, or historical force. Some refer to these as *power within.*

- ▪ Power that is relational but not dominant: An example is *co-powering,* which refers to individual leaders who work mindfully to support the power of others through modeling, validating, and feedback. Another example is the energy generated by *collaborative power*—partnership with people in pairs, teams, organizations, communities, coalition, and movements.[71]

Sometimes, we are able to see power and name it as such. At other times we need culturally based capacity builders to help us. Sojeila Silva illustrates this fact:

> I do financial management support with organizations. I've found a connection between a leader's relationship with money and the organization's culture regarding money and finances.

> When I grew up, we had no extra money. Everyone knew how much we had and where it went. In organizations where more affluent people are in leadership, they often have guilt about their salaries, so they don't want to disclose finances to the rest of the organization. It translates into mistrust, which sometimes leaks into other areas beyond finances.

> I help leaders see how their personal issues with money spill over into the organization. Everyone knows it, even when the leaders don't acknowledge it. It gets translated into secrecy. They might be subsidizing one program because it's a higher priority, but [they] don't acknowledge it. Or they keep salaries secret. So now, I just tell the leaders when I think they have distorted relationship with money.

Sojeila's story reminds me of ways that money has held power in my own life. When my grandparents had no money beyond necessities, everyone received just what they needed—nothing extra. And when there was a little disposable money, my grandparents talked about fairness and sharing equally with all. Yet we knew that they were actually more generous with their favorite grandchildren. It would have been better if this had been openly acknowledged.

"That's exactly what I'm talking about," says Sojeila. "If we could give your grandparents a financial report, they'd see the reality. That's what I do with organizations. I help them to see by putting it on paper how they are playing out their distorted relationships with money."

Cultural competency involves a deep level of honesty in digging for the facts. Sojeila reflected on this point: "I find it's about communication: What are the power relationships? Who is held accountable and for what? I pay attention to formal and informal relationships in doing that analysis. I gather financial information from the past three to five years. Where they've been says a lot about where they are and where they are going."

Challenge Conventional Beliefs about Power

People in the most privileged positions often hold most tightly to the belief that their power is completely earned and deserved. Power brokers benefit by believing that poor people are poor because they do not have the drive or the intelligence to be rich. This cultural dynamic is highly resistant to analysis and change. It is difficult for people to accept that at least some of their power results from culturally allocated privilege based on membership in a favored race or class.

During World War II, women were brought into the workforce in massive numbers while men were off soldiering. Women, including those without a lot of education or training, often discovered they could do the work that the men left behind. Most learned right on the job. Yet after the war, many women were moved out of the workforce, and even now there are jobs filled almost exclusively by men.

Today we see massive failures among small businesses and significant public resources used to prop up corporations. Yet there remains a belief that the private sector is more efficient and effective than the public sector. This seldom-explored belief lingers because it is accepted by people with power. Similar prejudices about ethnic groups remain unexamined, and for the same reason.

For capacity builders in the nonprofit sector, this dynamic hits close to home. Foundations are in positions of power because they control needed resources. Yet those resources are allocated on the basis of a narrow range of views about why the world is the way that it is. Rarely do foundations challenge conventional viewpoints.

Exercise Power Deliberately

As demographics change, so do power dynamics. Although heterosexual White males dominate corporations and Congress, the faces of leadership and power are changing at other levels of the public, private, and third (nonprofit or community benefit) sectors. Unless the new faces are intentional about changing the status quo, however, institutional power can overwhelm them. If we expect it to overturn historical patterns, we must exercise personal power in deliberate ways.

I live in Oakland, California, where for more than a century the power brokers, including the city council, were White men. In the mid-1970s the council gained an African American majority. Yet few of the new leaders were intentional about doing business differently. They were so pleased with getting into power that they did not change many policies. The city power dynamics did not change much either. Developers still had their way and neighborhoods were largely overlooked.

As a result of the 2006 election, five women won Oakland council seats. During the campaign, we heard lots of promises about how different things would be if women were in the majority. Even today, it is hard to find evidence of the feminization of the council or its policies.

The need to engage on a deeper, systemic level is one area that distinguishes cultural competency from "diversity." A study from the Applied Research Center found that increased diversity in a foundation's program officers did not lead to increased funding for organizations led by people of color.[72] Program officers reported that they were expected to represent their community *and* assimilate to mainstream foundation culture, making it harder to do their job.

A peer dialogue in Atlanta brought us this personal story:

> I once sat on a funding committee making major grants to organizations. We noticed that no women of color organizations were receiving grants, and there were a majority of women of color making the decisions. Not only was there internalized oppression but double standards . . . the theory is that we get people of color in those power positions where they could determine people's fates, and the outcomes would be different.

Changing this dynamic requires strong leadership and a commitment from the top. In his keynote address to the Alliance for Nonprofit Management's 2005 Annual People of Color Gathering in Chicago, Ron McKinley reminded us to see the places where race, class, and power intersect with community development. He described these intersections as community resources, public policy, nonprofit capacity, and foundation resources. We often focus on one of these elements but rarely see them as integrated. Instead, we must pay attention to all of them and their implications for cultural competency in capacity building.

Ultimately we minimize power differences by recognizing that they exist and by responding with intentional action. This calls for critical thinking, political analysis, and a strong measure of empathy. When we "get it" that we are all connected, we are more likely to see the differentials and to eliminate them, no matter what the cost. Change comes when power differentials are addressed and rectified.

Notice and Name the Various Forms of Oppression

It is important to notice and name oppression when we see it. This includes internalized oppression, which occurs when people who are targets of a dominant worldview take on the assumptions embedded in that worldview. For example, people of color might work hard to eliminate all vestiges of their first (non-English) language. They might chemically process their hair to eliminate curls. Some go as far as skin lighteners and cosmetic surgery that reshapes the nose or eyes.

When someone accepts a negative categorization, the results can be harmful and deeply disturbing: poor job performance, inability to work on teams, and more. This is unhealthy for individuals, organizations, and communities.

In the nonprofit world, we have seen funders fuel this phenomenon by looking for the "greatest needs." Nonprofits often respond by describing communities from a deficit perspective, trying to prove that their constituent group is more disadvantaged than others. In this way we have seen a wedge drawn between immigrant rights and racial justice, reinforcing rigid racial hierarchies.[73] This is deadly to social change.

As capacity builders, we ask ourselves: What does my internalized oppression look like? How am I dealing with it? How can I engage this particular

Dealing with Power Differentials

Dealing with power differences in an honest and open way is key in community building and creating justice. Some strategies include

■ Orient new members sufficiently so there is less tension between "insiders" and "outsiders." Often those who come late to the table miss the opportunity to know each other and the rest of the group.

■ Use ground rules. Those developed by the group as a whole are most effective in generating ownership of the process.

■ Reach out to people with less power. Invite voices that have not been heard and groups that have not been at the table.

■ Make your process accessible to those whose power you want to increase. If necessary, change the meeting time and place. Provide transportation, child care, and even stipends. Those with power tend to be paid for their participation in community building; those without power usually are not.

person, organization, or community to address its own internalized oppression? What are the strategies they need to develop for dealing effectively with internalized oppression?

Our work is to create space so that communities can notice and name internalized oppression. The organizational and community rewards that can erupt are sometimes phenomenal. When privilege and internalized oppression are openly addressed, people may experience a burst of creativity. Energy that had been bottled up is released to good use and greater enjoyment. I compare it to what left-handed people would feel if they suddenly entered a world where chairs, tools, and door knobs were designed specifically for them. Life would suddenly become easier as they entered this new world of privilege. The energy that had gone into coping with everyday obstacles could now be channeled into creating social change.

Examine Systems and Structures

Another principle that guides our work is a commitment to examining structures of oppression. It is not unusual for a group of wonderful and well-intended people to unconsciously participate in racist institutions. If we analyze only individual behaviors, we miss the larger framework, one that transcends individual attitudes and their manifestation.

How Language Intersects with Power

In any setting where multiple languages are spoken, there are power differentials. Sojeila Silva, from the Northern California Community Loan Fund, tells this story:

Usually, all meetings are carried on in English, with some translation to and from Spanish; the union members sit on one side of the table, owners on the other. Owners have formal education; union members are phenomenal leaders and are largely informally educated. Owners don't listen, refuse to negotiate; workers walk out. Eventually contracts get signed.

My approach: I mixed people up around the room, did team-building exercises, and matched the lead union person with the lead owner. We gave everyone two matches and told them they could talk only as long as the match was burning and couldn't talk more than twice. Everyone spoke in their first language, and we translated it for the nonspeakers. They agreed to *all* go through conflict resolution training, based on a plan we created together in that room. There's been no walkout since then (six years ago). They have more real relationships.

Frank Lopez is an experienced capacity builder based in a Texas community bordering on Mexico. When leading a nonprofit organization, he insisted that staff members consider linguistic issues carefully. This priority applied to meetings, to program publications, and even to the issue of whether to publish board bylaws and minutes in English. Key questions to ask are: What will be most useful for keeping an organization well grounded in its mission? What will keep constituents engaged? What will keep the work sustained and effective?

In her contribution to Part One of this book, Beth Applegate captures the tension between personal behavior and institutional racism: "Understanding the systemic nature of White supremacy affirms that I can be the subject of discrimination based on gender and sexual orientation. Being a White lesbian raises my awareness of oppression."

It is easy to miss the larger institutional framework. For example, one seasoned group of capacity builders involved in a race, class, and power workshop came to this conclusion:

> Clearly, approaches to addressing issues of race, class, and power must focus on the people involved, honoring their human dignity, and creating processes and norms that support full, broad-based participation. These principles and values are essential for the work of capacity building in a manner that addresses differences of race, class, and power. Moreover, since so much of the work involves helping rooms full of people find ways to listen to one another, learn from one another's perspectives, and determine how to move forward together in the face of differences, a focus on listening, interpersonal interactions, and group dynamics is warranted.[74]

Few of this group's comments focused on the issues of difference and power at the level of organizations, institutions, or systems. This might be explained, in part, by the way we asked the questions. Yet the results are consistent with a pattern that the workshop organizers have observed in the field as a whole.

A point that's repeated in a wide range of publications about racism in the nonprofit sector is well stated by john a. powell:

> [T]he patterns for racial inequality have been set. Persistent racial disparities are not dependent upon racial animus or ill will; this is why they are termed "structural." This is the racism that is built into all of our structures; it is the status quo, and will only be undone in a lasting way when structures are reformed. . . . [R]acism in motion stays in motion unless forces counteract it.[75]

According to powell, nonprofits can counteract racism through a variety of measures aimed at equity, particularly in community economic development and education.

In an interview with Leroy Moore, a disability advocate of color, we learned about the frustrations capacity builders encounter when they ask organizations to address structural racism. Here is a story that he shares:

With a nonprofit organization, we did a hands-on event/experience. Without telling the agency that we were doing it, we sent in two people [as testers]—one being Caucasian and the other one African American. Of course, we found that the African American person came out as soon as he went in; he was sent away without help. The Caucasian came out like about a half hour later having received services and resources and everything.

We wrote it up and we gave it to the agency. And they were very, very closed off about the results at first, but they came through and they saw that . . . they didn't have it [a process to make treatment equitable]. So it was: are you going to deal with this or not? Because of that they had a little town hall meeting to be more inclusive, but although I was excited about the town hall, I just didn't think it really went deeply on how to become inclusive.

Power and privilege are in the underlying framework that leads to structural racism. Our original research did not delve directly into structural racism, but our interviews and literature review uncovered important insights for capacity builders. Frank Lopez, a Texas-based leader of a capacity-building organization, with Latino ancestry and a previous career in law, shared a story from his own experience as a law school professor:

It was clear that the White faculty there had a perception of people of color, both students and faculty, unless they were part of the same-thinking group, that was negative. I arrived as new faculty at the law school. While I was on the admissions committee, I discovered that there was a systemic problem that guaranteed that 80 percent [of applicants being accepted] would always be White. I raised the issue; when I did that, they took me off admissions. That was my fall from the club.

Juan Cruz asked some provocative questions about cultural grounding and how it reaches beyond individual practice to the institutional:

By me being curious, open to them, not making assumptions about them, I am embodying cultural competency. Can institutions reflect that kind of behavior? I don't know; are they constitutionally set up to be open to people who are not like them? As people and institutions get together, are they calcified? Everybody be like the building: There are only certain ways to come in and out!

Looking for Structural Racism

Capacity builders can raise courageous questions about how structural racism plays out in an organization. Following are examples that relate to two crucial aspects of nonprofit operations.

Volunteer management

■ How are volunteers recruited? Where are ads placed? In what languages?

■ Who does recruitment? Are they trained in cultural competency? Language skills?

■ How are volunteers being used? What kinds of roles and opportunities are available?

■ What are the demographics of the volunteers? What are the demographics broken down by roles of volunteers?

■ Do all volunteers have advancement and development opportunities?

■ Do volunteers provide input for decision making?

■ Is there feedback on services and programs?

■ Are volunteers serving on the organization's board?

■ Are "VIP volunteers" treated differently than other volunteers?

■ Can volunteers become board members?

■ How are volunteers spoken of? (For example, what volunteers do is sometimes described as "magical." No, it's the application of hard work.)

■ Are volunteers recognized and honored in a community way?

■ Are community leaders being developed? Is the community putting its demands on the table, or is the community accepting the oppression of being excluded?

■ How do volunteers talk about what they do?

Board activity

■ Does the board reflect the community it represents?

■ When does the board meet? Who can attend at that time? (People earning hourly wages may be financially penalized for leaving work during business hours.)

■ Are child care and food provided at board meetings?

■ Does the board membership include consumers of the organization's services?

■ Does the board only use Robert's Rules of Order or a process for decision making that works more effectively in non-Western cultures?

■ Are board members chosen based only on the technical skills and formal education or other criteria (such as ability to speak clients' language, leadership skills recognized within their communities, cross-cultural effectiveness, and shared experience with clients)?

■ Are board members chosen only for their "diversity quotient"?

■ Does the board specifically recognize its accountability to the community members, viewing them as the stakeholders of the corporation?

■ Do historical factors or current practices make potential board members from "other" communities feel less welcome?

■ When "others" are recruited and their attendance drops off, do board members check for policies and practice that may drive people away? Do board members assume a lack of interest or simply dismiss the question (*We invite them, but they don't show up.*)?

■ Do we check in with "others" who leave the board with an exit interview that invites them to explore structural racism with us?

Note: A tool based on the above questions is included in the Resource E. See Strategies for Dealing with Internalized Oppression and Structural Racism on page 199.

Match Individual Change with Institutional Change

Some programs designed to engage the emotional aspects of cross-cultural relationships focus on diversity for its own sake. These programs are mostly designed to promote changes in personal behavior. They generally do not look at organizational and community systems. Other interventions designed to support organizations and communities, such as planning processes and assessments, do so without paying attention to culture. Only when we combine the two can we move toward real social change.

In culturally competent capacity building, this moves us beyond personal behavior change to systems change. We work on several layers at the same time. During strategic planning, we pay attention to how systems reinforce or break down patterns of racism and oppression. We move beyond a zero-sum approach and come from a perspective of abundance. Privilege is extended to everyone, not simply moved from one group to another.

The goal is to create a just and equitable society that develops enough resources for everyone. And the path to this ultimate goal may include compensatory realignment—granting privilege to people who have been historically underprivileged. However, this is a short-term strategy, not a permanent solution. In the best processes, this helps us take our work beyond the realm of personal behaviors and begin moving it to structural change that in the end benefits everyone.

Cynthia Parker, a colleague who reviewed an early draft of this book, notes the importance of stakeholder analysis. The challenge for capacity builders, she says, is to identify and bring the full range of stakeholders into planning and decision making. Stakeholder analysis, like power analysis, requires significant investment. As the analysis takes shape, however, it becomes easier to minimize power differences; everyone knows where everyone else stands. When we invite all the voices to the table and see accommodations as a path to justice, we move closer to breaking through structural racism.

Cynthia elaborates on this point:

> Related issues include making space for traditionally less influential or less organized groups to come together and explore their thinking apart from the broader collaborative. Sometimes you have to do work outside and alongside the collaboration to make sure the playing field is as level as possible—from simple things like prepping young people

who are participating in adult decision-making bodies to creating caucuses and opportunities for people to "explore their own stuff" alongside a multi-stakeholder process.

Beyond having everyone at the table to ensure equity, we need to ensure that their voices are heard and respected. In turn, this means that all parties have to be informed about each other and the existing power dynamics.

Examples of organizations that successfully address institutional racism are few and far between. However, we did find some. One foundation took intentional steps to change its board of direc-

Building Capacity for Advocacy: Eight Key Principles

One key component to creating a just society is advocacy. A working group from the People of Color Affinity Group (POC), part of the Alliance for Nonprofit Management, looked at cultural competency in building advocacy. Group members drew from their own experiences as well as path-breaking work from several sources. One is the article "Building Capacity for Policy Change: The Racial Justice Lens" by Makani Themba-Nixon, a national nonprofit executive. Another source is research conducted and disseminated by PolicyLink in the 2003 report *Leadership for Policy Change: Strengthening Communities of Color through Leadership Development*.[77]

Advocacy Working Group members Margo Bailey, Gita Gulati-Partee, Sida Ly-Xiong, Brigette Rouson, and Daryl Thompson drafted the following principles that were presented and affirmed at an annual POC gathering.

Why do we need these principles?

One key function of the POC is to be a voice for truth, all the truth, recognizing that truth is plural, multifaceted, and sometimes paradoxical. With these principles, we are naming some truths. Specifically, we are acknowledging that advocacy capacity building is not always done in a culturally competent way, thus limiting its social change impact. We also recognize the historic lack of investment in building the capacity of POC-led organizations and in advocacy efforts that fully engage people of color as leaders. Yet advocacy efforts in and related to communities of color continue to have great value and make important contributions to their communities.

How do we use these principles?

The working group intentionally chose not to create a template of policy agendas, as we recognize that communities and the organizations and leaders who serve them must drive their own agendas. Rather, we offer these principles to help communities of color achieve their own advocacy agendas, whatever they may be. Further, we hope that these principles not only build our collective knowledge base and advance the advocacy field but also catalyze other efforts to define and articulate culturally competent capacity building—for example, culturally competent fundraising.

Culturally competent capacity builders

1. Believe in the inherent right of people of color to drive their own policy agendas and recognize that lasting social change requires capacity building at three levels: individual leaders, organizations, and constituencies.

2. Meet people where they are, develop multiple strategies to help them achieve their own policy goals, and recognize that a variety of organizational structures can successfully integrate advocacy efforts. All policy discussions to benefit all communities require the voices and perspectives of people of color.

3. Employ a racial justice and systems lens to organizational development and advocacy. With a landscape perspective as described by Makani Themba-Nixon, we look beyond culture to a contextual analysis that includes changing structures and building power to achieve social change.

tors to reflect the grassroots constituencies it was funding. This foundation also listened when grassroots leaders urged the creation of an entirely new organization to be fully owned by the grantee community. That foundation created a plan for turning over its assets to that new entity, over time and with technical support. The result was the Southern Partners Fund. (See Janice Gow Petty's book *Cultural Diversity in Fundraising* for a detailed treatment of the impact of culture on funding.)[76]

I worked with an organization committed to becoming a genuine multiracial organization with shared leadership, including promoting leadership development of people of color. One of their strategies was to create caucuses—one

4. Draw out and build upon the myriad strengths and assets of people of color that can be applied in the advocacy arena. These strengths and assets include

   ■ A history of resistance and courage

   ■ An inclination toward inclusivity and real stakeholder involvement

   ■ An ability to facilitate bottom-up engagement

   ■ Two-ness: the ability to operate in the majority culture and one's own

   ■ Adaptive capacity that comes from being bilingual or bicultural

5. Help people of color confront and dismantle internalized oppression and address the complex dynamics of power, privilege, and oppression within and between communities of color. This must be done even as we must continue to expose the barriers that exist for people of color with majority-led organizations. Without this internal analysis and attention, efforts for social change will replicate the oppressive aspects of the dominant culture.

6. Help nonprofits move beyond the tendency to diversify by including only one or two people of color in their leadership. This assumes that all people of color share a uniform advocacy experience or policy perspective, and it creates an unfair, limiting, and potentially tokenizing experience. We must help nonprofits expand their own understanding and leadership pool while also building the capacity of people of color to say *no* to these types of situations.

7. Help organizations work together to build their collective capacity to identify, develop, and better connect people of color to the advocacy work of nonprofits. Collective capacity building could include, for example, shared board recruitment and development with an advocacy focus. As capacity builders, we have the unique opportunity to see trends across organizations and the community. These trends include recurring challenges as well as untapped resources.

8. Pay attention to developing the following skills needed for effective advocacy:

   ■ Mentoring and succession planning helps to actively identify and cultivate potential leaders.

   ■ Access, collect, analyze, and use quantitative and qualitative data to support advocacy positions. Advocates of color need to be comfortable talking numbers as well as putting faces and stories to those numbers.

   ■ Create win-win collaborations by knowing your own competitive advantage as well as the benefits of the relationship.

   ■ Work across traditional political boundaries. In the advocacy arena, there are no permanent enemies and no permanent friends.

for people of color staff and one for White staff. After a year, each caucus gave an update. I was struck by the results: The White people focused on changes in their individual behavior, while the people of color focused on the need for systemic changes. Both aspects need attention from everyone.

It takes an investment of both time and money to create accountability for producing sustainable, long-term, systemic change. However, a growing contingent of funders, fund-raisers, and nonprofit leaders are committed at this deeper level. They understand that paying attention to culture adds a new dimension to their processes and are willing to make the additional investment.

Chapter 9
Continuing the Conversation about Cultural Competency

In this final chapter we look at the $64,000 question: So what? What can result from cultural competency in capacity building? Why do it, and to whom is it really important?

We've offered several answers to these questions, and more are emerging from the continuing conversation about cultural competency. This book is intended to open a dialogue on the topic, not to be the last word. There are publications by other authors with important perspectives on this topic. More resources will emerge from programs and members of the Alliance for Nonprofit Management, including interactive institutes that allow practitioners to share rich stories and practical tips. Many in the field area already doing great work on this topic (see the Resources Section; it's more than a simple list of good books and articles. It's got more stories, showing how people are resources too).

We won't come to any complete conclusions. This work is ongoing, and the world around us is in flux. International events influence our work, and every shift in the larger community affects our capacity to support constructive change. Hurricane Katrina and the levees breaking in New Orleans, for example, reshaped the context of our conversation. The influx of immigrants from particular parts of the world affects the way we do business as well.

Keep Asking Questions

Questions help us continue the conversation about cultural competency and access the transformational power of language mentioned in the introduction to this book. By asking questions we can make new distinctions, create new possibilities, and re-examine our assumptions.

We can continue the conversation about cultural competency with the following questions from Makani Themba-Nixon of the Praxis Project:

> We have a number of benchmarks, a lot of them integrated in what the folks actually do. So there's the process stuff that is key: How do people feel about it? Do they feel heard? Do they think we paid attention? What do they see? Did they pay attention? Part of the insight is: What did we learn? How did we prepare them to do their work? Were we able to provide support that shows people that the folks who look at them see that they know what they're doing? That's part of capacity building.

One of our peer reviewers for this book was Guadalupe Pacheco, a public health advisor and special assistant to the deputy assistant secretary for minority health, U.S. Department of Health and Human Services. He challenges us to understand and apply cultural competency as a practical matter by asking even more questions:

> From a capacity-building perspective, what does [cultural competency] mean? Does it mean having staff within any organization that is reflective of the service delivery area? In other words, does having the right patient and provider racial and ethnic mix improve service delivery or produce better outcomes [in a health care context]? Does it mean hiring bilingual-bicultural staff? Does it mean hiring interpreters, trained interpreters? Does it mean having health promotion materials that are translated in the languages of the community?

How about from an organizational standpoint: Does it mean having policies and procedures regarding the implementation of cultural competency practices? How about the collection of racial and ethnic and language data? How do you use this data to improve service delivery? How about organizations' ability to incorporate cultural competency into their quality improvement processes? How about governance and community involvement? When it's all said and done, does it make a difference? Does the community really benefit when these cultural competency principles are operationalized? We need to start thinking about measurements to determine the impact of culturally competent principles. What's the value to the community or to the organization?

In this book we have responded to some of these questions; we still need to grapple with the rest.

Review Some Answers

If you read this book from cover to cover, we hope that you will find yourself further along in your journey than when you started. A large part of the journey is about creating awareness, understanding, and a new way of being. We hope the stories and models presented in these pages assist you in that process.

In the foreword to this book, Tangie Newborn mentioned the process of unleashing existing capacity. We hope that we have presented ways to do that. We looked at what can go wrong when we bring cultural perspectives to capacity building, but we have also mentioned where things are going right and ways to learn from that.

Above all, we laid out an overall framework from which the work can be done. For example,

■ We emphasized that if we don't start from shared definitions, we can end up in very different places. Imagine starting out very near to someone at the center of a map. You choose trajectories that are close but not the same. The farther you move out from the center, the greater the distance that will separate you from each other. In the same way, taking the time to clarify our key terms can create more common ground in our theory and practice of cultural competency.

■ We shared slices of the cultural landscape from several communities: African American, Asian American, Caucasian, Indigenous, and Latino communities. We explored the role of capacity builders in each landscape, whether engaging as insiders or outsiders.

■ We emphasized that our work takes place in multiple contexts. The most basic one is that differences between people are always present and ways of talking about them vary significantly across different regions of the United States and in other places. A constant challenge is to develop intimacy with the "other," even when a person's cultural norms conflict directly with our own. In addition, whatever culture dominates in a certain time and place is only one of many—an insight that comes alive as each of us locates our own culture. Personal identity springs from a place in our minds and hearts where many cultures intersect. Even so, our research confirms that in the United States, race is the major fault line in how we see differences between people. A look at American history confirms that the racial fault line is embedded in our institutions.

■ We looked at cross-cultural collaboration, staying mindful not only of the *product* but also the *process* of engaging in this work. We shared insights from the process of creating this book, which represents the work of practitioners who are passionate about social change that happens through the lens of culture.

■ We heard that cultural competency is a long-term investment rather than a set of parlor tricks. Culture has to become part of the fabric of our work. It cannot be reduced to a "topic" to be covered, a set of "diversity exercises," or even a list of skills to be developed. Cultural competency springs from a new way of seeing and a new way of being in the world.

■ We looked at institutional racism and power dynamics, stressing that this enterprise is about changing personal behavior, and much more. What we are really talking about is changing systems and structures.

■ We looked at the impact that culturally based capacity building might have on the capacity builder, the individuals, the organizations, and the communities we work with, as well as the field of capacity building itself.

■ We pointed to the significance of a values-based perspective that is rooted in a social justice agenda.

For more details on the above points, see the Summary of Research Findings on page 155.

Speak Your Vision of Justice

That final point in the above list deserves more emphasis. It is about imagining the kind of society that might be born from our efforts. The essence of our work is to promote social change that enhances life for everyone in our communities. Ray Charles sang it in simple words: "None of us [is] free while one of us is chained." We can arrive at a just society only if we practice justice along the way—if we "walk the talk." We ask you to join us on that path.

This might call for a paradigm shift for many capacity builders who see their work as being more neutral. Yet the view of cultural competency in capacity building as a way to advance social change emerged in nearly every aspect of our research: the literature review, the peer dialogues, and the interviews.

Any community-development project includes a visioning process that poses a question: What does a sustainable, socially just society look like? In my experience, the vision always has room for everyone. Race and culture are seen as assets that strengthen communities and organizations. In this vision, the goal of capacity building is to create a society of equity in rights, resources, life chances, and outcomes for all people, regardless of their membership in the majority or mainstream culture. This is a society in which both equity and the earth itself are sustained for the long term.

Capacity builders recognize that we are both *participants* in creating just societies and *resources* for this process. Just societies take shape as we support informed civic engagement where culture is central. Sometimes it is a transformed neighborhood; sometimes it is an organization better prepared to play its role in the larger community. Even the work we do with individuals influences the communities in which they live.

As culturally based capacity builders, we need to stay open to the opportunities that social change presents. We can support the status quo, where power remains in the hands of a few and where we "fix" people. Or we can support the changes that create more equity and justice.

Achieving this vision poses a challenge that we need to take up individually and collectively. We have a lot of power as capacity builders. We decide how we use it. I invite you to use your power to build the beloved community.

Part Three
Resources

BRIGETTE ROUSON

Resource A
Key Terms for Cultural Competency

Numerous terms used in connection with cultural competency as defined in this book are worth a closer look—not necessarily for creating final agreement but rather for distinguishing between various meanings. Following are definitions relating to nine key terms in the emerging conversation about cultural competency.

Capacity Building

This term often refers to nonprofit support through technical assistance, funding, and learning opportunities. The goal is to promote nonprofit impact, adaptability, and sustainability. More specifically, capacity building is the process of developing and strengthening the skills, instincts, abilities, processes, and resources that organizations and communities need to survive, adapt, and thrive in the fast changing world of the late twentieth and early twenty-first centuries. The term commonly refers to an array of measures that organizations take to strengthen their ability to operate effectively over the long term.[78]

Cultural Competency

In capacity building for the nonprofit sector, we speak often of *competencies* as a combination of basic skills, core knowledge, and an orientation to continuous learning. With those elements in mind, we prefer to use the term cultural *competency*. This is in contrast to *competence,* which may be heard to suggest a static quality or condition, as if one absolutely *is* or *is not* competent.

Also, capacity builders committed to cultural competency necessarily have a broader reach in the way that we hold the process and the end results we seek. Certainly, our work invites techniques that hold promise to eliminate disparities. But an even more important movement has surfaced within the Alliance for Nonprofit Management, where we ask, capacity building for what? We are calling one another to honor intention as well as method. The cultural competency of which we speak is about building communities and creating an equitable society (with domestic tranquility and liberty and justice for all) that cannot be limited by any one set of indicators.

At the Alliance for Nonprofit Management, the Cultural Competency Initiative operates with the understanding that

> Culturally competent capacity building is a community-centered process that begins with an understanding of historical realities and an appreciation of the community's assets in its own cultural context. The process works to enhance the quality of life, create equal access to resources, and promote community partnerships resulting in strategic and progressive social change.[79]

Building on widely accepted ideas, the Minority Executive Directors' Coalition of King County (based in Seattle, Washington) offers this definition:

> MEDC believes that cultural competency is critical to the success of the delivery of health and human services in an ever diverse environment. The respect of an individual's cultural domains and their experiences is essential to their engagement with service providers, consultants, trainers, researchers, and funders. Through an organization's recognition of cultural[ly] competent services, staff, and volunteers, it will be much better able to meet the diverse needs in all communities throughout King County. Organizations that embrace the . . . guiding principles of Cultural Competency must be willing to accept them throughout their organization's services, policies, and practices. Cultural Competency is a journey by which an agency must commit itself to a process of continuous improvement.[80]

Based on the work of Terry Cross and colleagues, the National Center for Cultural Competence (NCCC) refers to a five-part model:

> Cultural competence requires that organizations and their personnel have the capacity to (1) value diversity, (2) conduct self-assessment, (3) manage the dynamics of difference, (4) acquire and institutionalize cultural knowledge, and (5) adapt to the diversity and cultural contexts of individuals and communities served.

NCCC supports the concept that cultural and linguistic competence are developmental processes and evolve over extended periods of time. Both organizations and individuals are at various levels of awareness, knowledge, and skills along a continuum. There are numerous benefits of self-assessment that positively impact consumers, practitioners, organizations, and communities. Assessing attitudes, practices, structures, and policies of programs and their personnel is a necessary, effective, and systematic way to plan for and incorporate cultural and linguistic competency within organizations.[81]

The National Community Development Institute emphasizes a perspective that goes beyond skills:

We see culture as dynamic, with the lens changing as people's experiences expand. As we engage across differences, our worldview also expands to include a deeper understanding of other people's and communities' experiences. Moving beyond cultural competency, our culturally based approach is not a topic, but rather a methodology. More than a skill set, it is a perspective that shapes and informs how we arrive in communities, how we participate in the process of facilitating transformation, and how we leave tools, resources, and capacity behind for community members to continue their own processes of growth, change, and development. Culturally based technical assistance ensures that community residents lead their own change processes; that consultants come from or have extensive, well-received experience in the communities they serve; and that communities are left with the tools and resources to continue their own transformation and growth process after the intervention is completed. The goal of the work is to transfer knowledge into specific policies, practices, and standards to enhance the quality of their lives.[82]

In addition to the definitions already shared, other prominent sources are worth considering. Most works that we consulted, especially in connection with the health field, use the term *competence* (rather than *competency*) but the concept is related and useful. Examples include

Cultural competence is the organizational ability to have and utilize policies, appropriately trained and skilled employees, and specialized resources to *systematically* anticipate, recognize, and respond to the varying expectations (language, cultural, and religious) of customers and employees of diverse backgrounds.[83]

[A] process of learning that leads to an ability to effectively respond to the challenges and opportunities posed by the presence of social cultural diversity in a defined social system.[84]

Culture

The National Center for Cultural Competence presented the following definition of *culture* at the Alliance for Nonprofit Management's regional meeting in New England during May 2005:

An integrated pattern of human behavior which includes but is not limited to thought, communication, languages, beliefs, values, practices, customs, courtesies, rituals, manners of interacting, roles, relationships, and expected behaviors of a racial, ethnic, religious, social, or political group; the ability to transmit the above to succeeding generations; dynamic in nature.

We are also influenced by other definitions that are relevant to practicing cultural competency in the nonprofit sector. For example,

[C]ulture should be regarded as the set of distinctive spiritual, material, intellectual and emotional features of society or a social group, and that . . . encompasses, in addition to art and literature, lifestyles, ways of living together, value systems, traditions, and beliefs.[85]

Culture, as a body of learned behaviors common to a given human society, acts rather like a template—rather predictable in form and content—shaping behavior and consciousness within a human society from generation to generation. It includes

■ Systems of meaning, of which language is primary

■ Ways of organizing society, from kinship groups to states and multi-national corporations

■ Distinctive techniques of a group and their characteristic products[86]

Diversity

Diversity refers to a range of identities, practices, perspectives, and experiences being present in one situation, group or organization, or geographic area. In the for-profit environment, the term *diversity* is often used as shorthand for practices designed to increase the ability of teams with varying identities to work together in a way that enhances the profitability of an enterprise—for marketing appeal, preventing litigation, or other purposes. Diversity is increasingly considered important to building a public image and otherwise succeeding in the marketplace.

Based on a Cultural Competency Initiative review conducted by Elise Wong in 2006, this growing reality is suggested by the success of the *DiversityInc* magazine and online news service and is underscored by the many corporate diversity policies available online.[87] For example, two policies define *diversity* as "the collective mix of people's differences and similarities" (General Motors) and "varied skills, styles, perspectives, and backgrounds" (General Mills).

In the nonprofit sector, there is less open talk of diversity and fewer official policies to cultivate it. Where nonprofits and capacity builders recognize and invest in diversity, often the view is that mission impact and resource development are both at stake—the dual bottom line.

Inclusiveness

Inclusiveness is a term preferred by many in the nonprofit sector who are seeking to lift up a positive goal to hold in common and then encouraging new practices to achieve that goal. It is a concept that, through cultural competency in capacity building, can become a reality.

In the words of a publication from the Denver Foundation: "Inclusive organizations not only have diverse individuals involved; more importantly, they are learning-centered organizations that value the perspectives and contributions of all people, and strive to incorporate the needs and viewpoints of diverse communities."[88]

Internalized Oppression

Internalized oppression is a phenomenon in which members of a group adopt a negative view of themselves based on the prejudices of other groups. As an example from anti-racism work, here are descriptions offered by a leading capacity builder, the People's Institute for Survival and Beyond:

> **Internalized racial inferiority:** The acceptance of and acting out of an inferior definition of self, given by the oppressor, is rooted in the historical designation of one's race. Over many generations, this

process of disempowerment and disenfranchisement expresses itself in self-defeating behaviors.

Internalized racial superiority: The acceptance of and acting out of a superior definition of self is rooted in the historical designation of one's race. Over many generations, this process of empowerment and access expresses itself as unearned privileges, access to institutional power and invisible advantages based upon race.[89]

Racial Equity

Informed by the human rights concepts in the international arena, and no doubt also by human and civil rights work over several generations in the United States, the People's Movement for Human Rights Education goes beyond the typical first layer of equal access to opportunities and looks more specifically at standards and results. In this vein, racial equity is meant to be the path and the destination of the entitlement to adequate standards of living, wages, safe and healthy working conditions, basic social services, medical care, and free primary education without regard to race, culture, gender, or sexual orientation.[90]

Structural Racism

Structural racism describes the ways that multiple institutions and social practices maintain a hierarchy of privilege and power. As explained by the Aspen Institute,

> Many of the contours of opportunity for individuals and groups in the United States are defined—or "structured"—by race and racism. The term *structural racism* refers to a system in which public policies, institutional practices, cultural representations, and other norms work in various, often reinforcing ways to perpetuate racial group inequity. It identifies dimensions of our history and culture that have allowed privileges associated with "Whiteness" and disadvantages associated with "color" to endure and adapt over time.

Significant numbers in the current generation of adult White Americans, along with their parents, grandparents, and other forebears

- Benefited from access to good educational institutions
- Had access to decent jobs and fair wages

■ Accumulated retirement benefits through company programs, union membership, and Social Security

■ Benefited from home ownership policies and programs that allowed them to buy property in rising neighborhoods

By contrast, significant numbers in the current generation of adults of color, along with their parents, grandparents, and other forbears

■ Came from a background of slavery or labor exploitation

■ Were limited by *de jure* or *de facto* segregation

■ Were generally confined to jobs in areas such as agricultural, manual, or domestic labor and excluded from jobs that allowed them to accumulate savings and retirement benefits

■ Were discriminated against by lending institutions and were excluded from owning homes in economically desirable locations through redlining and other policies

In other words, at pivotal points in U.S. history when socioeconomic factors produced abundant opportunities for wealth and property accumulation—such as the G.I. Bill and home mortgage subsidies—White Americans were positioned to take advantage of them, whereas Americans of color were systematically prohibited from benefiting from them.[91]

White Privilege

Numerous practices and ways of thinking have tended to reinforce unequal power relationships based on racial and ethnic identity. In a report specific to community building, Potapchuk and colleagues share and use the following definition:

> White privilege is about the concrete benefits of access to resources and social rewards and the power to shape the norms and values of society that Whites receive unconsciously or consciously, by virtue of their skin color in a racist society.[92]

This phenomenon is also explored in Beth Applegate's chapter in Part One of this book (see page 17).

BRIGETTE ROUSON

Resource B
Summary of
Research Findings

This book is based on findings from research that include

- A literature review
- Peer dialogues (similar to focus groups) in San Francisco, Chicago, and Atlanta
- Articles from five contributing authors
- Interviews
- Case stories

The initial research includes an emphasis on race and ethnicity as an entry point but also brings into consideration many aspects of cultural identity. In particular, this work offers answers to three questions as they pertain to capacity building in nonprofit organizations within the United States:

- How does cultural competency differ from mainstream practice, and why is it important?
- How can cultural competency be applied in practice?
- What are long-term implications for the capacity-building field?

Following is a summary of answers to those questions. For more details about insights from the literature review, see page 161. And for specific comments gleaned during interviews, see Voices from the Field: Stories from Peer Dialogues on page 187.

How Does Cultural Competency Differ from Mainstream Practice, and Why Is It Important?

There is no wide acceptance yet of cultural competency in capacity building for nonprofits generally. Conventional thinking minimizes its importance. Nonprofit subsectors such as health and education have begun systematically paying attention to cultural identity and dynamics in service delivery. But the majority of the nonprofit sector and the capacity-building field have yet to identify cultural competency as vital to nonprofit effectiveness.

Institutional forms of racism and other institutional biases are more difficult to address than interpersonal relations. Practitioners using a cultural lens often find that people rooted in the dominant culture have a tendency to focus on interpersonal aspects of racism, as compared to the impact of policies and practices, which is often more evident to others.

One central tenet of cultural competency is to honor the precept "First, do no harm." Without attention to cultural identity and dynamics, capacity builders tend to feed into a system that disadvantages certain people and privileges others, based in part on membership in groups and the history of relations between groups.

Power and privilege are central to understanding current realities in the nonprofit world and advancing change. The capacity builder's role is important in reinforcing or changing power relations among people in different roles such as consultant, funder, constituent or community stakeholder, nonprofit executive or staff, and nonprofit board member.

A "revolving door" and unintentional exclusion persist for people of color and often for younger people in nonprofits and in the capacity-building field, both in management support organizations and independent practice. Bilingual staff are often narrowly pegged as "outreach workers" and rarely groomed for leadership or other capacity-building roles. Low retention of young workers and people of color continues to be a challenge for organizations across the nonprofit sector. Many communities have few readily identified people of Latino, Latina, Asian, or Native ancestry who hold formal paid roles as capacity builders when placed in the context of their numbers in the general population; there tends to be an even greater gap here than is found with African Americans.

Two dynamics—internalized oppression and hierarchy of oppression—are often at play. Cultural competency involves understanding these dynamics and how to name them and work through them on individual, organizational, and community levels.[93]

All capacity builders encounter cultural differences woven throughout their work, whether they recognize it or not. Culture is a factor constantly at play. It relates to experiences of being a person of color or White, Baby Boomer or next generation, gay or lesbian, bisexual or transgender or heterosexual, able-bodied or differently able, immigrant background or U.S.-born, having significant wealth or power or being less well endowed, and so on. Diverse backgrounds contribute to different ways of communicating, managing conflict, defining success, and designating as insiders or outsiders.

A challenge: The nature of mainstream capacity building itself may be problematic if it moves people too far from their cultural base and inhibits their ability to be at their best: creative, energized, focused, connected.

An opportunity: Shared background, or proven sensitivity and cultural knowledge, can increase a nonprofit's willingness to enter into the work and make lasting change.

How Can Cultural Competency Be Applied in Practice?

Cultural competency is a way of being that translates into practice. It is not merely a set of skills, a checklist of activities, or collected units of education. It is a lifelong commitment. Good practice requires continuous learning and deep involvement on the part of the capacity builders and nonprofit leaders.

In our framing document for this book, we outlined basic elements of culturally based work. We shared stories and insights. It is our hope that this work will give the readers food for thought. We are clear that it does not provide sufficient information for someone to "hang a shingle" as a culturally competent practitioner. Cultural competency means doing the work of identifying your own cultural location and cultivating a deep appreciation for the richness that cultural diversity brings to an organization or community.

Defining characteristics of cultural competency in capacity building include the following:

Focus on social change as the motivating force. Look at institutions, structures, patterns, and the interplay of forces influencing community change. By contrast, a "recipe" or checklist approach treats groups as if history and culture are the same for everyone across time and circumstance. This approach also assumes that capacity can be built by addressing a person, organization, or issue in isolation.

Actively explore cultural biases, including geography, historical context, religion, socioeconomic background, and other aspects to guide the work. This practice requires taking account of major historical moments, culturally based assets, current issues, and aspirations. It also means paying attention to the complexity of each ethnic community and dispelling the notion of monolithic groups.

Share and build power in contrast to seeing privilege and power as a zero-sum proposition. Use strategies that allow everyone to feel valued, empowered, and fully engaged. Power sharing includes strategically addressing individual behaviors, institutional practices, and public policies to create equity.

Model and facilitate learning, with reflection, disclosure, and listening as key skills. The premium is on bringing yourself fully to the work while respecting others. This involves intentional learning to understand your own background and that of groups with whom you work, culturally locating yourself to be more attuned to choices about process, engaging everyone as a learner and a source of knowledge, and making the transfer of knowledge very intentional.

Break silence. Take responsibility to ensure full participation despite cultural barriers within a commitment to name and work through the "elephant(s) in the room." Realize that people often dance around deep issues and ensure full participation despite cultural barriers.

Build principled relationships intentionally with people who are different from us. This includes community leaders and bridge builders. Do this to increase the ability to work and live effectively across differences and to better understand and meet capacity needs in personal and professional settings.

Structure engagements with a cultural lens. Show a willingness to make the necessary time commitments and do the capacity building in a way that honors culturally based realities, such as the extraordinary demands on nonprofit leaders of color.

Recruit, retain, and develop diverse staff, board, and other stakeholders, such as volunteers and individual donors. Make an extra effort to reach out and involve members of particular groups that are not as often included; recognize the diverse ways that they can contribute.

Access and form diverse teams for consulting and grantmaking. Follow through on an intention to influence interventions and results. Increase information about the reality of power dynamics, and bring the diverse perspectives necessary for constructive "pushback" on all sides.

Be community-centered and client-centered. Yet don't do this with unqualified acceptance or support of all aspects of a culture and not as supposedly value-neutral.

Define *capacity builder* as a "critical friend" looking at the organization and beyond it for the collective interest. This requires engaging about values when forming a relationship with a nonprofit, though not necessarily disclosing all one's opinions. As a result, a practitioner might decline to start or continue a working relationship, or challenge a nonprofit to expand its view.

Make language accessible and an instrument of transformation. This may involve "code switching"[94] to correct for power inequality or keeping an accent to create a stronger bond and stay culturally grounded, especially in the South, immigrant communities, or in groups less taken with academic credentialing.

Routinely review capacity-building materials and delivery and interaction techniques with members of diverse groups to ensure effectiveness. Examples of such materials are training curricula, tools, questionnaires, manuals, books, articles, grant applications, and reports.

Remember that culturally based innovations allow for reshaping the work as practitioners draw from a wider array of sources and approaches. Change can be accelerated by approaches such as "spirit work" done as capacity building. (By "spirit work," we mean the ways in which spiritual beliefs and practices having to do with a higher power are adopted, which may influence what happens in the work.) Change can also be sparked by providing more substantive roles for constituents, support staff, or volunteers than a typical process allows—and genuinely working with ideas that emerge.

Understand generational differences as a key to leadership effectiveness. Valuing elders while supporting young people in leading roles can generate broad engagement and changed conditions through a unique balance of new and old practices. This may be particularly true for immigrant communities and groups. For young leaders, some touchstones are inclusion in decision making, less hierarchy, greater work-life balance, and constituent ownership.

Approach grantmaking as capacity building, which offers important opportunities and responsibilities to advance change. The selection process often has disparate outcomes, resulting from insufficient attention to cultural dynamics in stages such as initial access, relationship building, applications, and site visits. Organizations led by and for people of color, or rural White residents, often face high hurdles, garner fewer resources, and have a more fragile infrastructure than counterparts.

What Are Long-Term Implications for the Capacity-Building Field?

The long-term character of culturally competent work requires more than the usual arrangements. Capacity builders need to check assumptions about what it will take to realize change in nonprofit organizations and the sector. For all participants to understand their own place in cultural dynamics, capacity builders must find ways to help shift perceptions of White identity.

To be better positioned for effectiveness, capacity builders need to broaden and deepen relationships with a diverse network of colleagues and partners. All these voices will need to be heard when identifying the best ways to organize the work. Accountability means engaging constituents and extending beyond formal evaluation projects, other capacity building, or funding requirements.

BRIGETTE ROUSON

Resource C
Literature Review

Context for This Literature Review

In recent decades, we have witnessed an outpouring of books, papers, articles, training curricula, tools, and online sites—as well as conference sessions and conversations among colleagues—to guide organizational success using "diversity" principles, cultural competence, and multicultural or cross-cultural approaches. Much of the attention (and considerable financial and human resources) have been devoted to the corporate and government sectors. Strong currents are found in areas such as health care, education, community development, grantmaking, and fundraising. Definitions, purposes, and recommended approaches vary widely. A wealth of useful materials has been produced, providing valuable insights and tools. Periodicals such as *The Nonprofit Quarterly, Nonprofit Management and Leadership, Stanford Social Innovation Review,* and the Organization Development Network journal add to informed research and practice. Still, a great deal more attention is needed on the role of cultural dynamics in nonprofit leadership and organizational development and how to build capacity.

Most studies in recent years that focused on the nonprofit sector, even where cultural identity was a prominent feature, did not deal with it openly—or if they did, failed to bring an in-depth treatment. Examples include reports on the nonprofit role in disaster response, looking especially at the aftermath of Hurricanes Katrina and Rita[95] and a national report on nonprofit leadership development.[96]

This review is not comprehensive or exhaustive in the academic sense. Rather, it offers touchstones about cultural competency for the work of strengthening nonprofit effectiveness, starting with a core issue: racial equity. For our purposes, *organizational* includes groups, programs, initiatives, collaborations, and other forms of nonprofit activity. The intent is to encourage truth-telling and change-making, beginning with the community of practitioners who seek to influence nonprofit capacity building.

Sources highlighted here are widely accessible, provocative, and easily applicable. They get at a root analysis of how culture is relevant for those who identify as technical assistance providers (consultants and trainers) and other nonprofit support providers (funders, researchers, instructors in nonprofit management, and so on). A number of key resources are compiled on the Cultural Competency Resource Pages posted by the Alliance for Nonprofit Management, online at www.allianceonline.org.

Key Points

Researchers and writers have rarely addressed cultural competency in the nonprofit field. Until recently, what had been available mainly documented inequities in leadership, structures, outcomes, and in some cases success stories or strategies—typically based on a single aspect of identity. Race and ethnicity were perhaps most prominent, but now attention is increasing to gender, generation, class, sexual orientation, disability, geography, religious and political identity, and similar ways of understanding who we are.

The effects of leaving this set of issues outside of what most capacity builders and nonprofit leaders consider "core" issues of effectiveness and sustainability include the following:

- A disproportionate percentage of nonprofit executive directors and board members are White as compared to the general population and in business and government sectors, based on surveys conducted nationally and regionally.

- Indicators and outcomes for people of color show major disparities relating to race, even when controlled for other factors such as income level, insurance coverage, and employment.

- A common unstated assumption among funders and nonprofit leaders is that communities of color and individual people of color ought to have highly prescriptive interventions by people from outside their communities, rather than resources that support collective work and responsibility in their own cultural context.

- Increased professionalization of nonprofit management leads to a disconnect between nonprofit leaders and the communities they serve.

- Organizational culture dominated by the "mainstream" can hinder recruitment and retention of diverse staff, volunteers, and board members, particularly of young people and people of color who are strongly grounded in the grassroots.

Areas needing improvement and strategies to make those improvements that have been identified in the literature include the following:

- Understand structural and institutional racism as they relate to nonprofit organizations and the communities they serve.

- Promote "maximum feasible participation" of communities of color in programs and initiatives that affect them, including respect for differences in decision making and life circumstances and the role of community in solving personal and collective problems.

- Remember that nonprofit organizations need to listen and be accountable to the communities they serve.

- Promote an understanding that cultural sensitivity, while necessary, is not by itself sufficient to create change.

- Remember that power and agency need to be addressed in the approaches that an organization takes to defining challenges based on race and ethnicity, creating change processes, and envisioning results.

- See capacity building in communities of color and organizations led by people of color as a critical step toward promoting democracy, social justice, and equity for all.

- Make an explicit commitment to social change, including acknowledgment of institutional racism and cultural differences not measured against the "dominant culture."

- Provide accessibility in opportunities for service, training, and funding; avoid exclusion based on factors such as location, language, class sensibility and rank, and perspective.

- Determine whether the race or ethnicity of the capacity builder plays a role in supporting culturally competent leadership.

- Do further research and provide more documentation about the knowledge and skills capacity builders need to employ these strategies and approaches.

Many of these key issues are addressed in the literature of other fields, and have been for years. Only more recently has the attention turned to the nonprofit sector distinctly. It is an issue of public interest because nongovernmental organizations, by being tax-exempt—while not forbidden to make a profit—must invest any profits back into the primary work driven by a social purpose (rather than distribute it to owners as would happen in business).

Effectiveness as a Matter of Cultural Competency

The road to effectiveness has many markers, whether we are speaking of nonprofits or those dedicated to supporting their success with funds, technical assistance, or a knowledge base. At the Alliance for Nonprofit Management, the Cultural Competency Initiative (CCI) made a choice early to use language and practices that honor the origins of the Initiative (with the People of Color Affinity Group) and catalyze change toward cultural competency across the nonprofit sector. At the start, we looked at how to build racial equity as opening the way for the larger task. We operated with a specific mission and membership and with modest startup resources. As a result, our focus was on issues of effectiveness in the practice of capacity building, mainly consulting and secondarily funding and research, that serves nonprofits.

This review provides background for more work, including trainings and future publications. It identifies key subject areas, findings, and approaches. Guiding this review is the initiative's intent to increase awareness, will, and skill in the field. The aim is a grounded, results-oriented approach in which nonprofit effectiveness is closely tied to understanding what it takes to generate change at the level of community, nation, and world.

The term *cultural competency* (rather than *cultural competence*) expresses a consensus among practitioners involved in launching the CCI that continuous learning and growth is the key. The term offers an alternative to the idea that a person or organization can simply acquire and possess a level of practice ("competence") that is static, that is everywhere and always effective.

As used in this book, the concept of cultural competency is strongly aligned with the terms *culturally based capacity building* and *multicultural organizational development* written about by the authors of the California Endowment series *Organizational Development and Capacity in Cultural Competence: Building Knowledge and Practice*.[97] Three main themes from these papers resonate with our purpose and framework in this book:

■ Culture is simply too pervasive and powerful to be ignored in looking at nonprofit effectiveness; culture is relevant to multiple systems and a requisite for success.

■ Cultivating effectiveness is about creating equity.

■ Models of practice grounded in cultural competency will cast capacity builders in the role of peers and resources in a co-learning arrangement rather than experts directing the nonprofits with which they work.

As Anushka Fernandopulle, formerly of CompassPoint, notes, since culture encompasses "the beliefs, values, customs and behaviors of a particular group of people," it has significance not only for race and ethnicity or national origin "but also, for example, deaf culture, or the culture of urban gay men." In essence, the argument is that people *are* cultural, and people make up organizations, each "part of a unique ecosystem." Thus, cultural dynamics inevitably shape our ways of working and their impact. She argues that "improving cultural competency improves organizational effectiveness." Effectiveness has to do with ability to take on the work and carry it out—to attract, serve, and retain constituents; to deal with issues within staff; to recruit and retain board, staff, and volunteers; to work with other organizations. As such, "cultural competency cannot be dealt with in isolation from other parts of organizational systems but rather is a dimension of all including governance, finance and fundraising, program, human resources, information technology, and facilities."[98]

Frank J. Omowale Satterwhite and Shiree Teng note that although basic concepts of cultural competency have existed for centuries, newer ways of articulating and applying it emerged in the 1980s. In the work of the National Community Development Institute, capacity building with any group or initiative is centered in community change and firmly linked with broad social movements. Its approach "is rooted in the racial and cultural dynamics of communities, based on social equity principles, shaped by the voice of the community and focused on social transformation." Working with this culturally based method means "working as peers—not experts—who are facilitators, catalysts, resources, cheerleaders, and critical friends in the capacity building process." And given that the ultimate aim of social change requires "a long journey," capacity builders maintain ties and view their work together as part of building a just society.[99]

On a related note about multicultural organizational development, Laurin Mayeno writes that "human beings are not lumped into distinct and separate groups but have multiple identities and social experiences. Virtually everyone is affected by social inequities or targeted by oppression, and almost everyone benefits from some form of unearned privilege."[100] And with multiple identities, the dynamics of any one are interconnected with others. To address this reality, the capacity builder "starts with the assumption that oppression is institutionalized, systemic, and entrenched in public and private organizations." Diversity and equity are inseparable, and the responsibility is one of "questioning, and if necessary, dismantling existing patterns of power within the organization."[101]

This basic principle is also reflected in a report by the Movement Strategy Center, *Reflections on Organization Development for Social Change,*[102] which focuses on this question: How can our organizations be bold enough to alter the fundamental structural relationships in society, and wise enough to act according to the principles of organizational sustainability and community transformation? With a view beyond nonprofits, work such as Scott Page's research takes on the question: Why can teams of people find better solutions than brilliant individuals working alone? Page's work starts at the team level to connect effectiveness with diversity in the book *The Difference: How the Power of Diversity Creates Better Groups, Firms, Schools, and Societies.*[103] It is essential to note that Page builds on the wisdom of many practitioners, including Ron Chisom, Elsie Cross, Roosevelt Thomas, and others who shaped the field of diversity and racial equity.

This literature review aims to explore the tensions between goals, uncover potential points of unity, and develop a holistic framework for change. The road to this clarity of insight and intention has been made through a long line of efforts to learn the relevance of history, find patterns, and form strategies. These efforts are captured by attention to numerous other resources, a modest portion of which are described in the following sections.

Community Building—Race, Culture, History, and Power

With increasing recognition of the significance of cultural identity and dynamics, the history of the United States itself is being written anew. Inclusive perspectives provide a base for better understanding the very social issues for which nonprofits are founded to address. Numerous resources are important to this understanding. Ronald Takaki, in *A Different Mirror: A History of Multicultural America,* provides an in-depth historical portrait of communities of color that documents themes still present today. Takaki starts by noting some reasons for his project:

America has been racially diverse since our very beginning . . . and this reality is increasingly becoming visible and ubiquitous. [M]inorities are fast becoming a majority [and] already predominate in major cities across the country. . . . This emerging demographic diversity has raised fundamental questions about America's identity and culture. . . . What is lacking is historical context; consequently, we are left feeling bewildered. . . . What does our diversity mean, and where is it leading us?[104]

Documenting the issues at stake and effective approaches, current resources focused on nonprofits most often speak in terms of diversity, racism, or community engagement and empowerment. They point to a need to see differently what is going on within and at the hands of nonprofit organizations, especially to see that the impact nonprofits seek (or the missions they serve) cannot be achieved if the actions discount and suppress particular groups. However, historical patterns and collective memory are powerful forces that must be taken into account as greatly influencing what we see and experience today. This becomes clear from the work of scholars such as Takaki, Howard Zinn, and Mindy Thompson-Fulilove.[105]

As a resource about today's issues, *The Nonprofit Quarterly* (*NPQ*, www.nonprofitquarterly.org) is an ongoing repository of stories and analysis. This publication emphasizes issues that confront the vast majority of small to midsize nonprofits. For instance, in its groundbreaking issue on "Race and Power" (Summer 2002), *NPQ* explored the significance of immigration status, the underground nature of contemporary racism, initiatives to build cultural diversity in public life and in nonprofits, and experiences of transformation.

NPQ editors admitted that despite scouring extensive networks, few success stories emerged of organizational change that transformed race and power dynamics. Nonetheless, there are stories of organizations that had some success in becoming more racially equitable, including a public broadcasting station, a statewide Planned Parenthood, and a statewide multi-issue coalition. Strategies employed to bring about change in and by nonprofits included the following:

■ Create a team-based approach to change rather than rely on a single person or position as the champion. Create a safe environment for people to participate without fear of reprisal. Share information consistently and keep diversity on the agenda for board and staff meetings. Recognize and prepare for inevitable burnout or plateaus. Choose consultants with a track record for similar projects (Sidberry, pp. 28–33).[106]

■ Use a process of dialogue that balances structure with a free-flowing, meaningful engagement among participants, and document the effects over time of the shared insights and concrete actions (such as diversifying the board) (Rivero and Saunders, pp. 34–36).

■ Place a premium on diversity in the search for a new CEO and hire an executive committed to address issues of race and power in leading organizational transformation. Strategically plan with an inclusive process that involves a cross-section from community, staff, and board. Institute interpretation training and expanding availability of interpreters to assist in direct service for Spanish, Portuguese, Vietnamese, Laotian, and Creole speakers. Develop goals at every organizational level. Reach out and form more collaborations (Innocencio and Gravon, pp. 36–40).

■ Understand the reality of aversive racism in the nonprofit workplace, fed by subtle biases that affect access and performance by people of color (Dovidio and Gaertner, pp. 22–27).

■ Take account of structural racism in selecting local issues on which to work and go beyond the usual attention to one's own government funding or issues that have a direct effect on program (powell, pp. 6–11).

■ Bridge the gap between immigrant rights and racial justice to advance beyond a stagnant approach of rigid racial hierarchies blocking change (Quiroz-Martinez, pp. 18–21).

■ Form learning communities to transform the way people deal with issues of race, class, and gender and promote collective responsibility (Guinier, pp. 12–17).

Especially telling was the issue's review of many current disparities along racial lines in the United States, with consistently worse outcomes for people of color as compared to White people. According to john powell, a scholar and advocate of racial equity, some important counteracting forces are nonprofit efforts aimed at equitable regional development in many areas: housing and zoning, public schools and higher education, faith-based economic development, employment access, transportation planning, and a variety of neighborhood support measures. A cross-cutting factor in bringing about change is participatory governance—in institutions, neighborhoods, and society. "The nonprofit sector has a crucial role to take in ensuring that policies and programs . . . truly enhance equity within our regions," powell writes. "There are many entry points for nonprofits; this work is not limited to policy advocacy."

And as Lani Guinier and Gerald Torres point out, racialized groups have a "diagnostic" function like the canary in the mine, alerting us to conditions that affect everyone, as indicated when an intensive search for stories about successful transformation in nonprofits yielded "few noteworthy examples of profound change." William Diaz finds that the charitable and nonprofit sector distributes few of its resources to the poor to "address the issues of poverty, disadvantage and social injustice faced by communities of color, immigrants, and others in need"—which ultimately raises questions of leadership.[107]

Aspen Institute's groundbreaking work, most notably the Project on Structural Racism and Community Revitalization in its Roundtable on Community Change,[108] provides in-depth analysis in several commissioned papers of the link between race and racism and building communities. This work vividly addresses the importance of advancing beyond "cultural sensitivity" to "power and agency" in defining challenges, creating change processes, and envisioning results. A core premise: structural racism is neither natural nor inevitable; it is an infrastructure of privilege accumulated over generations and actively maintained in institutions, producing unequal outcomes.

Seen in this light, racial inequity—similar to inequities along lines of generation, gender, sexuality, disability, or geographic base—often is both entrenched and subject to change. As a result, all those working on community development—in which nonprofits play a significant role—need to tailor responses accordingly to be effective. Aspen Institute's overarching analysis of structural racism and community building points to the importance of capacity building to bolster the work of community change agents, particularly nonprofits. As the report explains,

> Currently, for the most part, local-level community development, social service and other community-building organizations are strapped for resources and, as a result, can barely attain modest programmatic results in fairly narrowly defined arenas. Yet these thousands of organizations, staffed by millions of workers, [are] a potentially powerful network for achieving significant change. Viewed in this light, investment in their capacity is a critical step toward promoting true democracy, social justice, and racial equity.[109]

This work has had substantial support and partnership from the Annie E. Casey Foundation, which is among a number of foundations striving for racial equity internally and externally. Numerous resources developed by the foundation (and available at its Web site, www.aecf.org) provide a structural racism and cultural-competency analysis—and share promising practices in such areas as health care and education, workforce development, and employment needs of formerly incarcerated people.

Finding the Ways Forward

As evidenced by the resources discussed above, institutional and structural racism are a reality in the nonprofit sector. This understanding is significant because analysis of race and power in the "diversity" framework has often dealt only with interpersonal relationships and diversifying the faces in organizations. Diversity approaches previously did not include an analysis of institutional factors. For example, a diversity frame did not necessarily go beyond recruitment to address *retention* of people of color as staff and board members. Nor did this frame take account of other dimensions of identity—gender, sexual orientation, socioeconomic background, disability, geographic base—and whether board or staff functioning are inclusive.

Yet, as important as it is to have a comprehensive view of issues that influence race and power in organizations and the communities they serve, the literature only begins to identify the way forward to create change.

The *NPQ* has published a series of pieces by people of color in the nonprofit world looking at community-based nonprofits or national philanthropy and lifting up solutions. For example, Bob Agres recounts that Hawai'i Alliance for Community Based Economic Development has grounded its efforts in the native Hawai'ian concept that wealth (*waiwai,* literally "water water") is communally shared.[110] Processes developed by his nonprofit and others to address land, housing, and a range of social and economic issues must attend to ways for people to align cultural traditions with innovative strategies.

In a similar vein, Gus Newport called on his experience as a nonprofit leader in a largely Black and Latino community of Boston to spotlight the need to cultivate community involvement—often neglected by government, whether citywide, state, or federal.[111] While this article does not include an explicit race and power analysis, it does point out a major disconnect between the interests and ambitions expressed by community residents and those of the nonprofit leaders. This occurs when nonprofits attempt to squeeze out resident decision-making authority in favor of professional roles.

Otis Johnson, mayor of Savannah, Georgia, challenged public interest agencies—government and nongovernmental—to reclaim from earlier community action days the guiding concept of "maximum feasible participation." Johnson noted that the concept was decimated as government policy evolved but also as many foundations and nonprofits failed to take it seriously. At cause is "a kind of brainwashing that many ascribe to: the elites, in a *noblesse oblige* kind of mentality, must tell these folks what they need." As he explained, some public and nonprofit leaders "clearly believe if people are poor or if they are of color in this society, they don't have the intellectual ability required to engage productively in the collective work and responsibility of making our communities whole. It goes back to slavery. The rationalization about why slaves should obey their master was that . . . the master is the smartest and has your interests in mind."[112]

This orientation, even if unconscious, limits the effectiveness of nonprofits and the capacity-building support on which they rely. Program design, resource development, board governance, and other aspects all suffer. This has even broader implications if certain trends continue: professionalization of the sector, increasing tendency to define accountability in terms of financial or legal compliance, or a sense that equity is achieved when nonprofits have added variety in faces, languages, or economic background.

Nesly Metayer analyzed the need for cultural competency in assisting immigrant organizations—specifically Haitian American. Ethnic-based organizations should be seen, he noted, in terms of "the interaction between external cultural pressures and the internal dynamics of the organization in its community."[113] Three key findings related to organizations he studied in three U.S. cities with a large Haitian population. Metayer notes

- The reproduction of old patterns of organizing and managing organizations
- The extension of social conflict and social competition inside the organization
- Predispositions about Haitian leadership and cooperative behaviors

Metayer found that the power structure and positioning tend to carry over old class divisions from Haitian society, which "actively play out in the practices of Haitian nonprofits here in America." Examples include an enormous investment in leaders as the authorities and knowledge repositories, heavy constraints on open discussion or questioning in staff meetings, limited staff involvement in decision making, and a great deal of maneuvering to be closer to the boss. "These practices are the grammar of everyday actions," he says, "jeopardizing the organization unity and team spirit inside the organization. This, of course, jeopardizes the quality of information the leader is working with."

Metayer, who is of Haitian ancestry, poses an alternative model of servant leadership. He also offers a warning: "Without understanding these stakes, the contextual politics of the community, and the cultural 'markers' of class or power position embedded in a particular political history, a management consultant may be nearly oblivious to cues that might otherwise be essential guides to our work."[114]

NPQ's Fall 2006 issue focuses on socioeconomic class and the way it influences nonprofit dynamics. Its stories of class-based power explore the importance of class consciousness, distinctions between good intentions and unwitting ways that power difference is reinforced, and even "battered agency syndrome"—a dilemma of social service agencies that find themselves facing similar challenges to their constituents.

In a similar vein, an article by Adrie Kusserow in the *Stanford Social Innovation Review* suggests that class issues are rooted in different notions of the individual and appropriate socialization. The impact is seen throughout a variety of settings, from education to human services to politics. Indeed, the "rift between hard and soft individualisms," writes Kusserow, "can . . . undermine very well intentioned social sector attempts at building cross-class coalitions." For those who are willing to take on being class bridgers, "An important step is becoming aware of one's own culture-based style of individualism and the ways in which it unconsciously seems natural, right, true, and inevitable." Further steps are to acknowledge that different goals and values may be legitimate, and to experience other worlds in order to understand their own integrity. Essentially, this is a call to shake up assumptions about class and bring the questions into "the broader American discourse on social change."[115]

Cultural Grounding for Effective Nonprofit Support

A number of organizations and individuals have begun translating the work of structural racism into a larger frame of reference: culturally based, or culturally competent, work. Among them are the National Community Development Institute (NCDI), Patricia St.Onge and Seven Generations Consulting, the Minority Executive Directors Coalition, the Building Movement Project, and Interaction Institute for Social Change. St.Onge, in *Through the Lens of Culture*, written for NCDI, described the historical basis for culturally based consulting and related practices.[116]

One application that shows the difference of being culturally based is found in documentation of work done by Seven Generations in partnership with the Praxis Project, which generated a useful approach to tobacco reduction among technical assistance providers in Montana's Native American communities.[117] A central lesson was that invoking the tradition of "tobacco as sacred" was far more compelling than "just say no" methods. The key was empowering the people most involved and affected to develop their own solutions.

The Minority Executive Directors' Coalition of King County (based in Seattle) found a need to define cultural competency and guiding principles for implementing it as the county seeks to improve human services delivery and technical assistance. Goals include being "much better able to meet the diverse needs in all communities throughout" the county. Key principles are

■ Commitment to social change, including acknowledgment of institutional racism and cultural differences that mean the "dominant culture" cannot always be the measure

■ Accessibility of opportunities for service, training, and funding that are not exclusionary by factors such as location and language

■ Relevance, including respect for differences in decision making and life circumstances and for the role of community in solving personal and collective problems[118]

Nonprofit Leadership and Diversity

Speaking in terms of diversity, the for-profit and government sectors are in some ways ahead of the nonprofit sector in developing systems and institutionalizing practices that ensure leadership for an evolving context. A common premise is that faces and perspectives must reflect the markets that businesses are trying to reach—the consumers or residents ("we the people") that governments are supposed to be by and for.

While much wisdom is available to be tapped in the business and government sectors, nonprofits focus on a different "bottom line" of hugely ambitious social goals and complex paths to achieving them. Building and supporting culturally competent leadership specifically for nonprofits allows them to function well as essential players in realizing those goals—and to be better partners (even instigators) for private and government sector leadership.

Issues of nonprofit sector leadership are being documented in clearer terms. For one, research confirms that people of color are underrepresented in executive director positions. A major study by CompassPoint Nonprofit Services found 75 percent of executive directors in a national sample were White. In a local area such as Washington, DC, population ratios are in dramatic contrast to executive directorships. *Daring to Lead 2006* stated that 80 percent of executive directors in the Washington, DC, area are White; the general population is 60 percent White. Equally telling is that, nationally, only 18 percent of nonprofit executives under the age of forty-five are people of color. The work of Building Movement Project and Nonprofit Sector Workforce Coalition, calls attention to intersections of generation, race/ethnicity, and socioeconomic status. CompassPoint concluded: "[E]fforts to identify, develop, and support nonprofit leaders of color, and organizations based in communities of color, are essential . . . low percentage of executive directors of color is in part a reflection of the difficulties faced by community-based nonprofits in communities of color."[119]

Expanding knowledge about those difficulties and means of addressing them—not just at the level of individuals or single organizations but with a clear sense of the sectoral and societal—will be increasingly important for study and practice. Even in the field of community development, where a common working assumption is that the community context, including cultural identity and demographics change, will be routinely taken into account, recent research documents "a lack of fair racial and ethnic representation."[120]

As a leverage point in changing social conditions, race and ethnicity in the United States has yet to be linked sufficiently to nonprofit leadership, including analysis and action strategies. St.Onge has documented the difference that culturally based coaching makes.[121] Slowly, intentional practice and even research are developing on this form of coaching. A Grantmakers for Effective Organizations (GEO) report on coaching noted that a network of Black coaches has formed. Its members specifically work with Black executive directors of nonprofits. The GEO report does suggest a set of questions on diversity as part of a protocol for nonprofits interviewing potential coaches. A subsequent report—*Listen, Learn, Lead*—clearly conveys the importance of transforming the power imbalance between grantmakers and nonprofits. The message is that cultural competency is no longer optional.[122]

Increasingly, nonprofit leaders and capacity builders recognize the importance of board diversity. As numerous sources document, the composition of nonprofit boards has over-represented White members as compared to the population and constituent base and under-represented people of color. Boards have also overrepresented women, but this finding is specific to smaller organizations. The reverse reality of underrepresentation is pronounced with Hispanic or Latino members (rivaled only by people who identify as "other" than the major categories ethnically), followed by board members of Asian and African ancestry. In all likelihood, the Native or American Indian representation is least of all. Also, the overwhelming majority of board members are age forty or older. Among the findings from an Urban Institute study released in August 2007, with more than 5,100 responding (a 41 percent response rate), are[123]

◾ On average 86 percent of board members are White "non-Hispanic," 7 percent African American or Black, and 3.5 percent Hispanic or Latino.

◾ Of all nonprofit boards, 51 percent are exclusively White "non-Hispanic," although larger nonprofits with budgets of more than $10 million are more diverse, with 31 percent being all White. Similarly, boards in large metropolitan areas are 45 percent White versus 66 percent outside the big cities.

◾ About 25 percent of those responding to the survey said that racial or ethnic diversity is somewhat important, and only 10 percent say that it is very important.

Another Urban Institute study focused on the boards of midsize nonprofits.[124] After studying 2005 data on 1,862 midsize organizations, the institute found the following:

◾ "On average, 83 percent of trustees are White (non-Hispanic), 9 percent are Black, and 4 percent are Hispanic, with the balance from other groups. Thirty-six percent of boards have no minority members. Furthermore, 48 percent of midsize nonprofits say that racial or ethnic diversity is not an important criterion when they select new board members.

◾ "Nonprofits whose clientele include higher percentages of ethnic or racial minorities are more likely to include board members from those groups. Still, many nonprofit boards have no minority representation, even among organizations serving a high percentage of minorities.

■ "Other groups underrepresented on nonprofit boards are those under age thirty-five or over age sixty-five. On average, only 6 percent of board members are under thirty-five and only 13 percent are over sixty-five."

The report suggests directing attention to recruiting, although how likely that is to happen and be effective seems questionable if board members themselves do not see a need for change. The Alliance for Nonprofit Management and BoardSource, along with numerous member organizations, have started to address diverse cultural identity in who serves on boards *and* in the ways in which boards are structured, commissioned, and operating. BoardSource has produced a governance index report on demographics by race and ethnicity, age groups, and gender, based on responses from more than 1,200 CEOs and nearly 1,200 board members. Reports also addressed satisfaction with board diversity, finding about half were somewhat or very satisfied and only 13 percent very dissatisfied.[125]

The Board Governance Affinity Group from the Alliance for Nonprofit Management has been at work on alternative governance models that emphasize community engagement. This work from the first part of 2007 is documented in the *NPQ* and is decidedly in favor of a close connection to a nonprofit's constituency or community, which could facilitate being more in tune with cultural values and traditions.[126] A useful perspective by Ellen Bryson in *Foundation News & Commentary*[127] offers tips for foundations to build boards that better reflect the diversity in their communities.

Where present, persons who bring more diverse backgrounds face challenges: isolation, being called upon so much that they become overextended, and not having sufficient recognition for leadership styles that differ based on cultural experience. As a result, nonprofit leadership on policy matters is far from being at its most effective in and for communities of color.[128] Studies point to varying views and experiences but a growing sense that increased diversity has significant value for nonprofit boards.[129]

Similar and related issues can be found in all areas of capacity building: strategic planning, advocacy, executive transitions, collaboration, technology, and more. However, systematic research on the cultural dimensions of these capacity-building areas and the historical-cultural context that affects them has not been done. Thus, the vast majority of leadership-development efforts have not been sufficiently grounded in the principles of cultural competency. The learning that has been documented is not often shared in ways likely to reach and empower a diverse network of nonprofit capacity builders.

Informing Practice, Making Change

Multiple resources and initiatives have cropped up in recent years to inform practice and increase cultural competency, including many that focus on equity and inclusiveness with racial and ethnic identity. A new turn is to confirm cultural competency as a requirement of good practice, as is done in Alliance for Nonprofit Management's ethical standards for capacity builders, approved in 2006. Parallels include ethical standards of the National Association of Social Workers (NASW) and the NASW Standards for Cultural Competence in Social Work Practice.[130] Also in 2006, the Alliance's People of Color Affinity Group developed "Principles of Culturally Competent Advocacy Capacity Building," published in the online Cultural Competency Resource Pages. And a special Alliance newsletter edition about the aftermath of Hurricanes Katrina and Rita raised issues of cultural identity and effectiveness as relevant to nonprofit capacity building.[131]

Denver Foundation, with its Expanding Nonprofit Inclusiveness Initiative, articulates reasons for working toward greater inclusiveness in nonprofits: "Regardless of the mission of an organization, becoming more inclusive will help nonprofits be more successful based on higher job satisfaction, retention, and productivity; better problem-solving; increased creativity and innovation, and less vulnerability to legal challenges."[132]

The Annie E. Casey Foundation, with its *Race Matters Toolkit,* makes explicit several motivating factors. Most important are that "almost every indicator of well-being shows troubling disparities/disproportion by race," and it is "only possible to close equity gaps by using strategies determined through an intentional focus on race." The core analysis holds up for re-examination the "dominant model of thinking about 'race' in the U.S.," which stresses progress already made, individual will, and assimilation.[133] The intention is to encourage nonprofits toward higher awareness, equity action plans, and tracking organizational progress. As with the Denver Foundation's initiative, attention is called to the importance of nonprofit leaders recognizing the need for change, and their relying on knowledgeable, skilled capacity builders to support the change process. The Casey Foundation also has commissioned numerous reports that shed light on cultural dynamics and the extraordinary importance of gaining proficiency in matters of identity.[134]

An important caveat to these discussions is the reality that concepts such as "people of color" are still unsettled or embraced slowly. Tensions come with the natural process of identifying by national origin and, in particular, with groups or communities based on experiences outside the United States. Rinku Sen and Lori S. Robinson are among the writers who have captured these complexities.[135]

Although our emphasis at the outset has been on race and ethnicity, certainly other dimensions of identity are as important. A growing body of resources provides closer attention to supporting faith-based organizations and non-profit work in the interest of equity around generation, sexual orientation, disability, gender, and geography. Examples of useful material include research reports by

■ The National Gay and Lesbian Task Force, providing data on the presence, challenges, and contributions of homeless youth, aging Americans, and spe-cific ethnic groups (with some attention to religious identity and politics as well as demographics and culture) within the LGTBQ community[136]

■ The Building Movement Project, sponsored by the Annie E. Casey Founda-tion, the Movement Strategy Center, and American Humanics in connection with the Nonprofit Sector Workforce Coalition—all offering key points about generational issues in the nonprofit sector[137]

Opportunity gaps persist in the field of capacity building for nonprofits, which raises cultural-competency concerns. At stake are questions about who is typically named as high profile, referred to by colleagues, understood as available and capable, actually employed in positions of great authority or autonomy, and who has adequate or even generous levels of resources to offer nonprofit support.

Cultural Competency in Money Matters

There is a growing body of literature in relation to philanthropy and fundraising. The foremost message is that success in investing time, talent, or treasure—as well as in securing those resources—requires paying close attention to cultural patterns and working toward greater equity.

The Council on Foundations' special report *Cultures of Caring* largely sets the stage for fostering cultural awareness by one of the first scans of culturally based philanthropy.[138] This report observed that much of institutional philanthropy has relied on stereotypes, mistakenly tagging African Americans, Asians, Latinos, and Native Americans "as recipients of charity—not as donors."

While acknowledging that income and asset gaps continue along racial and ethnic lines, the report encouraged people in philanthropy to understand various forms of giving, note the influence of geography with increasingly diverse communities, and act on recommendations to expand diverse philanthropy in the United States.

Ultimately, it is not only the individuals but the institutional practices and results—in terms of grant distribution—that matter. In *Shortchanged,* a groundbreaking work that more specifically addresses inequities in grants made, the Applied Research Center (ARC) presents an analysis of foundation giving that shows declining funds for organizations led by people of color that concentrate on civil rights and anti-racism work. The decline, in percentage and dollars, came at a time when the presence of people of color in foundation grantmaking staff positions was increasing. ARC found that "although people of color [made] up nearly one-third of the general U.S. population, grants explicitly targeted to benefit them constituted only 7 percent of foundation giving in 2001." Even as foundation giving was on the rise, and more people of color were coming into positions at foundations, many racial justice organizations were hit by a significant loss of foundation grant support.[139]

The Greenlining Institute released a pair of studies in November 2005 and November 2006 about the lack of diversity in philanthropic giving.[140] The first, *Fairness in Philanthropy,* found that independent foundations nationally award only 3 percent of grant dollars to nonprofits led by people of color. Based on advocacy to change this record, state legislators in California in 2007 began to consider proposed legislation that would require that data be reported on giving to organizations with a majority of people of color on the board and staff. Based on an agreement among some major California foundations to invest more in such organizations, sponsors decided not to move the legislation forward in 2008.

The second annual report, *Investing in a Diverse Democracy: Foundation Giving to Minority-Led Nonprofits,* ranks major foundations according to the diversity in their grantmaking. The premise for the research has to do with three points: that "the foundation sector wields enormous influence in matters impacting American democracy," that the "nation's pressing issues need the input of all the nation's citizens," and that changing practices in philanthropic investments—like financial institutions' investments in business—can better realize the promise of democracy.[141]

A key finding is that only 3.6 percent of philanthropic dollars from a sample of major national and California foundations in 2004 went to organizations led by people of color. (The 3.6 percent purposely leaves out of consideration a single unusual grant—$535 million to United Negro College Fund by the Bill and Melinda Gates Foundation.) Five, or about one-fifth of the twenty-four foundations studied, gave less than 1 percent of their dollars to "minority-led" organizations. The significance of the issue becomes apparent when considering that nonprofit (or nongovernmental) organizations led by people of color have made unparalleled contributions leading change in the United States.[142]

Rockefeller Philanthropy Advisors in 2008 offered two in a series of reports adding to the knowledge base about diversity in philanthropic giving and leadership. *Philanthropy in a Changing Society: Achieving Effectiveness through Diversity* recounts how the focus on diversity has emerged and some key strategies. *Diversity and Inclusion: Lessons from the Field* provides a further grounding with voices of experience from philanthropic institutions and a review of research on the link of diversity to effectiveness.[143]

In other materials

■ The Joint Affinity Groups of the Council on Foundations explored *The Meaning and Impact of Board and Staff Diversity in the Philanthropic Field,* devoting a section to the less-known world of corporate philanthropy and the business case as well as business approaches for diversity.[144]

■ The National Network of Grantmakers (NNG) conducted research and provided a paper as an information base for its 2005 annual conference: "Pursuing Racial Equity Through Civic Engagement and Mass Media." NNG listed resources specific to capacity building and leadership, several of them readily applicable to developing cultural competency and supporting nonprofits to do so.[145]

■ A 2007 report by Marga Inc., for the Race and Equity in Philanthropy Group—*Profiles in Foundation Giving to Communities of Color*—and a 2005 earlier report by Marga for the Annie E. Casey Foundation—*Race, Class, Power in Philanthropy: Promising Practices*—document innovative practices by foundations to reshape race, class, and power dynamics. The reports identify structural barriers to equity and inclusion and ways to move beyond them through internal practices (board composition, staffing, consulting relationships, and vendor selection) as well as externally (replacing "charity" with "strategic" approaches).[146]

■ A paper for the Ford Foundation, *Community Philanthropy and Racial Equity: What Progress Looks Like: Results of a Preliminary Inquiry*, offers a richly layered portrait of historical and current practices that benefit racial equity and rural community change. Highlighted are community foundations and the southeastern United States. The Effective Communities Project, which authored this paper, also provides numerous other resources and tools.[147]

■ The Philanthropic Initiative for Racial Equity (PRE) prepared with the Ford Foundation's Grantcraft initiative a guide on racial equity in grantmaking, published in 2007.[148] PRE is also at work with Applied Research Center (ARC) on specific tools to promote racial justice through philanthropic institutional and grant practices.

The W. K. Kellogg Foundation[149] has continued initiatives to expand philanthropy in communities of color designed to "support and expand the resources of communities of color by focusing on the designated funds, philanthropic organizations, and giving practices of four major ethnic groups: African Americans, Latinos, Asian Americans/Pacific Islanders, and Native Americans," as noted in a report published online.[150] The Kellogg Foundation work is based on recognition that most institutions and individuals widely seen as major players in mainstream philanthropy are older, affluent, and White, and that communities of color "often referred to as 'minorities'" are fast becoming the majority in the United States.

Other documentation from Kellogg gives a sense of how organizational capacity issues are at play. For instance, one of the conclusions from a networking meeting among the "Emerging Philanthropy" initiative grantee organizations was that

> Support by majority philanthropies through the development of practices and policies which would enhance the infrastructure of these community organizations is needed for the preparation and implementation of community support. Participants in the networking meeting were clear in their beliefs that support from philanthropic agencies was a prerequisite for their success. Participants were clear also that such support needed to be implemented; the need, in their view, for further discussion has been surpassed by the imperative for action.[151]

A resource guide documents numerous culturally based philanthropic programs and practices. The guide was prepared by Grassroots Leadership for a plenary at the National Network of Grantmakers 2006 annual conference, co-sponsored by the W. K. Kellogg Foundation and NNG's People of Color Caucus.[152]

Background on racial and ethnic traditions for fundraising can be found in works of Janice Gow Pettey and Diana Newman, with collaborating authors. Pettey offers a rare, in-depth assessment of the U.S. historical-cultural context for ancestry groups of color and responsive strategies. Newman was involved with and tracks findings from the Council on Foundations' *Cultures of Caring,* adding practical guidance. In related work, the National Center on Black Philanthropy's conferences and research advance knowledge and power of Black-led grantmaking. The intersections come to the fore in Mary Ellen Capek and Molly Mead's book *Effective Philanthropy: Organizational Success through Deep Diversity and Gender Equality.*[153]

Numerous organizations have developed training materials to accompany their own specific programs, such as the Academy for Fundraising by People of Color (CompassPoint and *Grassroots Fundraising Journal*) and Grassroots Institute for Fundraising Training.[154] As an example, a literature review published in 2002 pulls together source material on "communities of color and the role that foundations have played in social movements," as a means of rethinking the history of giving and the influence of foundations. Grantcraft also has an important guide on gender equity in grantmaking.

There are numerous resources on grantmaking that focus on the phenomenon of immigrant "integration" into U.S. communities and in the interest of equity based on sexual orientation. A prominent example is the Funders for Gay and Lesbian Issues' work, including *Out for Change: Racial and Economic Justice Issues in Lesbian, Gay, Bisexual and Transgender Communities* dealing with support for promising practices in which nonprofits' work addresses the intersections of identity and justice issues.[155] Another example is *Expanding Opportunities: A Grantmaker's Guide to Workplace Policies for Lesbian, Gay and Bisexual Staff,* documenting funders' institutional practices.[156]

Capacity-Building Strategies

Practices central to culturally based capacity building, based on the work of NCDI, include building trust with community members, using project teams that understand the culturally based process, co-designing the change strategy, working as peers rather than experts, developing a learning agenda linked to community action plans, developing shared vision and goals, and building sustainable organizations. The method aims to fulfill these main roles

- Identify and use indigenous wisdom
- Broker knowledge and resources
- Build bridges across cultural identity groups
- Provide technically superior capacity-building support

Fernandopulle shares that CompassPoint's work to build the cultural competency of nonprofit clients has been based on multicultural organizational development principles such as the following.[157] The work of building cultural competency is best done at the organization level rather than through short-term trainings of large cohorts. A team is essential, and it needs to include different cultural lenses and different types and levels of responsibility and formal authority across the organization. In forming the team, a "skilled facilitator can act as a partner in developing a unique work plan for ongoing attention." The team must develop the focus for the work, gathering data to assess what would be most useful, drafting a work plan, then consulting about it and finalizing it, deciding an evaluation process, and dealing with implementation as well as monitoring success. Participants in the change work must envision practical effects such as improvements in service or better relationships with the community. These may result from new, culturally authentic approaches to donor cultivation. The example of donor relationships is drawn from CompassPoint's experience running the Fundraising Academy for Communities of Color.

Multicultural organizational development strategies recommended by Mayeno[158] focus on assessing environmental forces relating to change and then working to increase organizational readiness, gain commitment across organizational levels, support change agents, engage the community, and establish accountability. Also important are modeling desired behaviors, values, and skills; creating a climate of dialogue and trust; sustaining the work through an ongoing process with a clear vision and benchmarks; and recognizing the impact and responsibility beyond the boundaries of an organization. In addition, Mayeno calls attention to the stages of organizational development in a multicultural framework: guiding the group to select a change goal, identifying critical and facilitating actors, making an analysis of the driving and restraining forces, and establishing a process led by a change team that continues analysis of the force field and refinement of goals and strategies.

With Kellogg Foundation support, Grand Valley State University's Johnson Center on Philanthropy published a report on cultural competency in nonprofit mental health organizations that identifies the needs of nonprofits and offers recommendations on developing a culturally competent environment in organizations.[159] A related report addresses "strategic diversity" for nonprofit and governmental human capital.[160]

In addition to cross-cutting practices, numerous identity-specific approaches are being documented. Heather M. Berberet offers guidance on needs assessment specifically to develop services for LGTBQ youth.[161] Alexandra Pierce researched factors that affect capacity building with immigrant- and refugee-led organizations.[162]

Background on racial equity practice is cited in several resources. The Web site Evaluation Tools for Racial Equity provides tips, tools, resources, and stories with an evaluation focus.[163] And, effective ways to intergroup relations are explored in works by Potapchuk, Kien Lee, and others.[164]

Lessons from Other Arenas

The health care field remains the most prolific source of materials, including standards, studies, tools, and other resources that fall increasingly under the banner of cultural competency. A major reason for such an explosion of resources is the recognition of demographic changes and stark disparities in health outcome. This often comes with an admission that any service provider operates with a limited sense of values, and the goal is achieving equal access and quality. The California Endowment papers mentioned earlier are prime examples. Without a doubt, the health arena will continue to produce an abundance of materials.

Numerous online sources function as resource bases, offering bibliographies, lists of assessment tools and methods, books and reports, and even e-lists for discussion. Prominent examples include Web sites from the National Center for Cultural Competence, U.S. Department of Health and Human Services (HHS) Office of Minority Health, HHS' Substance Abuse and Mental Health Services Administration, and DiversityRx. Among the guides that address nonprofit capacity building is *Building Coalitions among Communities of Color: A Multicultural Approach,* which emphasizes the primacy of relationships and equitable footing.[165]

The National Center for Cultural Competence (NCCC) has collected resources, provided online access to reference lists for relevant publications, developed trainings and tools, and documented stories about cultural competency—primarily but not exclusively focused on health care institutions and providers.[166] One of the NCCC tools provides a means of self-assessment for health care practitioners. In its information base and work, NCCC pays attention to policy development as well as staff development and planning processes and service delivery. As keynote speaker for the spring 2005 England regional meeting of the Alliance for Nonprofit Management, the center's director, Tawara Goode, spoke to the importance of immigration and language groups as communities are changing. She also noted the influence of a range of cultural factors, such as "family constellation."

A great tribute is owed to educators and advocates for equity in education. Early on, these efforts were named in terms of "multicultural" education or African-centered studies, with Molefi Asante of Temple University having established the first related Ph.D. program and consulting to school systems across the United States. In recent years, *cultural competence* or *cultural competency* are terms used in education (Jerry Diller and Jean Moule's *Cultural Competence: A Primer for Educators,*[167] for example) and across fields. Arenas such as politics and law may employ other words for closely related ideas. For instance, "political race" and consequences of cultural identity are explored in *The Miner's Canary* by Lani Guinier and Gerald Torres. This analysis relates not only to electoral politics or public policymaking but to broader not-for-profit (and, indeed, for-profit) endeavors.[168]

The community development field, which is woven together with the capacity-building field that is the focus of this book, deserves particular note for being in the forefront on structural racism. Although many community development organizations and a substantial part of their fundings are based within the nonprofit sector, these organizations represent a mixed arena, with for-profit and not-for-profit organizations occupying the same space. That reality will likely promote cross-sector insights and techniques.

Finally, a critical arena for lessons learned is that of the arts and humanities world, where organizations are typically nonprofit. Though they focus explicitly on cultural matters, these organizations exhibit all the promise and peril of other social institutions around cultural dynamics. Indeed, a book on cultural equity seeded the Cultural Competency Initiative: *Voices from the Battlefront: Achieving Cultural Equity,* edited by Marta Moreno Vega and

Cheryll Y. Greene.[169] Among the classic perspectives it includes is Bernice Johnson Reagan's "Battle Stancing," a glimpse of the ways that people carry historical perspective, hopes, and determination into all their work, whoever the employer may be. Similarly, Dudley Cocke's "Appalachia, Democracy, and Cultural Equity" identifies the richness and the ruin of this cultural and geographic territory within the United States. He signals the importance of moving past mainstream approaches in which outsiders do the community planning and decision making through processes that stereotype, demoralize, and divide residents—and the need to move toward appreciation and self-determination.

Conclusion

Cultural competency is growing up as more "buzz" is generated and the "tipping point" reached. The result is increasing visibility and viability as an important aspect of all work to advance the nonprofit sector. The intention of this book is to continue a collective journey and invite more people on that journey. We stand on the path to bring excellence to support nonprofit effectiveness, realize greater nonprofit impact, and ultimately transform society toward equity.

BRIGETTE ROUSON

Resource D

Voices from the Field: Stories from Peer Dialogues

The following are insights and experiences, many of them in the form of direct quotes, from capacity builders who participated in Cultural Competency Initiative research sessions sponsored by the Alliance for Nonprofit Management. These peer dialogue sessions were conducted during the first half of 2006 in San Francisco, Chicago, and Atlanta.

Matters of Time, Commitment, and Resources

Good practice requires extended, deep involvement. Unfortunately, that level of involvement is unusual, largely due to available resources and how nonprofits view capacity building:

> We're all limited by the kind of time we have with our clients. It's kind of misleading to say cultural competency is a lifelong process, then to say we're going through a strategic planning process and by the end we'll have a completely different organization. So how do we, when we approach this work, raise the capacity of the people in the organization to continue to do it? . . . It's ideal to have a lifelong partnership, but that's not real.

One practitioner shared from the experience of working with an alliance of service providers on a two-year contract that was renewed for another two years. The specific focus was cultural diversity:

> I started working with leadership first to get full buy-in, because otherwise it's not going to go anywhere. I started with the [executive director] and board, and then staff, with multicultural training,

bringing tools, and started asking them: What are some good strategies that you have taken? Out of that came a lot of interviewing with people being served . . . focus groups, etc. We learned a lot. [The program] came a lot from White women's perspective . . . food was not culturally appropriate . . . staff needed to be trained: Look at the people you serve, and here's what way that people would like to be greeted, etc. . . . There is a required level of commitment to this training, and ongoing commitment to looking at this work. Because if the [executive director] sees it [mainly] as a way to get grant money, it falls on the shoulder of one staff member who's committed to the process but can't [succeed].

A lot of times an organization will say *let's do multicultural training,* and they fix on the interpersonal. They don't want to review the policy level. If we are truly going to do it, we would have to do it at all levels. At this point, no one's really funding it.

Strategies for Matching Cultural Identity

A diverse consulting team can make a difference, both in (a) the opportunity for role assignments such as creating a cultural identity match for subgroups formed as part of organizational or program assessment, or the use of power dynamics relating with the client organization and in (b) the diversity of perspectives and even necessary "pushback" from within the consulting team.

In providing technical assistance to one initiative, a consultant worked as part of a team that was ethnically diverse: "One of the things we do is try to match the [consultant for a] focus group with whatever racial-ethnic identity." Another consultant whose ancestry and language matched that of an immigrant group she was serving found her background "really helpful" based on "ways of saying things" and an understanding of how to enter in:

> I used a lot of cultural knowledge that's really hard to define. For instance, you don't go and just start asking questions. You talk about the children, what's happening [in the family or community], then thirty minutes later, you say, "By the way, we want to improve this program."

A White woman on our team came from the women's liberation movement. She struggled with providing services to the family [versus individuals]. So there were some ways we had to shift to understand another culture. I could understand people from my cultural background, but I couldn't readily understand the Indian women coming in.

◆

We have White people on our team because a lot of times I'll say something but the White [executive director] may not hear it. We make sure that when we're confronting power, we have somebody [who] can take on that level of authority.

Cultural competency is increasingly recognized as a requirement for capacity builders—including funders, whose views carry great weight—as well as the nonprofits they support. The key is not to assume that this requirement is met by looking only at obvious characteristics of nonprofit executives and their constituencies, or of capacity builders and clients or grantees. In working with nonprofits, a willingness to locate oneself culturally and take a stand are both vital:

They [nonprofits] will accept what you bring them as a consultant. If they were able to talk about . . . concerns, there would be a lot more movement in terms of cultural competency. When you have minority-led organizations, a lot of times as minorities, we naturally believe we are culturally competent because we were born into this community. But if I am an urban Mexican-born woman, or American-born Mexican woman, I don't know everything about a Mexican-born woman in a small rural area who's bringing her experience. Agencies that are minority-managed do a lot of excellent work, but you encounter sometimes agencies who feel they're on the right path but are not open to change. It [the program] may not be culturally appropriate.

The point is that differences along socioeconomic lines or geographic boundaries can be just as significant as ethnicity, national origin, or gender.

Grounding the Capacity-Building Relationship

Typically, it is important to engage about values in developing the support relationship with a nonprofit. However, in some cases, considering a consultant's value base, it is appropriate and advisable not to bring up views likely to conflict with those of the client:

The fact [is] that we enter this work with values. We're never objective.

◆

What is the way groups choose their consultants or not? Is it gut level? People here get calls and sometimes refer them. Is it a checklist? The relationship with the consultant is so central. And yes, you can list your values, but how do they [play out]?

◆

It is important to have the values conversation up front—transparency. Because you have the choice to do the work, to say, "Well, the way I like to do the work is. . . ." With certain disclosure, that can be a conversation stopper and relationship blocker. We have to really honestly believe in the power of relationship building.

◆

It's complex, the shared values thing. Because I worked with ministers in the valley, I know they're not down with the whole gay-lesbian thing. But they weren't working on an explicitly homophobic project.

◆

I have learned the hard way with Salvadoran American groups. [El Salvador] had that long war for years. What you get here [in the U.S. among most Salvadoran immigrants] is either FLN sympathizers or Republican sympathizers. Opening up my value set as a college-educated Bay Area resident can be a hindrance to helping them move along in the direction they need to be moving in. If I say, for instance, that I'm pagan, that's the end of that—for a lot of American clients, much less Salvadoran. [The question is] how we utilize disclosure.

Honoring Culture, Transforming Dynamics

Appreciating culture is not the same as reinforcing all its typical practices or popular concepts. Nor does it mean accepting at face value the dominant portrait of cultural identity. In some cases, the capacity builder's responsibility is to open people up to changing those practices that undermine the broader vision of healthy communities and a just society: "Culture is one thing. Appreciating it is one thing. On the other hand, culture can be oppressive in the community."

One consultant, a young woman working with an Asian ancestry organization, had experiences that raised issues of age, gender, language, and power. She was introduced at a board meeting by the executive director with great emphasis on her formal education and experience. (This was a board whose members had been extremely deferential to the chair because of his community standing as a top business executive.) She found that her critical task at the outset was to create a participatory process. Her consulting approach took into account that traditional cultural practices can be hierarchical and patriarchal. The consultant succeeded with "subversiveness" by bringing in humor and by switching languages to show respect and the ability to speak as an insider—and yet had to avoid being overly deferential. There were moments when she used English to reinstate some power balance and encourage board members to create a new participatory climate.

Capacity builders who are dedicated to cultural competency find it necessary to learn about the complexity of cultural heritage. One practitioner, a Latina, points to a recent museum exhibit on Africans in Mexico's heritage. To her this suggests "a whole other concept to go on. Mexico has excluded the whole African experience in Mexico from its history, though it's very apparent in some states. And so we have to have these conversations, and there are conversations that go on in areas [of Chicago]. . . . You have to figure out what you don't understand and what are the questions that can help you relate to other people."

Place, Politics, and Past in Cultural Identity

Many practitioners suggested that the textures of neighborhood base, rural or urban settings, and national, ethnic, and racial origins deserve serious consideration in capacity building. These dimensions are relevant whether one's work is seeding unified efforts at community change or the usual assessment and planning process at the organization level. Neighborhood and ethnic dynamics are complex and interwoven, as a Chicago practitioner related:

> You can understand the interesting challenges of working in a place like Humble Park, where on the East Side it is largely Latino . . . and on the other side, largely African American, where they're trying to come together. In the Latino community, there is an interesting range of identities. You think Humble Park, you think Puerto Rican; you see flags. But East Side is not only Puerto Rican, and the West Side is not only African American. There is a lot of dialogue of my staff when we think about what we're trying to do over there. Where does culture come in? What does it mean? I just try to push to sharpen the language.

Racial and ethnic relations take shape in ways particular to geography. Chicago's Black-Brown relations were built largely on people coming to live side by side who had not previously. A previous mayor—the late Harold Washington—rose to the top by forming political coalitions of African Americans and Latinos within and across neighborhoods. Yet White ethnic identities and neighborhood politics are also influential. Peer dialogue participants observed that, along with directional divides in Black and Brown communities, there is a North Side–South Side split among Chicagoans as well. In an organizational assessment, a capacity builder may locate herself or himself culturally—or be located by a client or grantee—in the process of establishing trust.

> Chicago is interesting. I was really shocked at how there is a divide in the African American community—East Side and West Side. I was quickly educated, and it impacted how I did my work and how I approached it, because the first time I walked into a group on the West Side, they said, "Oh, you're from the South Side."

A consultant identified the importance of taking specific steps in early stages of a capacity-building assignment. For instance, a useful practice was to ask who nonprofit staff, board, or constituents looked to as leaders, past *and* present, and also to ask questions to get at different versions of community or organizational history. This approach is a key to understanding views presently held by people involved in the organization—or who left it but still have an impact. It also may offer cues to individual behaviors and the organizational culture:

> My first time being in that same part of the city, I learned quickly there were certain names you could not bring up without half the room starting [fussing]. They could actually connect the dots to certain things that happened in their community and they could trace it to certain people; i.e., this is why that happened, because so and so cut

a deal with some people. And it's almost like [Black residents] were conditioned to believe that the enemy was really Latinos—"Oh, the city gave Hispanic contracts to do some housing, but didn't give it to Black organizations." But did anybody Black bid on it? Oh, that's not the point. It cuts across by part of the city and it cuts across race; and people can't even put their finger on it. It's as if that's just the way it is and will be; and you don't even have the conversations challenging people to do community building that notices and works through the tensions.

Insider-Outsider Dynamics

The act of responding in a culturally competent way involves every effort to understand historical context and intent on all sides. The insider-outsider dynamic comes through clearly.

After an extended period of traveling to a rural Southern area to guide strategic planning for a nonprofit board, one consultant—in this instance an African American woman—was concluding the work. All along, she received detailed feedback that was constructive, balanced, and overwhelmingly positive. Time upon time, participants commented that good results were achieved. Also, it was significant that she had managed to become more of an insider than when the work began—as shown by the fact that after a while in this small town it was no longer widely noticed when she came into town, where she lodged, where she ate, and the like.

At this closing point, the client group wanted to give her a memento made of marble, which was popular and plentiful in the area. What did they choose?

A small replica of the old county jail—and proceeded among themselves to talk about how many people had been hung in the jail over the years. It was really fascinating. . . . I had to make a decision, and the decision I made was based on going through a very rapid thinking—like Rolodex flipping—OK, what's their intent, what's my intent, what would happen if I say that? I didn't say, "Thank you very much for this jail." I took the gift and said, "Oh, this is very interesting. I really appreciated this time working with you." I decided that there were many intents. In the ground were all these racial issues and historical issues. All that stuff was sitting there in the ground of that event. . . . One intention was to say, "You are an outsider in a number of different ways—based on your race, education and training, your experience, based on [having been] a Yankee." Not just [that I was from the city]. They were communicating big time to me. In that one gesture they were telling me a lot about themselves. And so I had to do some boundary management—like who am I in this, and who am I not in this, and what is it that I need to happen here. . . . It's all about making real contact with people.

A less subtle statement was being made to a woman of color who served as a trainer for White women in a rural area. She worked with them in a quilting circle to begin making a cultural space in which they could inform and organize themselves against domestic violence.

The entire two days I was with them—and I didn't want to be *the* Black person on that mountain at night, it was in 1992—they kept calling me "the colored girl." I remember my own cultural competency being called into question because [I had to remind myself] this was the best they could do. I had to process it as to how they meant it, given that these were the wives of men in the Klan, who felt they were being nice to me by calling me "the colored girl."

A value of culturally competent support is bringing oneself fully to the work while respecting others, building trust that allows participants to manage and move beyond their resistance to change. One trainer who served as part of a multi-ethnic team described bringing openness into an agency training and locating herself in the process, which made all the difference to success:

In a workshop I did, most of the employees where White men. In the room there were a few Black people, a few [White] women. We had already worked with the senior leadership team, all White men. Three guys, including [a supervisor], decided they were going to critique our leadership in the guise of intellectual querying. I was there with another White woman and an African American man [on the consulting team]. We always work in teams; two people are always up front. That day we were looking for the exit! I was sitting in back on the edge of my seat, just waiting. At one point, they both looked at me like, "OK, we're out of here." I said, "We're going to take a break, and you're welcome not to come back. But if you do, here are the rules." It was a mandated workshop, but I certainly wouldn't have told if some did not come back. They'd been sitting in rows; I said we need to get in a circle. It was huge. I began to ask, "What was good about growing up? What was challenging?" And asked them to offer an appreciation about somebody else in the circle. We [facilitators] were in the circle.

It was fascinating listening to these stories—a number of guys who couldn't think of anything good growing up, who were raised poor; some hadn't finished high school. They experienced a lot of physical violence. You just started to hear these stories come out. Some people couldn't even speak what was challenging, it was so hard. Then appreciation. And, of course, a lot of guys in this small town knew each other. They did an amazing job of appreciating somebody across the circle. For me, my big "ah ha, oh my gosh" was these are my people too. They got to notice, too, what really happened in their lives that got them to where they are today, and how oppressive that was, and how poor they were, and how hard it was. At the end of the day, one guy who'd been doing this hard thing [said he] appreciated that I held the container. Because part of what they were trying to figure out is: Is it really safe for them to go where we were asking them to be? There has to be this bigness about you get to be in this space, but also there are rules. There were all these rich learnings that had racism, sexism, and class issues. We were coming from [the city], and however we looked or dressed that was slightly different, they were in a rural area. And we really had to be in the room—our whole selves, in order for things to work well.

Religion, Family, and Other Distinctions

Another distinctive piece is religious identity and family background, and it varies from location to location. This reality was echoed in an exchange among capacity builders from various roles and venues—all pointing to the importance of making connections, with some striking parallels from one cultural group to another:

I don't know any other part of the country that has to deal with organized religion as much as in the Deep South. You're living in a community where when you're introduced, they say, "Are you churched or not?" The unchurched, the undefined identity, is so much a part of belonging [when you move beyond] the Black-White paradigm, which of course is the primary relationship.

When I go outside [a large urban] area, people will want to figure out
who my people are. I find that more when I'm way out than in the
metro area. People really try to connect. That's part of the grounding of, Can I really make some kind of contact with you; is there a
way that I can know you by your family? If I just look at you, there's
no connection.

◆

They're asking you what your values are, because you're being located
on a subtle set of value clues. If you can't relate quickly, then you're not
embedded in your family. If you can't name your church . . . then there
is not enough of a values match.

◆

You go into many immigrant communities, you're going to get those
same questions, so they can see how you are and also so they can build
a connection, and they're going to see how much you're going to share
with them. . . .

Cultural Competency in Grantmaker Practice

The grantmaker's role brings a unique possibility of cultural competency. The
same role carries risks of reinforcing inequities and inefficiencies. Many nonprofits "find their decisions being driven not necessarily by what they want,
but what they perceive their funders want," a practitioner observed:

It seems that a lot of what is pushed upon the sector is driven by
funders. Part of my frustration is that for organizations working in
communities of color, if they are designated organizations of color or
"minority," the funding levels are never the same [as for their counter-
parts], and it's always much more of a struggle to get them to capacity.
They can propose the same project as someone outside the community,
but the funding level is almost never the same. Funder discussions
can seem so logical, rational, but they don't say some of these things
about organizations in the "majority" community and still give them
the same funding year after year. . . . Funders don't really appreciate
the different cultures in the community. . . . You want everybody to

function the same—and for some reason there's a sense that that will make the world a much better place.

One organization revised its grant guidelines and found, on further review, that many Latino organizations no longer were being funded, even though their work was known to be effective. The funder came up with creative ways to revamp the site visit process and took on the role of translating—culturally, not just linguistically. This allowed organizations to express themselves authentically and still meet the needs of funding decisions.

**PATRICIA ST.ONGE
AND WILSON RILES,
SEVEN GENERATIONS
CONSULTING**

Resource E

Strategies for Dealing with Internalized Oppression and Structural Racism

The first step in dealing with any problem is the recognition that there *is* a problem. This book presents many ways to help individuals and organizations take this step.

The next step is to recognize that there is no magic bullet or elixir that will cure a problem permanently. As individuals and organizations in the United States, we swim in a sea of racism that leads from the past into our future, shaping every aspect of our lives. The dominant culture's language (English) and other languages are imbued with racially biased concepts. These influence our thinking and expressions without much critical thought on our part. Many of the assumptions that stand behind our business, political, community, and personal roles and structures are also racially biased.

It would be irrational to assume that structural racism and oppression could be eliminated through a weekend seminar. As organizations and as individuals, we need to commit to long-term institutional change work and regular rituals that remind us to continually pay attention to the cultural waters in which we swim. When the "carriers" of racism are as continuously confronted with the impacts of structural racism and oppression on a conscious level as are the "targets," then we can say that sufficient commitment has been made. Real change is possible.

Also critical is the capacity to forgive but not to forget. This needs to be exercised with others (including organizations) so that we can forgive ourselves. It is well known in the social sciences that those who cannot forgive themselves for inappropriate and harmful past behaviors can become so stuck on that bad identity that they struggle to embrace hopeful, positive views of self that allow for change. The same is true of interpersonal, societal, and organizational relationships where there is no capacity or process for the giving and the acceptance of forgiveness.

There is no question that the request for forgiveness must be accompanied with real change that "repairs" the damage done and goes a long way toward curtailing potential damage in the future—reparations. There must also be the capacity to give forgiveness once it is properly requested. If the "target" is *invested* in being a target—internalized oppression—then forgiving can be difficult. The request for and giving of forgiveness *must* be accompanied from all sides with the commitment not to forget and the construction of personal rituals and organizational mechanisms to accomplish this. These rituals and mechanisms become the concrete, visible signs of change.

This is a change from unconscious, blind immersion to recognition of bias and distortion. It is not a change from being a racist organization into being a non-racist organization. The work is about innovating, updating, and accomplishing ongoing behavioral changes. The goal is to monitor the evolution of oppression in the external environment and blunt the negative impacts of this evolution on the individual and the organization.

Because structures are more than the sum of their members, it is important to look at the whole constellation of elements that make an institution or organization run. Analysis of every element is critical to unearthing the inequities and dealing with them. The following template provides the framework for that analysis. This is only a sample, not by any means an exhaustive list of the kinds of questions we can ask in doing a power analysis.

Template:
Strategies for Dealing with Internalized Oppression
and Structural Racism

Overarching questions to ask about each area of assessment listed below:

Does this aspect of our organization actively work to erase inequity?

Does it seek to create justice?

Is this aspect of our work part of the greater building movement to create and support social change?

What are the power dynamics at play?

Is there a single cultural lens through which things get interpreted for the group?

Whose voices are at the table? Whose are not?

Who benefits from the way things are currently done?

Who is hurt by things the way they are?

Are differences celebrated or tolerated?

What other questions do we need to ask?

Area of assessment	Power analysis (Asks the questions on page 201.)	Inequities unearthed (What are the results of the analysis? What do we find?)	Internalized oppression indicators (Is there evidence that the group is playing out the way it does because some members struggle with their roles as minor?)	Redress recommendations (What concrete actions can be taken by individuals and by the institution to address the issues and concerns raised?)	Additional considerations and action steps
Mission/vision/values					
Communications					
Information management					
Technology					
Organizational structure/ systems					
Decision making					
Planning/priorities					
Policy/advocacy					
Programs					
Human resources					
Personnel management					
Volunteer management					
Constituency					
Governance					
Board					
Committees					
Board/staff relations					
Operations					
Insurance					
Legal					
Facilities					
Fiscal management					
Sustainability					
Fund development					
P.R./marketing					
Media relations					
Evaluation					
Programs					
Organizational effectiveness					

Area of assessment	Power analysis
Governance board	Does the board reflect the community it represents?
	When does the board meet?
	Who can attend at that time? (Hourly waged people can rarely get away from work during the day without getting financially penalized; this is often not the case with salaried workers.)
	Are child care and food provided at the meetings? (Single parents can only attend if there is child care.)
	Are there consumers of the organization's services on the board?
	How are decisions made? (Do we only use Robert's Rules of Order? Do we make room for decision making that works more effectively in non-Western cultures?)
	Are board members chosen only because of formal education (for example, as a banker, lawyer, accountant)? Or are other skills (the ability to speak the language of clients, indigenous leadership skills) recognized by communities (cross-cultural effectiveness, shared experience with clients, and so on)?
	Are board members chosen *only* for their "diversity quotient"?
	Does the board recognize its accountability to the community, understanding that it represents the community as the "stakeholders/shareholders" of the corporation?
	Is there a periodic review of historical factors and current practices that might make potential board members from communities feel less welcome?
	When we recruit hourly workers and their attendance drops off, do we check ourselves to see if the organizational systems and structures may have driven them away or made them feel unwelcome, or do we assume they aren't interested? Do we say, "We invited them, but they don't show up"?
	Do we check in with people who leave the board or drop out without saying much with an exit interview that invites them to explore structural racism with us?

Using the board of one organization as an example and asking questions from the above template, we came up with the set of answers shown to the right. These are based on the following dynamics: Board meetings are held at noon, downtown, to accommodate the "professionals" who don't want to come to our offices (which are in the neighborhood we serve) in the evening. Some board members cite inconvenience as the reason for the meeting time and location; others acknowledge that they are afraid to be in that neighborhood at night.

	Inequities unearthed	Internalized oppression indicators	Redress recommendations	Additional considerations and action steps
	We've recruited a good balance based on gender and sexual identity but not race, class, or age diversity. Professionals feel welcome; hourly workers may not. Professionals can walk from work to the meetings; hourly workers may not be able to. Professionals' attitudes of fear at being in the neighborhood we serve are accommodated; hourly workers live and work in the neighborhood and are made to feel that their neighborhood isn't even worth visiting, let alone living in. Professionals can afford to buy their lunch in downtown venues; hourly workers may not be able to afford that.	Pay attention to when a member of the hourly workers' group is quick to agree with the inequity. Acknowledge the possibility that internalized oppression may be at play.	Poll the whole board to see what time and place is best for each person. Move the meetings to accommodate those with less power historically, or at least rotate the meetings so that everyone has greater access on an equitable basis. Provide lunch or dinner (and child care if the meetings are in the evenings).	There are budget implications for providing food. Action steps to address them: Put a basket out for people to contribute what they can. Modify the organizational budget to pay for the lunch or dinner and child care. Ask volunteers to provide the meals.

PATRICIA ST.ONGE

Resource F
Self-Assessment in Three Parts

Power and privilege play out in a full array of factors. Your capacity to pay attention to the whole constellation of factors at play in a given situation increases your capacity to address it in a culturally competent way. It's important to ask yourself three questions in particular:

- What's going on with me?
- What's going on in the room—that is, with the other people who are present with me right now?
- What historical and structural issues are at play?

Following are more details about each of these questions:

What's going on with me?

- What am I wearing?
- How am I talking?
- Where am I looking?
- What cultural lens(es) do I bring with me?
- What are the power positions and dynamics that I bring to the table, based on the factors listed above?
- What language do I use?
- What are my first impressions of people?
- What assumptions do those impressions spark?

What's going on in the room?

- How are the seats arranged?
- Who is sitting where?
- What are the power dynamics embedded in the group dynamics?
- Is there a plan for movement that stretches people beyond the usual practices and typical power relations?
- Who speaks more, or with a greater sense of confidence?
- Who speaks less, or more tentatively?
- Who likely feels welcome? Who might not?
- How am I working to bring equity into the room?
- Where is the privilege in the room based on the factors listed above?

What historical and structural issues are at play?

- Describe the practices of this organization or community as they relate to power and privilege based on:
  - Race and ethnicity
  - Education
  - Socioeconomic status (class)
  - Language
  - Immigration status, national origin
  - Gender
  - Gender identity
  - Sexual identity
  - Physical ability and disability
  - Age
  - Generation
  - Religion
  - Culture
  - Family constellation
- Who has had to overcome what to be sitting here?

➻ Where are there likely points of internalized oppression?

- Do I recognize them for what they are?

- Do I address them in their historical context, seeing beyond who is in front of me *and* recognizing the many shoulders on which we all stand?

The diagram on this page presents a way to visualize the above factors and their possible interactions.

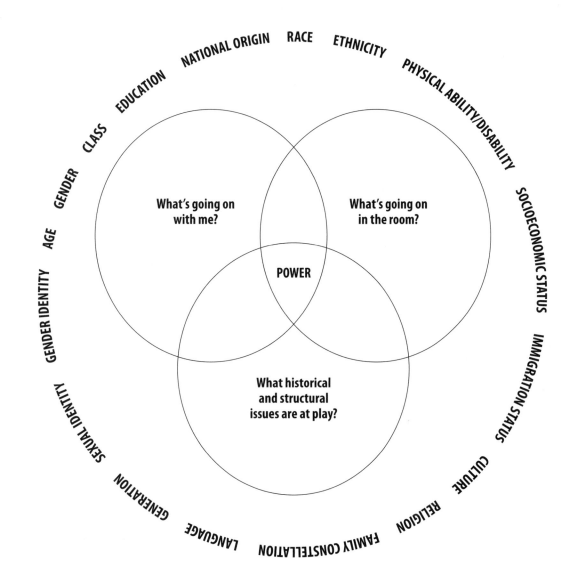

Resource G
Bibliography

Abrams, Jeremiah, and Connie Zweig. *Meeting the Shadow: The Hidden Power of the Dark Side of Human Nature.* Los Angeles: Tarcher, 1991.

Adams, John D. "Building a Sustainable World: A Challenging OD Opportunity" in *Understanding Organization Development: Foundations and Practices.* Edited by B. Jones and M. Brazzel. San Francisco: Pfeiffer/Wiley, 2006.

Adams, Maurianne, Lee Anne Bell, and Pat Griffin. *Teaching for Diversity and Social Justice: A Source Book.* New York: Routledge, 1997.

Advocacy Working Group (led by Gita Gulati-Partee, People of Color Affinity Group). *Principles for Culturally Competent Advocacy Capacity Building.* Washington, DC: Alliance for Nonprofit Management, 2006.

Agnes, Michael, ed. *Webster's New World College Dictionary,* fourth edition. New York: Wiley, 1999.

Allen, Theodore. *Invention of the White Race I and II.* New York: Verso Books, 1997.

Annie E. Casey Foundation. *Race Matters.* http://www.aecf.org/KnowledgeCenter/PublicationsSeries/RaceMatters.aspx, 2006.

Applied Research Center. *Mapping the Immigrant Infrastructure.* http://www.arc.org/content/view/243/48/, 2002.

Applied Research Center and Philanthropic Initiative for Racial Equity. *Racial Justice Grantmaking Assessment Tool,* www.arc.org.

Asian American Justice Center and Asian Pacific American Legal Center of South California. *A Community of Contrasts: Asian Americans and Pacific*

Islanders in the United States. Washington, DC: Asian Pacific American Justice Center, 2006.

Bakhtin, M. *The Dialogic Imagination.* Austin: University of Texas Press, 1982.

Baldwin, James. *Notes of a Native Son.* New York: Vintage, 1955.

———. *Nobody Knows My Name.* New York: Vintage, 1962.

Bates, Valerie. *Is Reconciliation Possible? Lessons from Combating Modern Racism.* http://www.visions-inc.org/Is%20Reconciliation%20Possible.pdf.

Bell, Ella, and Stella Nkomo. *Our Separate Ways: Black and White Women and the Struggles for Professional Identity.* Boston: Harvard Business School Press, 2001.

Benne, K. D. "History of the T-Group in the laboratory setting," 80–136, in *T-Group Theory and Laboratory Method: Innovation in Re-education,* edited by I.. P. Bradford, J. R. Gibb, and K.D. Benne. New York: Wiley, 1964.

Brinckerhoff, Peter C. *Generations: The Challenge of a Lifetime for Your Nonprofit.* St. Paul, MN: Fieldstone Alliance, 2007.

Bryson, Ellen. "Building Board Diversity," *Foundation News and Commentary,* 45, no. 6 (November/December 2004).

Butler, Shakti. "Conversations That Matter: Making Whiteness Visible." White Privilege Conference Workshop, St. Louis, MO, 2006.

———. *Mirrors of Privilege: Making Whiteness Visible.* Oakland, CA: World Trust Educational Services, 2006.

Capek, Mary Ellen, and Molly Mead. *Effective Philanthropy: Organizational Success through Deep Diversity and Gender Equity.* Boston: MIT Press, 2006.

Center for Assessment and Policy Development and MP Associates. Evaluation Tools for Racial Equity Web site, http://www.evaluationtoolsforracialequity.org/, 2005.

Center for Social Inclusion and Kirwan Institute for the Study of Race and Ethnicity. *Thinking Change: Race, Framing, and the Public Conversation on Diversity. What Social Science Tells Advocates about Winning Support for Racial Justice Policies.* http://www.diversityadvancementproject.org/media/ThinkingChange.pdf, 2005.

Chang, H., D. Salazar, and C. Leong. *Community Building and Diversity.* Oakland, CA: California Tomorrow, 1997.

———. *Drawing Strength from Diversity.* Oakland, CA: California Tomorrow, 1994.

Chao, Jessica, Julia Parshall, Desirée Amador, Meghna Shah, and Armando Yañez. *Philanthropy in a Changing Society: Achieving Effectiveness through Diversity.* New York: Rockefeller Philanthropy Advisors, 2008.

Clark, Christine, and James O'Donnell. *Becoming and Unbecoming White: Owning and Disowning a Racial Identity.* Westpoint, CT: Bergin & Garvey, 1999.

Coalition of Community Foundations for Youth and California Tomorrow. *Leading by Example: Diversity, Inclusion and Equity in Community Foundations.* http://www.ccfy.org/toolbox/docs/LBE_CA.pdf.

Community Development Institute. *White Paper: Transforming Philanthropy in Communities of Color: Key Issues and Recommendations from the Field.* Denver: Community Development Institute, 2007.

Community Foundations of Canada. *Building Bridges: A Tool for Engaging Diverse Communities.* Ottawa, Ontario: Community Foundations of Canada, 2006.

———. *Diversity Scanning Tool for Community Foundations.* Ottawa, Ontario: Community Foundations of Canada, 2006.

CompassPoint Nonprofit Services. *Organizational Development and Capacity in Cultural Competence,* Monograph series. San Francisco: CompassPoint Nonprofit Services and Los Angeles: The California Endowment, 2007.

Council on Foundations. *Cultures of Caring: Philanthropy in Diverse American Communities.* Arlington, VA: Council on Foundations, 1999.

———. "Statement on Inclusiveness." http://www.cof.org/learn/content.cfm?ItemNumber=1083&navItemNumber=6540, 2008.

Crossroads. *A Strategy for Building Anti-Racist Collectives.* Matteson, IL: Crossroads, n.d.

Dang, Alain, and Cabrini Vianney. *Living in the Margins: A National Survey of Lesbian, Gay, Bisexual and Transgender Asian and Pacific Islander Americans.* New York: National Gay and Lesbian Task Force Policy Institute, 2007.

Dismantling Racism Project, The. "Assessing Organizational Racism" in Western States Center. *Views,* Winter 2001.

Donors Forum of Chicago, Minnesota Council on Foundations, New York Regional Association of Grantmakers, and Northern California Grantmakers. *Building on a Better Foundation: Toolkit for Creating an Inclusive Grantmaking Organization.* http://mcf.org/mcf/resource/diversitytoolkit.htm, 2001.

Dovidio, John, and Samuel L. Gaertner, "Color Blind or Just Plain Blind? The Pernicious Nature of Contemporary Racism." *Nonprofit Quarterly* 9, no. 2, 22–27. www.nonprofitquarterly.org.

Drabek, Alisha, and Carrie Rothburd. "Approaches to Tribal Grant Writing and Project Planning." *CharityChannel,* November 9, 2005.

Dubois, W.E.B. *The Souls of Black Folk.* New York: Library of America, 1986.

Emarita, Betty. *Just Philanthropy: Becoming a Catalyst for Social Justice: A Tool for Aligning Internal Operations to Produce Progress.* Minneapolis: Effective Communities, 2006.

Epstein, Steven. "Gay Politics, Ethnic Identity: The Limits of Social Constructionism." *Socialist Review* 17, 3-4 (1987): 9–54.

Espinoza, Robert. *Building Communities: Autonomous LGBTQ People of Color Organizations in the U.S.* New York: Funders for Lesbian and Gay Issues, 2008.

Expanding Non-Profit Inclusiveness Initiative. *Inside Inclusiveness: Race, Ethnicity and Non-Profit Organizations.* Denver: Denver Foundation, 2003.

Fellner, Kim, Terry Keleher, Elisa Ortiz. *Work with Me: Intergenerational Conversations for Nonprofit Leadership.* Washington, DC: National Council of Nonprofits.

Fernandopulle, Anushka. "A Capacity Building Approach to Cultural Competency: Improving Cultural Competency Improves Organizational

Effectiveness" *Organizational Development and Capacity in Cultural Competence.* Los Angeles: The California Endowment and San Francisco: CompassPoint Nonprofit Services, July 2007.

Forum of Regional Associations of Grantmakers. "Racial, Ethnic, Tribal Philanthropy Knowledge Base." http://www.givingforum.org/s_forum/sec.asp?CID=1478&DID=3782, 2009.

Foundation for the Mid South. *Where Hope and History Rhyme: Reflections and Findings from the Mid South Commission to Build Philanthropy.* Mississippi: Foundation for the Mid South, 2005.

Freire, Paulo. *Pedagogy of the Oppressed.* New York: Continuum, 2007.

Frye, M. *The Politics of Reality: Essays in Feminist Theory.* Berkeley, CA: Crossing Press, 1983.

GrantCraft and Philanthropic Initiative for Racial Equity. *Guide to Grantmaking with a Racial Equity Lens.* http://www.grantcraft.org/index.cfm?fuseaction=Page.viewPage&pageID=893, 2007.

The Greenlining Institute. *Investing in a Diverse Democracy: Foundation Giving to Minority-Led Nonprofits.* Berkeley, CA: The Greenlining Institute, 2006.

Helfand, Judy, and Laurie Lippin, "Understanding Whiteness and Unraveling Racism," White Privilege Conference, St. Louis, MO, April 29, 2006.

Jensen, Robert. *The Heart of Whiteness: Confronting Race, Racism and White Privilege.* San Francisco: City Light Books, 2006.

Jessie Smith Noyes Foundation. *Diversity Policy Brochure.* http://www.noyes.org/admin/noyes_brochure13.pdf.

Johnson, Allan G. *Privilege, Power, and Difference.* New York: McGraw-Hill, 2005.

———. "Unraveling the Knot of Privilege, Power and Difference," White Privilege Conference, St. Louis, MO, April 29, 2006.

Jones, Brenda, and Michael Brazzel, eds. *The NTL Handbook of Organization Development and Change: Principles, Practices, and Perspectives.* Hoboken, NJ: Pfeiffer, 2006.

Khan, Surina, and Marcia M. Gallo. *Out for Change: Racial and Economic Justice Issues in Lesbian, Gay, Bisexual and Transgender Communities.* New York: Funders for Lesbian and Gay Issues, 2005.

Kivel, Paul. *Uprooting Racism: How White People Can Work for Racial Justice.* British Columbia, Canada: New Society Publishers, 2002.

Klein, D., with K. Morrow. *New Vision New Reality: A Guide to Unleashing Energy, Joy, and Creativity in Your Life.* Center City, MN: Hazelden, 2001.

Kunreuther, Frances. *Up Next: Generation Change and the Leadership of Nonprofit Organizations.* Baltimore, MD: Building Movement Project and Annie E. Casey Foundation, 2005.

Kunreuther, Frances, Helen Kim, Robby Rodriguez. *Working Across Generations: Defining the Future of Nonprofit Leadership.* San Francisco: Jossey-Bass, 2008.

Lawrence, Keith, Stacey Sutton, Anne Kubisch, Gretchen Susi, and Karen Fulbright-Anderson. *Structural Racism and Community Building.* Washington, DC: Aspen Institute, 2004.

Leary, Joy DeGruy. *Post-Traumatic Slave Syndrome: America's Legacy of Enduring Injury and Healing.* Milwaukie, OR: Uptone Press, 2005.

———. "Post-Traumatic Slave Syndrome." White Privilege Conference, St. Louis, MO, 2006.

Lewin, Kurt. *Field Theory in Social Science.* New York: Harper, 1951.

Lippit, R. *Training in Community Relations.* New York: Harper, 1949.

Lopez, Ian Haney. *White by Law: The Legal Construction of Race.* New York: NYU Press, 1999.

Lorde, Audre. *Sister Outsider.* New York: Crossing Press, 1984.

Love, Barbara, "Amazing Grace How Sweet Youth Sound: Strategies for Youth Empowerment and Liberation," White Privilege Conference, St. Louis, MO, 2006.

Marrow, Alfred J. *The Practical Theorist.* New York: Basic Books, 1969.

Mayeno, Laurin Y. "Multicultural Organizational Development: A Resource for Health Equity." In *Organizational Development and Capacity in*

Cultural Competence: Building Knowledge and Practice. Los Angeles: The California Endowment and San Francisco: CompassPoint Nonprofit Services, 2007.

Mayer, Steven E., Vanessa McKendall Stephens, and Betty Emarita. *Introduction and Overview: Three Tools to Assist Progress: Moving Philanthropy Closer to Racial Equity and Social Justice.* Minneapolis: Effective Communities Project, 2006.

McGregor, A. *The Philanthropy Index for Small Towns and Rural Areas of the South.* Asheville, NC: Southern Rural Development Initiative, 2003.

McIntosh, Peggy. "White Privilege and Male Privilege: A Personal Account of Coming to See Correspondences through Work in Women's Studies." In *Race, Class, and Gender: An Anthology,* edited by M. L. Andersen and P. H. Collins. Belmont, CA: Wadsworth, 1992.

McLemore, S.D. *Racial and Ethnic Relations in America,* fourth edition. Boston: Allyn & Bacon, 1993.

Miller, Jean Baker. *Toward a New Psychology of Women.* Boston: Beacon Press, 1976.

Minnesota Council on Foundations. *Diversity Framework.* http://www.mcf. org/mcf/resource/DivFramework.htm, 2009.

Mosaica: The Center for Nonprofit Development and Pluralism with Southeast Asia Resource Action Center. *Standing Up and Speaking Out for Refugees: An Advocacy Toolkit.* Washington, DC: Mosaica, 2009.

———. *Choosing the Right Structure for Your Community-Based Organization: Organizational Develop Toolkit.* Washington, DC: Mosaica, 2009.

National Center for Cultural Competence—Georgetown University Center for Child and Human Development. *Cultural and Linguistic Competence Policy Assessment.* Washington, DC: National Center for Cultural Competence, 2006.

National Gay and Lesbian Task Force. *Setting Up In-Person Volunteer Recruitment Actions.* http://www.thetaskforce.org/downloads/resources_ and_tools/IPVR-TrainingOutline.pdf, 2009.

New York Regional Association of Grantmakers. NYRAG's Policy on Diversity and Inclusiveness. http://www.nyrag.org/info-url2323/info-url_show.htm?doc_id=97975, December 12, 1990.

Nonprofit Quarterly editors. "Tracking the Miner's Canary: An Interview with Lani Guinier," *Nonprofit Quarterly* 9, no. 2, 12–17. www.nonprofitquarterly.org.

Opportunity Agenda. American Opportunity: A Communications Toolkit. http://www.opportunityagenda.org/atf/cf/%7B2ACB2581-1559-47D6-8973-70CD23C286CB%7D/American%20Opportunity%20-%20A%20Toolkit.pdf.

Palmer, Helen. *The Enneagram in Love and Work: Understanding Your Intimate and Business Relationships.* San Francisco: Harper Collins, 1995.

Parker, Cynthia. *Values and Guiding Principles for Addressing Issues of Race, Class and Power in Capacity-Building Work.* Boston: Interaction Institute for Social Change, 2007.

Parker, Cynthia, Linda N. Guinee, and Andrea Nagel. *Leveraging Diversity and Building Power.* Boston: Interaction Institute for Social Change, 2007.

Parker, R., and Smith, P. "Revealing the Invisibles of White Privilege." White Privilege Conference, St. Louis, MO, 2006.

Pease, Katherine, et al. *Inclusiveness at Work: How to Build Inclusive Nonprofit Organizations,* Modules 1 and 8. Denver: Denver Foundation, 2005.

Peters, Jeanne, and Timothy Wolfred. *Daring to Lead: Nonprofit Executive Directors and Their Work Experience.* San Francisco: CompassPoint Nonprofit Services, 2001.

Pettey, Janice Gow. *Cultivating Diversity in Fundraising.* New York: Wiley, 2002.

Pfeffer, Jeffrey. *Managing with Power: Politics and Influence in Organizations.* Boston: Harvard Business School Press, 1992.

Pierce, Alexandra. *Factors in Successful Capacity Building with Immigrant- and Refugee-Led Organizations (IRLOs).* St. Paul: Fieldstone Alliance, 2006.

Pittz, Will, and Rinku Sen. *Short-Changed: Foundations Giving and Communities of Color.* Oakland, CA: Applied Research Center, 2004.

Pompey, Pam. *Ujamaa: Building African American Philanthropists and Fundraisers.* Charlotte, NC: Grassroots Leadership, 2007.

Portes, Alejandro, and Rubén G. Rumbaut. *Immigrant America: A Portrait,* third edition. Berkeley, CA: University of California Press, 2006.

Potapchuk, Maggie. *Concentric Circles: Unpacking Privilege and Power— Diagnostic Tip-sheet.* mpotapchuk@mpassociates.us.

Potapchuk, Maggie, Sally Leiderman, Donna Bivens, and Barbara Major. *Flipping the Script: White Privilege and Community Building.* Silver Spring, MD: MP Associates, and Conshohocken, PA: Center for Assessment and Policy Development, 2006.

powell, john a. "Does Racism in Motion Have to Stay in Motion? Nonprofits as a Force Against Structural Racism," *Nonprofit Quarterly* 9, no. 2, 6–11. www.nonprofitquarterly.org.

———. *Talking the Walk: A Communications Guide for Racial Justice.* Oakland, CA: AK Press, 2006.

Praxis Project, The. *Building Diverse Community Based Coalitions.* Washington, DC: http://www.thepraxisproject.org/tools/Coalition_ Building_2.pdf

Quiroz-Martinez, Julie. "Missing Link," *Nonprofit Quarterly* 9, no. 2. www.nonprofitquarterly.org.

Quiroz-Martinez, Julie, Lori Villarosa, and Anne Mackinnon. *Grantmaking with a Racial Equity Lens.* New York: Grantcraft, 2007.

Rockefeller Philanthropy Advisors. *Diversity and Inclusion: Lessons from the Field.* New York: Rockefeller Philanthropy Advisors, December 2008.

Romero, S. *The Honest Truth: Lessons Learned from the Stories of People of Color in Philanthropy (NNG).* Minneapolis: Native Americans in Philanthropy, 2006.

Ryan, William. *Grantmaking with a Gender Lens.* Grantcraft, 2004. Said, Edward W. *Culture and Imperialism.* New York: Knopf, 1993.

Satterwhite, Frank J. Omowale, and Shiree Teng. "Culturally Based Capacity Building: An Approach to Working in Communities of Color for Social Change." In *Organizational Development and Capacity in Cultural Competence*. Los Angeles: The California Endowment and San Francisco: CompassPoint Nonprofit Services, July 2007.

Scheie, D. M., T. Williams, and J. Foster. *Improving Race Relations and Undoing Racism: Roles and Strategies for Community Foundations*. Minneapolis: Rainbow Research, 2001.

Segrest, Mab. *Memoirs of a Race Traitor*. Boston: South End Press, 1994.

Senge, Peter. *The Fifth Discipline Field Book*. New York: DoubleDay, 1994.

Shapiro, Ilana. *Training for Racial Equity and Inclusion: A Guide to Selected Programs*. Washington, DC: The Aspen Institute, 2002.

Sidberry, Tyra. "Building Diversity in Organizations," *Nonprofit Quarterly* 9, no. 2, 28–33. www.nonprofitquarterly.org.

Social Justice Fund N.W., Western States Center, and the Nonprofit Assistance Center. *Opening a Dialogue: Invitation for Community Action*. Seattle: Washington State Immigrant and Refugee Scoping Project, 2004.

Stephens, Vanessa McKendall. *Moving Past the Silence: A Tool for Negotiating Reflective Conversations about Race*. Minneapolis: Effective Communities Project, 2006.

St.Onge, Patricia, Breonna Cole, and Sheryl Petty. *Through the Lens of Culture: Building Capacity for Social Change and Sustainable Communities*. Oakland, CA: National Community Development Institute, 2003.

St.Onge, Patricia, and Virginia Kellogg. "Culture Matters," *Coaches Training Institute Newsletter*. San Rafael, CA: Coaches Training Institute, 2006.

Tatum, Beverly D. *Why Are All the Black Kids Sitting Together in the Cafeteria?* New York: Basic Books, 1997.

Tong, R. *Feminist Thought: A Comprehensive Introduction*. Boulder, CO: Westview Press, 1989.

Vygotsky, L. *Mind in Society*. Cambridge, MA: Harvard University Press, 1978.

W. K. Kellogg Foundation. *Cultures of Giving Cluster.* http://www.wkkf.org/default.aspx?tabid=75&CID=299&NID=61&LanguageID=0.

———. *Emerging Philanthropy in Communities of Color: A Report on Current Trends.* http://www.wkkf.org/default.aspx?tabid=102&CID=12&CatID=12&ItemID=120687&NID=20&LanguageID=0.

Wijeyesinghe, Charmaine, and Bailey Jackson, eds. *New Perspectives on Racial Identity Development: A Theoretical and Practical Anthology.* New York: New York University Press, 2001.

Wildman, S. *Privilege Revealed: How Invisible Preferences Undermine America.* New York: New York University Press, 1996.

Wise, T. "Disasters, Natural and Otherwise: What Hurricane Katrina Tells Us about Race, Class and Privilege in the U.S." White Privilege Conference, keynote address, 2006.

Wright, Kai. "Twenty Years Later: James Baldwin's America Hasn't Changed." RaceWire: The Color Lines Blog, http://www.racewire.org/archives/2007/12/twenty_years_later_james_baldw_1.html, December 12, 2007.

Young, I. M. "Gender as Seriality: Thinking about Women as a Social Collective." *Signs* 19, no. 3 (Spring 1994): 713–38.

Zinn, Howard. *A People's History of the United States.* New York: Harper and Row, 1995.

Note: This list of publications includes sources originally compiled for the Global Equity Organization's 2008 Annual Conference by Ron McKinley, project director of the Kellogg Action Lab at Fieldstone Alliance.

Notes

1. Internalized oppression involves turning on oneself or the members of one's own group the same negative thinking or treatment experienced from other groups that have maintained a higher level of authority and resources.

2. Robert Kegan and Lisa Laskow Lahey, *How the Way We Talk Can Change the Way We Work* (San Francisco: Jossey-Bass, 2001), 7.

3. These are among strategies outlined in a series of articles about race and power in *Nonprofit Quarterly* 9, no. 2 (Summer 2002), www.nonprofitquarterly.org.

4. "Mental Health Plan Definitions," Seattle: King County Department of Community and Human Services, http://www.metrokc.gov/dchs/mhd/mhp/definitions.htm, January 1, 2005.

5. Ann Philbin, *Capacity Building in Social Justice Organizations* (New York: Ford Foundation, 1996).

6. This definition came from the Alliance for Nonprofit Management Cultural Competency Initiative, May 2005, and is based on conversations at the People of Color Affinity Group's gathering at the Alliance annual conference in Houston, 2003.

7. It is important to note that these starting efforts were encouraged by Vincent Hyman in his capacity at Fieldstone Alliance (then Wilder Publishing) and were grounded in the work of Alliance for Nonprofit Management member organizations, particularly the National Community Development Institute and Seven Generations Consulting.

8. James Baldwin, *Nobody Knows My Name* (New York: Vintage, 1962).

9. Crossroads, *A Strategy for Building Anti-Racist Collectives,* http://www.crossroadsantiracism.org/index.sxml.

10. W.E.B. DuBois, *The Souls of Black Folk* (New York: Library of America, 1986).

11. Christine Clark and James O'Donnell, *Becoming and Unbecoming White: Owning and Disowning a Racial Identity* (Westpoint, CT: Bergin & Garvey, 1999).

12. Robert Jensen, *The Heart of Whiteness: Confronting Race, Racism and White Privilege* (San Francisco: City Light Books, 2006).

13. Ibid.

14. Barbara Love, "Amazing Grace How Sweet Youth Sound: Strategies for Youth Empowerment and Liberation," White Privilege Conference, St. Louis, MO, 2006.

15. Allan G. Johnson, *Privilege, Power, and Difference* (New York: McGraw-Hill, 2005).

16. Howard Zinn, *A People's History of the United States* (New York: Harper and Row, 1995).

17. Ibid.

18. Johnson, *Privilege, Power, and Difference.*

19. Audre Lorde, *Sister Outsider* (New York: Crossing Press, 1984).

20. Beverly D. Tatum, *Why Are All the Black Kids Sitting Together in the Cafeteria?* (New York: Basic Books, 1997).

21. Marianne Adams, Lee Anne Bell, and Pat Griffin, *Teaching for Diversity and Social Justice: A Source Book* (New York: Routledge, 1999).

22. John D. Adams, "Building a Sustainable World: A Challenging OD Opportunity" in *Understanding Organizational Development* (San Francisco: Pfeiffer/Wiley, 2006).

23. Peter Senge, *The Fifth Discipline Field Book* (New York: Doubleday, 1994) 125–29.

24. Valerie Bates, *Is Reconciliation Possible? Lessons from "Modern Racism,"* http://www.visions-inc.com/is%20reconciliation%20possible%20document.htm.

25. Asian American Justice Center and Asian Pacific American Legal Center, *A Community of Contrasts: American Asians and Pacific Islanders in the United States,* http://www.advancingequality.org/files/ComCont.pdf.

26. Ibid.

27. Meizhu Lui, Barbara Robles, Betsy Leondar-Wright, Rose Brewer, and Rebecca Anderson, *The Color of Wealth: The Story Behind the U.S. Racial Wealth Divide* (New York: New Press, 2006).

28. Social Justice Fund N.W., Western States Center, and the Nonprofit Assistance Center, *Opening a Dialogue: Invitation for Community Action* (Seattle: Washington State Immigrant and Refugee Scoping Project, 2004) 6.

29. Jeff Kibler, *The Vietnamese Experience: Twenty Years After, A Reflection of Fact and Experience,* 1994, unpublished manuscript.

30. Social Justice Fund N.W., *Opening a Dialogue,* 28.

31. Jennifer Sullivan and Christine Clarridge, "Man Sentenced for Attack on Seattle Cab Driver," *Seattle Times,* April 18, 2008, http://seattletimes.nwsource.com/html/localnews/2004359233_webhatecrime18m.html.

32. Kibler, *The Vietnamese Experience.*

33. Janice Gow Pettey, *Cultivating Diversity in Fundraising* (San Francisco: Wiley, 2002).

34. Applied Research Center, *Mapping the Immigrant Infrastructure* (http://www.arc.org) 63.

35. Tsuguo Ikeda, *Ike's Principles* (self-published, 2007), available from Atlantic Street Center, Resource Development, 2103 South Atlantic Street, Seattle, WA 98144, 206-329-2050.

36. Charles Mills, *The Racial Contract* (Ithaca, NY: Cornell University Press, 1999), 30–33.

37. United Nations, *Report on the World Social Situation 2005: The Inequality Predicament,* 1, http://www.un.org/esa/socdev/rwss/docs/Executivesummary.pdf.

38. Hazel DeGruy-Leary, *Post-Traumatic Slave Syndrome: America's Legacy of Enduring Injury and Healing* (Milwaukie, OR: Uptone Press, 2005).

39. Hummel, Ray Jr. *Southeastern Broadsides Before 1877: A Bibliography* (Richmond, VA: Virginia State Library, 1971), 215, http://digital.tcl.sc.edu/cdm4/item_viewer.php?CISOROOT=/bro&CISOPTR=250&REC=19.

40. Pew Charitable Trusts, *One in 100: Behind Bars in America* (Washington, DC: Pew Charitable Trusts, 2008), http://www.pewcenteronthestates.org/uploadedFiles/One%20in%20100.pdf.

41. This gathering was sponsored by the Praxis Project. Patricia St.Onge facilitated it as part of a process of trying to define what it means to do capacity building in a culturally based way.

42. Alisha Drabek and Carrie Rothburd, "Approaches to Tribal Grant Writing and Project Planning," CharityChannel, November 9, 2005, 5, http://charitychannel.com/Articles/NonprofitConsultingReview/DetailPageNCR/tabid/1703/xmid/1056/BioID/1515/Default.aspx.

43. There are many good sources of historical data related to Native America. One that looks at the history through the lens of philanthropy is by Janice Gow Pettey: *Cultivating Diversity in Fundraising* (New York: Wiley, 2002).

44. Howard Zinn, *A People's History of the United States* (New York: HarperCollins, 2001).

45. Drabek and Rothburd, "Approaches to Tribal Grant Writing and Project Planning," http://charitychannel.com/Articles/NonprofitConsultingReview/DetailPageNCR/tabid/1703/xmid/1056/BioID/1515/Default.aspx.

46. This consulting work was sponsored by the Praxis Project as part of a Robert Wood Johnson Foundation initiative to increase the presence of communities of color in tobacco policy. See a fuller illustration of this story at "Tobacco Policy: Capacity Building That Honors Culture," (Washington, DC: Alliance for Nonprofit Management and

Seven Generations Consulting), www.allianceonline.org/Members/Library/diversity/tobacco_policy.pdf/file?agree=I+Agree.

47. The Native American Tobacco Coalition of Montana Web site is www.keeptobaccosacred.org.

48. Drabek and Rothburd, "Approaches to Tribal Grant Writing and Project Planning," CharityChannel, 5, http://charitychannel.com/Articles/NonprofitConsultingReview/DetailPageNCR/tabid/1703/xmid/1056/BioID/1515/Default.aspx.

49. "Hispanic Americans by the Numbers: From the U.S. Census Bureau," Information Please Database, 2007, http://www.infoplease.com/spot/hhmcensus1.html.

50. "African-Americans," *The History Channel* Web site, 2008, http://www.history.com/encyclopedia.do?articleID=200351.

51. Tim Padgett, "A Pro-Choice Movement in Mexico," *Time,* March 30, 2007, http://www.time.com/time/world/article/0,8599,1605054,00.html.

52. Shari Turitz and David Winder, "Private Resources for Public Ends: Grantmakers in Brazil, Ecuador, and Mexico," in *Philanthropy and Social Change in Latin America,* Cynthia Sanborn and Felipe Portocarrero, eds. (Harvard University Press, 2003), http://www.synergos.org/knowledge/03/privateresourcespublicends.pdf.

53. Edgar Schein, *Process Consultation: Its Role in Organization Development* (Reading, MA: Addison Wesley, 1969).

54. The data are available online with a subscription at www.freedemographics.com.

55. In an intervention that promises to help expand dialogue beyond the Black-White dichotomy, the Southeastern Network of African Americans in Philanthropy (an affiliate of Association of Black Foundation Executives) collaborated with the local chapter of Hispanics in Philanthropy to explore culturally based philanthropy, including assessments of what needs to be addressed and how, together. This experience was detailed at the 2007 Annual Conference of the Alliance for Nonprofit Management in a discussion led by Milano Harden.

56. This phenomenon has been described by Pat Vivian and Shana Hormann in "Organizational Trauma and Healing," *OD Practitioner* 34, no. 4 (Winter 2002).

57. American Civil Liberties Union, *Race and Ethnicity in America: Turning a Blind Eye to Racial Injustice,* 2007, 61, http://www.aclu.org/pdfs/humanrights/cerd_full_report.pdf.

58. *The Race to Rebuild: The Color of Opportunity and the Future of New Orleans* (The Center for Social Inclusion: New York, 2006), 3, http://www.soros.org/resources/articles_publications/racetorebuild_20060908.pdf.

59. Social Justice Fund N.W., *Opening a Dialogue,* 8–9.

60. William Lamb, "Officials: End Federal Monitoring of State Police," March 31, 2008, NorthJersey.com, http://www.northjersey.com/news/Are_we_past_profiling.html.

61. ACLU, *Race and Ethnicity in America: Turning a Blind Eye to Racial Injustice,* 2007, http://www.aclu.org/pdfs/humanrights/cerd_full_report.pdf.

62. Jack Weatherford, *Indian Givers: How the Indians of the Americas Transformed the World* (New York: Crown, 1988).

63. Hippocrates, *Of the Epidemics,* Book 1, Section 11 (Whitefish, MT: Kessinger, 2004).

64. This reality is affirmed by provisions included in a working draft of "Ethical Standards in Nonprofit Capacity Building" from the Alliance for Nonprofit Management. For example, "Capacity builders shall be cognizant of the cultural dimensions of their work and the relationship between their own cultural identity and that of clients and communities."

65. Jared Diamond. *Guns, Germs, and Steel: The Fates of Human Societies* (New York: W. W. Norton, 1997).

66. Pratap Chatterjee, *Gold, Greed, and Genocide: Unmasking the Myth of the '49ers* (Berkeley, CA: Project Underground, 1998).

67. Peggy McIntosh, "White Privilege: Unpacking the Invisible Knapsack," presented at Understanding Whiteness, Recognizing Privilege: A Conference Toward Racial Justice, Hampshire College, 1988.

68. Known as PDC for short, this is a program created and run by National Community Development Institute. It has since been renamed to reflect the focus on community builders.

69. John Dovidio and Samuel L. Gaertner, "Color Blind or Just Plain Blind? The Pernicious Nature of Contemporary Racism," *The Nonprofit Quarterly* 12, ,no. 4 (Winter 2005), http://academic.udayton.edu/race/01race/racism10.htm.

70. Paul Kivel, *Uprooting Racism: How White People Can Work for Racial Justice* (Gabriola Island, BC, Canada: New Society Publishers, 2002).

71. Rockwood Leadership Program, Berkeley, CA 94703.

72. Will Pittz and Rinku Sen, *Shortchanged: Foundations Giving and Communities of Color,* http://www.philanthropy.iupui.edu/Millenium/Short%20Changed%20(Fdn%20giving%20to%20POC).pdf.

73. Julie Quiroz-Martinez, "Missing Link," *Nonprofit Quarterly* 9, no. 2 (Summer 2002): 18–21.

74. This statement was offered in the overview for a compilation of participants' comments, prepared by Cynthia Parker of Interaction Institute for Social Change after co-leading a session at the Alliance for Nonprofit Management Conference in 2005. The compilation is included in this book as "Voices from the Field: Stories from Peer Dialogues."

75. john a. powell, "Does Racism in Motion Have to Stay in Motion? Nonprofits as a Force Against Structural Racism," *Nonprofit Quarterly* 9, no. 2 (Summer 2002): 6–11.

76. Pettey, *Cultivating Diversity in Fundraising.*

77. Dwayne S. Marsh, Milly Hawk Daniel, and Kris Putnam, *Leadership for Policy Change* (Oakland, CA: PolicyLink, Fall 2003), www.policylink.org/publications.

78. Ann Philbin, *Capacity Building Work with Social Justice Organizations: Views from the Field,* 1997 [Prepared for Ford Foundation, available through online resource center from Alliance for Nonprofit Management, http://www.allianceonline.org].

79. People of Color Affinity Group, *CCI Concepts and Definitions* (Washington, DC: Alliance for Nonprofit Management, 2005), http://www.allianceonline.org/cci.ipage/cci_definitions.page.

80. Minority Executive Directors' Coalition of King County, Seattle, WA, "A Working Definition of Cultural Competency," http://www.evansforum.org/nonprofit/seventh_annual/pdf/medc.pdf.

81. "Conceptual Frameworks: Models, Guiding Values and Principles" (Washington, DC: National Center for Cultural Competence), http://www11.georgetown.edu/research/gucchd/nccc/foundations/frameworks.html.

82. Patricia St.Onge, Breonna Cole, and Sheryl Petty, *Through the Lens of Culture: Building Capacity for Social Change and Sustainable Communities* (Oakland, CA: National Community Development Institute, 2003).

83. "A Roadmap for a Culturally Competent Organizational Culture," National MultiCultural Institute workshop, April 2004.

84. J. Cox and R. Beale, *Developing Competence to Manage Diversity: Readings, Cases, and Activities* (San Francisco: Berrett-Koehler, 1997).

85. United Nations Educational, Scientific and Cultural Organization, UNESCO, "Universal Declaration on Cultural Diversity," 2002, http://www.unesco.org/education/imld_2002/unversal_decla.shtml.

86. Eric Miraglia, et al., "A Baseline Definition of Culture" (Pullman, WA: Washington State University, May 26, 1999), http://www.wsu.edu/gened/learn-modules/top_culture/culture-definition.html.

87. A summary is forthcoming at the Cultural Competency Resource Pages, Alliance for Nonprofit Management, http://www.allianceonline.org/about/cc_resources.page.

88. Katherine Pease, et al., *Inclusiveness at Work: How to Build Inclusive Nonprofit Organizations* (Denver: Denver Foundation, 2005), http://www.denverfoundation.org/images/IAW_intro.pdf.

89. *Anti-Racist Principles for Effective Organizing and Social Transformation* (New Orleans, LA: People's Institute for Survival and Beyond, 2006), http://www.pisab.org/anti-racist-principles/.

90. National Network of Grantmakers, "Pursuing Racial Equity through Civic Engagement and Mass Media: A Research and Discussion Paper" (2005), 3.

91. Keith Lawrence, Stacey Sutton, Anne Kubisch, Gretchen Susi, and Karen Fulbright-Anderson, *Structural Racism and Community Building* (Washington, DC: Aspen Institute, 2004), 11, 16.

92. Maurianne Adams, Lee Anne Bell, and Pat Griffin, ed., *Teaching for Diversity and Social Justice: A Sourcebook* (New York: Routledge, 1997), 97.

93. Internalized oppression is defined as attitudes and behaviors that adopt another group's negative view of one's own group. Hierarchy of oppression relates to the "race to the bottom" in which the system has encouraged and rewarded the practice of groups showing they are more disadvantaged than other groups as a way of gaining attention or resources to remedy disparities. More on these concepts is found in the CCI glossary.

94. Code switching refers to the use of different kinds of language—including nuances of phrasing, slang, accent, and voice tone—depending on audience or situation.

95. Albert L. May, *First Informers in the Disaster Zone: The Lessons of Katrina,* (Washington, DC: Aspen Institute, September 2006).

96. That report, by Grantmakers for Effective Organizations, fortunately has been followed up by subsequent works that do address cultural identity, including *Listen, Learn, Lead* (2006), which includes a statement that cultural competency is necessary and some very thoughtful approaches to power analysis in grantmaker-grantee relationships. See www.geofunders.org.

97. See, e.g., "Culturally Based Capacity Building: An Approach to Working in Communities of Color for Social Change" by Frank J. Omowale Satterwhite, Ph.D., and Shiree Teng, M.A., National Community Development Institute; "A Capacity Building Approach to Cultural Competency: Improving Cultural Competency Improves Organizational Effectiveness" by Anushka Fernandopulle, M.B.A., CompassPoint Nonprofit Services; "Multicultural Organizational Development: A Resource for Health Equity" by Laurin Y. Mayeno, M.P.H.; and "Organizational Forces and Multicultural Change" by Laurin Y. Mayeno, M.P.H., in *Cultural Competency in Capacity Building: Organizational Development and Capacity in Cultural Competence—Building Knowledge and Practice* (Los Angeles: The California Endowment and San Francisco: CompassPoint Nonprofit Services, July 2007).

98. Anushka Fernandopulle, "A Capacity Building Approach to Cultural Competency: Improving Cultural Competency Improves Organizational Effectiveness," *Cultural Competency in Capacity Building: Organizational Development and Capacity in Cultural Competence—Building Knowledge and Practice,* 15–17.

99. Frank J. Omowale Satterwhite and Shiree Teng, "Culturally Based Capacity Building: An Approach to Working in Communities of Color for Social Change," *Capacity Building: Organizational Development and Capacity in Cultural Competence—Building Knowledge and Practice,* 3, 5 (San Francisco: CompassPoint Nonprofit Services, July 2007).

100. Laurin Y. Mayeno, "Multicultural Organizational Development" and "Organizational Forces and Multicultural Change,", www.calendow.org/uploadedFiles/Mayeno.pdf.

101. C. A. Hyde, "Multicultural Organizational Development in Nonprofit Human Service Agencies: Views from the Field," *Journal of Community Practice* 11, no. 1 (2003): 39–59. Quoted in Laurin Y. Mayeno, "Multicultural Organizational Development: A Resource for Health Equity" and "Organizational Forces and Multicultural Change," *Cultural Competency in Capacity Building: Organizational Development and Capacity in Cultural Competence—Building Knowledge and Practice* (Los Angeles: The California Endowment and San Francisco: CompassPoint Nonprofit Services, July 2007).

102. Zak Sinclair, Lisa Russ, Susan Lubeck, et al., "Reflections on Organization Development Through the Lens of Social Justice Change Methodologies" (Oakland, CA: Movement Strategy Center, 2006), http://www.bevscott.com/OD%20%20Social%20Justice%20Change%20Methods.pdf.

103. Scott Page, *The Difference: How the Power of Diversity Creates Better Groups, Firms, Schools, and Societies* (Princeton, NJ: Princeton University Press, 2007).

104. Ronald Takaki, *A Different Mirror: A History of Multicultural America* (New York: Little, Brown, 1994), 4–5.

105. Zinn, *A People's History of the United States*; Mindy Thompson-Fulilove, *Root Shock: How Tearing Up City Neighborhoods Hurts America, and What We Can Do About It* (New York: Random House, 2004).

106. Specific sources cited in the *The Nonprofit Quarterly* Summer 2002 issue include "Building Diversity in Organizations," by Tyra B. Sidberry; "If You Stop Rowing . . . You'll Drift Back: An Interview with Marita Rivero and U.T. Saunders"; "Leading Change: Planned Parenthood of Rhode Island," by Miriam Inocencio with Clare Gravon; "Color Blind or Just Plain Blind? The Pernicious Nature of Contemporary Racism," by John F. Dovidio and Samuel L. Gaertner; "Does Racism in Motion Have to Stay in Motion? Nonprofits as a Force Against Structural Racism," by john a. powell; "Missing Link," by Julie Quiroz-Martinez; "Tracking the Miner's Canary: An Interview with Lani Guinier."

107. William Diaz, "For Whom and for What? The Contribution of the Nonprofit Sector," in Lester M. Salamon, *The State of Nonprofit America* (Washington, DC: Brookings Institution, 2002).

108. See Keith Lawrence, Stacey Sutton, Anne Kubisch, Gretchen Susi, and Karen Fulbright-Anderson, *Structural Racism and Community Building* (Washington, DC: Aspen Institute, 2004); "Applying a Structural Racism Framework: A Strategy for Community Level Research and Action," [Presentation slides] by the Aspen Institute Roundtable on Comprehensive Community Initiatives," December 2002. These and a wide variety of additional materials, original and referenced, are available at www.aspeninstitute.org .

109. Lawrence et al., *Structural Racism and Community Building*, 37.

110. Bob Agres, "Community Building in Hawai'i," *The Nonprofit Quarterly* 12, no. 2 (Summer 2005).

111. Gus Newport, "Why Are We Replacing the Furniture When Half the Neighborhood Is Missing?" *The Nonprofit Quarterly* 10, no. 3 (Fall 2003).

112. Otis Johnson, "Reflections of a Lifelong Civil Leader," *The Nonprofit Quarterly* 11, no. 3 (Fall 2004).

113. Nesly Metayer, "Considerations on Leadership in an Immigrant Population: Lessons from the Haitian Community," *The Nonprofit Quarterly* 11, no. 3 (Fall 2004).

114. Ibid.

115. Adie Kusserow, "The Workings of Class: How Understanding a Subtle Difference between Social Classes Can Promote Equality in the Classroom—and Beyond," *Stanford Social Innovation Review* (Fall 2005), http://www.ssireview.org/pdf/2005FA_feature_Kusserow.pdf.

116. St.Onge, Cole, and Petty, *Through the Lens of Culture.*

117. St.Onge, "Tobacco Policy: Capacity Building that Honors Culture" (Washington, DC: Alliance for Nonprofit Management and Seven Generations Consulting), www.allianceonline.org/Members/Library/diversity/tobacco_policy.pdf/file?agree=I+Agree.

118. Minority Executive Directors' Coalition of King County, Seattle, "A Working Definition of Cultural Competency," http://www.evansforum.org/nonprofit/seventh_annual/pdf/medc.pdf.

119. Jeanne Peters and Timothy Wolfred, *Daring to Lead: Nonprofit Executive Directors and Their Work Experience* (San Francisco: CompassPoint Nonprofit Services, 2001), 25, https://www.compasspoint.org/assets/5_daring.pdf.

120. Aida Rodriguez, *Bridging the Leadership Gap: Solutions for Community Development Corporations* (New York: Milano Management Information Exchange, 2004).

121. Patricia St.Onge with Virginia Kellogg, "Culture Matters," Coaches Training Institute newsletter, 2005, http://www.thecoaches.com/print/newsletter/culturematters.html.

122. Kim Ammann Howard and Jill Blair, *Coaching as a Tool for Building Leadership and Effective Organizations* (Berkeley, CA: BTW Consultants, 2006), http://www.pennconsultingllc.com/downloads/geo-blueprint.pdf; *Listen, Learn, Lead: A Report on Phase 1 of GEO's Change Agent Project, 2006* (Washington, DC: Grantmakers for Effective Organizations, 2006), http://www.efc.be/ftp/public/cpi/Newsletter_Feb07/ListenLearnLeadFinal.pdf.

123. Francie Ostrower, *Nonprofit Governance in the United States: Findings on Performance and Accountability from the First National Representative Study* (Washington, DC: Urban Institute, June 2007).

124. Francie Ostrower, *Boards of Midsize Nonprofits: Their Needs and Challenges* (Washington, DC: Urban Institute, May 8, 2008) http://www.urban.org/publications/901165.html.

125. *Nonprofit Governance Index 2007* (Washington, DC: BoardSource), http://www.boardsource.org/dl.asp?document_id=553.

126. Judy Freiwirth, "Engagement Governance for System-Wide Decision Making," *Nonprofit Quarterly* 14, no. 2 (Summer 2007).

127. Ellen Bryson, "Building Board Diversity," *Foundation News and Commentary* 45, no. 6 (November/December 2004), http://www.foundationnews.org/CME/article.cfm?id=3063&issueID=&authByte=33419&profileID=173727 . See also related articles, e.g., Henry A. J. Ramos, Constance Walker, and Gabriel Kasper, "Making the Case for Diversity in Philanthropy," 45, no. 6 (November/December 2004), http://www.foundationnews.org/CME/article.cfm?ID=3054.

128. The work of PolicyLink is informative in this regard. See Dwayne S. Marsh, Milly Hawk Daniel, and Kris Putnam, *Leadership for Policy Change* (Oakland, CA: PolicyLink, 2003), www.policylink.org/publications.

129. See John Michael Daley and Flavio Francisco Marsiglia, "Social Diversity within Nonprofit Boards: Members' Views on Status and Issues," *Journal of the Community Development Society* 32, no. 2 (2001).

130. *NASW Standards for Cultural Competence in Social Work Practice* (Washington, DC: National Association of Social Workers, June 23, 2001), http://www.socialworkers.org/sections/credentials/cultural_comp.asp .

131. Some articles were posted online at the Alliance for Nonprofit Management, www.allianceonline.org.

132. Katherine Pease, et al., *Inclusiveness at Work: How to Build Inclusive Nonprofit Organizations* (Denver: Denver Foundation, 2005), http://www.denverfoundation.org/images/IAW_intro.pdf.

133. The *Race Matters Toolkit,* and numerous resources that address cultural and linguistic competency, are available online at the Annie E. Casey Foundation Web site, http://www.aecf.org/KnowledgeCenter/PublicationsSeries/RaceMatters.aspx.

134. See the Annie E. Casey Foundation Web site, www.aecf.org. Resources include *Building Culturally and Linguistically Competent Services to Support Young Children, Their Families, and School Readiness,* by Kathy Seitzinger Hepburn (May 2004), providing a toolkit with self-assessment approaches, resource listings, and other information; *The Context and Meaning of Family Strengthening in America,* by the Harvard Project on American Indian Economic Development (August 2004), documenting the effectiveness of supporting organizations to address the "critical role of Native self-determination" as influencing legitimacy, which affects "everything from the managerial structure to the hours of operation, from the priorities of service delivery to the standards of personnel

review"; *The Role of Social Capital in Building Healthy Communities* by Jo Anne Schneider (November 2004), distinguishing the vitality of "cultural capital" and power dynamics in the life of a community, influencing organizational structures, social services, the economy, and public policy; and *Taking the Initiative on Jobs and Race: Innovations in Workforce Development for Minority Job Seekers and Employers* (2001), establishing the value of program approaches that build skills, offer placement and support services, in recognition of the "complex interplay of race and regional job markets."

135. See Lori S. Robinson, "Black Like Whom?" *The Crisis,* NAACP, January/February 2006; Rinku Sen, "Are Immigrants and Refugees People of Color?" *Colorlines,* Applied Research Center, July/August 2007.

136. Numerous research reports are available on the National Gay and Lesbian Task Force Web site, www.thetaskforce.org, including *An Epidemic of Homelessness,* by Nicholas Ray with chapters contributed by Colby Berger, Susan Boyle, Mary Jo Callan, Mia White, Grace McCelland, and Theresa Nolan (2006), identifying important distinctions in the situations faced by teens who become homeless as compared to other homeless persons—warranting different approaches to social services and public policy; *Make Room for All: Diversity, Cultural Competency, and Discrimination in an Aging America,* by the Task Force (2005), documenting the "explosive demographic" of Baby Boomers and other communities of elders, and presenting issues and strategies to promote quality of life; *Living in the Margins: A National Survey of Lesbian, Gay, Bisexual, and Transgender Asian and Pacific Islander Americans,* by Alain Dang and Cabrini Vianney (2007), offering analysis and data on demographics, including languages spoken as well as patterns of discrimination, public policy, and politics; *Hispanic and Latino Same-Sex Couple Households in the United States: A Report from the 2000 Census,* by Jason Cianciotto (2005), providing analysis of demographic data and profiles to illuminate new forms of the *familia.*

137. *Up Next: Generation Change and the Leadership of Nonprofit Organizations,* by Frances Kunreuther, *Building Movement Project,* published by the Annie E. Casey Foundation (2005); *What's Next? Baby Boom Leaders in Social Change Nonprofits,* by Helen S. Kim and Frances Kunreuther; *Building Movement Project,* published by Annie E. Casey Foundation (2007), www.buildingmovement.org; *ReGeneration: Young People Shaping the Environmental Justice Movement,* by Julie Quiroz-Martinez, Diana Pei Wu, and Kristen Zimmerman, published by the Movement Strategy Center (2005), www.movementstrategy.org. See also www.americanhumanics.org.

138. See *Cultures of Caring: Philanthropy in Diverse American Communities* (Washington, DC: Council on Foundations, 1999), http://www.cof.org/Learn/content.cfm?ItemNumber=842.

139. See Will Pittz and Rinku Sen, *Short-Changed: Foundations Giving and Communities of Color* (Oakland, CA: Applied Research Center, 2004), http://www.philanthropy.iupui.edu/Millennium/Short%20Changed%20(Fdn%20giving%20to%20POC).pdf.

140. See *Fairness in Philanthropy Part I: Foundation Giving to Minority-Led Non-profits* and *Fairness in Philanthropy Part II: Perspectives from the Field* (Berkeley, CA: The Greenlining Institute, 2005 and 2006), http://greenlining.org.

141. *Investing in a Diverse Democracy: Foundation Giving to Minority-Led Nonprofits* (Berkeley, CA: The Greenlining Institute, 2006), 7, 8.

142. Ibid., 7.

143. *Diversity and Inclusion: Lessons from the Field* (New York: Rockefeller Philanthropy Advisors, December 2008), http://rockpa.org/wp-content/uploads/2008/12/diversity-inclusion.pdf; Jessica Chao, Julia Parshall, Desiree Amador, Meghna Shah, and Armando Yanez, *Philanthropy in a Changing Society: Achieving Effectiveness from Diversity* (New York: Rockefeller Philanthropy Advisors, April 2008), http://rockpa.org/pdfs/Philanthropy_in_a_Changing_Society_full.pdf .

144. See Lynn C. Burbridge, William A. Diaz, Teresa Odendahl, and Aileen Shaw, *The Meaning and Impact of Board and Staff Diversity in the Philanthropic Field: Findings from a National Study* (Joint Affinity Groups, 2002), http://www.jointaffinitygroups.org/downloads/JAG_Research_Report.pdf.

145. See www.nng.org.

146. Contact Marga Inc. at www.margainc.com for the 2005 report and see the 2007 report and related materials available in PDF on its Web site.

147. *Community Philanthropy and Racial Equity: What Progress Looks Like: Results of a Preliminary Inquiry* (Minneapolis: Effective Communities Project, 2005), http://www.effectivecommunities.com/pdfs/ECP_CommunityPhilanthropy.pdf.

148. Resources are available at www.grantcraft.org and www.racialequity.org. See also www.arc.org.

149. See the W. K. Kellogg Foundation Web site at www.wkkf.org.

150. *Emerging Philanthropy in Communities of Color: A Report on Current Trends,* See W. K. Kellogg Foundation, http://www.wkkf.org/default.aspx?tabid=102&CID=12&CatID=12&ItemID=120687&NID=20&LanguageID=0.

151. See *Emerging Funds for Communities of Color Networking Meeting Proceedings Summary* (April 1999), http://www.wkkf.org/default.aspx?tabid=102&CID=2&CatID=2&ItemID=20594&NID=20&LanguageID=0.

152. Contact Grassroots Leadership, a Kellogg initiative grantee, at http://www.grassrootsleadership.org/. An important "footnote" to this session and resource: As of fall 2007, the NNG had closed its doors with plans to carry on the work through its network of people and institutions and through other organizations with shared goals.

153. Mary Ellen Capek and Molly Mead, *Effective Philanthropy: Organizational Success through Deep Diversity and Gender Equity* (Cambridge, MA: MIT Press, 2006).

154. See www.compasspoint.org and www.grassrootsfundraising.org.

155. Funders for Gay and Lesbian Issues, *Out for Change: Racial and Economic Justice Issues in Lesbian, Gay, Bisexual and Transgender Communities* (New York: Funders for Gay and Lesbian Issues, 2005).

156. These and other reports are available at www.lgbtfunders.org.

157. See Anushka Fernandopulle, "A Capacity Building Approach to Cultural Competency: Improving Cultural Competency Improves Organizational Effectiveness," *Organizational Development and Capacity in Cultural Competence* (Los Angeles: The California Endowment and San Francisco: CompassPoint Nonprofit Services, July 2007), http://www.calendow.org/uploadedFiles/NCDI.pdf.

158. Laurin Y. Mayeno, "Multicultural Organizational Development: A Resource for Health Equity" and "Organizational Forces and Multicultural Change," *Cultural Competency in Capacity Building: Organizational Development and Capacity in Cultural Competence—Building Knowledge and Practice* (The California Endowment and CompassPoint Nonprofit Services, July 2007), http://www.calendow.org/uploadedFiles/Mayeno.pdf.

159. George Grant, "Cultural Competency for Nonprofit Mental Health Organizations" (Johnson Center for Philanthropy, Grand Valley State University, September 2008), http://www.npgoodpractice.org/Resource/CulturalCompetencyforNonprofitMentalHealthOrganizations.aspx.

160. Maria Gajewski, "Strategic Diversity to Increase Human Capital in Public and Nonprofit Organizations" (Grand Rapids, MI: Johnson Center for Philanthropy, Grand Valley State University, 2005), http://www.npgoodpractice.org/Resource/ResourceFile.aspx?resourceid=8340.

161. Heather M. Berberet, "Putting the Pieces Together for Queer Youth: A Model of Integrated Assessment of Need and Program Planning," *Child Welfare* 85, no. 2 (March/April 2006).

162. Alexandra Pierce, *Factors in Successful Capacity Building with Immigrant- and Refugee-Led Organizations (IRLOs)* (Fieldstone Alliance, n.d.), http://www.fieldstonealliance.org/client/nexus_research_rept.cfm.

163. See "Evaluation Tools for Racial Equity" (Center for Assessment and Policy Development, 2005), http://www.evaluationtoolsforracialequity.org/.

164. Maggie Potapchuk with contributing writer Lori Villarosa, *Cultivating Interdependence: A Guide for Race Relations and Social Justice Organizations* (Joint Center for Political and Economic Studies, 2004), http://www.racialequity.org/docs/500393_0_cultivating-interdependence.pdf; Kien Lee, *Community Foundations/Intergroup Relations Program* (Gaithersburg, MD: Association for the Study and Development of Community, July 2002), http://www.capablecommunity.com/pubs/CFIR072002.PDF.

165. *Building Coalitions among Communities of Color: A Multicultural Approach* (U.S. Department of Health and Human Services, July 2004), http://www.shireinc.org/reports/Building%20Coalitions%20among%20Communities%20of%20Color.pdf.

166. See the National Center for Cultural Competence Web site, http://www11.georgetown.edu/research/gucchd/nccc/.

167. Jerry V. Diller and Jean Moule, *Cultural Competence: A Primer for Educators* (Florence, KY: Wadsworth Press, 2005).

168. Lani Guinier and Gerald Torres, *The Miner's Canary* (Cambridge, MA: Harvard University Press, 2002).

169. Marta Moreno Vega and Cheryll Y. Greene, eds., *Voices from the Battlefront: Achieving Cultural Equity* (Trenton, NJ: Africa World Press, 1993).

Index

More Results-Oriented Resources from Fieldstone Alliance

Practical books are just one of the resources Fieldstone Alliance has to offer. We also provide consulting, training, and demonstration projects that help nonprofits, funders, networks, and communities achieve greater impact.

As a nonprofit ourselves, we know the challenges that you face. In all our services, we draw on our extensive experience to provide solutions that work:

EXPERT CONSULTATION

Our staff and network of affiliated consultants are recognized nonprofit leaders, authors, and experts with deep experience in managing organizations, teaching, training, conducting research, and leading community initiatives. We provide assessment, planning, financial strategy, collaboration, and capacity-building services. Contracts range from short-term assessments to the management of multi-year initiatives.

PROVEN TRAINING

Training can be a powerful change strategy when well designed. Our experienced staff, authors, and network of experts from across the United States provide practical, customized training for nonprofits, foundations, and consultants. From one-hour keynote addresses to multi-session programs, we offer expertise in various aspects of capacity building, nonprofit management, leadership, collaboration, and community development. Coupling training with books and follow-up support increases retention and application of what is learned.

DEMONSTRATION PROJECTS

Fieldstone Alliance conducts research and hosts demonstration projects that have promise for improving performance and results in the nonprofit sector. Through this work we mine best practices, package the findings into practical, easy-to-apply tools, and disseminate them throughout the sector.

To find out more, call 1-800-274-6024. Or visit www.FieldstoneAlliance.org.

□ **SEE MORE BOOKS AND FREE RESOURCES**

Free Resources

GET FREE MANAGEMENT TIPS!

Sign-up for *Nonprofit Tools You Can Use,* Fieldstone Alliance's free e-newsletter. In each issue (arriving twice a month), we feature a free management tool or idea to help you and your nonprofit be more effective.

Content comes from our award-winning books, our consultant's direct experience, and from other experts in the field. Each issue focuses on a specific topic and includes practical actions for putting the information to use.

There are more than 70 great issues in the archive!

ONLINE RESOURCES

Here are other free resources you'll find on our Web site:

Articles
In-depth information on key nonprofit management issues.

Assessment Tools
See how your organization or collaboration is doing relative to characteristics of a successful nonprofit.

Research Reports
See research that was done to inform our demonstration projects and consulting practice.

Related Books

Seven Turning Points
Leading Through Pivotal Transitions in Organizational Life

To remain strong and effective, organizations must periodically adjust their leadership, management, structure, governance, and operating style to fit their changed circumstances. *Seven Turning Points* identifies key times when nonprofits must reassess the way they operate and make fundamental changes or risk decline.

by Susan Gross | 120 pp | 2009 | ISBN 978-0-940069-73-2 | order no. 069732

The Nonprofit Strategy Revolution
Real-Time Strategic Planning in a Rapid-Response World

This ground-breaking guide offers a compelling alternative to traditional strategic planning. You'll find new ideas for how to form strategies, and the tools and framework needed to infuse strategic thinking throughout your organization. The result: your nonprofit will be more strategic in thought and action on a daily basis. When the next opportunity (or challenge) comes along, you'll be able to respond swiftly and thoughtfully.

by David La Piana | 208 pp | 2008 | ISBN 978-0-940069-65-7 | order no. 069657

Generations
The Challenge of a Lifetime for Your Nonprofit

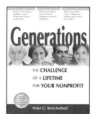

What happens when a management team of all Baby Boomers leaves within a five year stretch? Peter Brinckerhoff tells you what generational changes to expect and how to plan for them. You'll find in-depth information for each area of your organization—staff, board, volunteers, clients, marketing, technology, and finances.

by Peter Brinckerhoff | 232 pp | 2007 | ISBN 978-0-940069-55-8 | order no. 069555

Financial Leadership for Nonprofit Executives
Guiding Your Organization to Long-term Success

Provides executives with a practical guide to protecting and growing the assets of their organizations while accomplishing as much mission as possible with those resources.

by Jeanne Bell & Elizabeth Schaffer | 144 pp | 2005 | ISBN 978-0-940069-44-2 | order no. 06944X

Benchmarking for Nonprofits
How to Measure, Manage, and Improve Results

This book defines a formal, systematic, and reliable way to benchmark (the ongoing process of measuring your organization against leaders), from preparing your organization to measuring performance and implementing best practices.

by Jason Saul | 144 pp | 2004 | ISBN 978-0-940069-43-5 | order no. 069431

The Five Life Stages of Nonprofit Organizations
Where You Are, Where You're Going, & What to Expect When You Get There

Shows you what's "normal" for each development stage which helps you plan for transitions, stay on track, and avoid unnecessary struggles. Includes an assessment.

by Judith Sharken Simon with J. Terence Donovan
128 pp | 2001 | ISBN 978-0-940069-22-0 | order no. 069229

The Manager's Guide to Program Evaluation
Planning, Contracting, and Managing for Useful Results

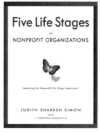

Explains how to plan and manage an evaluation that will help identify your organization's successes, share information with key audiences, and improve services.

by Paul W. Mattessich, PhD | 112 pp | 2003 | ISBN 978-0-940069-38-1 | order no. 069385

Nonprofit Stewardship
A Better Way to Lead Your Mission-Based Organization

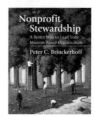

You may lead a nonprofit, but it's not your organization; it belongs to the community it serves. You are the steward—the manager of resources that belong to someone else. The stewardship model of leadership can help you make decisions that are best for the people you serve by keeping your mission foremost.

by Peter C. Brinckerhoff | 272 pp | 2004 | ISBN 978-0-940069-42-8 | order no. 069423

Strategic Planning Workbook, Revised and Updated

Chart a wise course for your nonprofit's future. This time-tested workbook gives you practical step-by-step guidance, real-life examples, and one nonprofit's complete strategic plan.

by Bryan W. Barry | 144 pp | 1997 | ISBN 978-0-940069-07-7 | order no. 069075